THERAPEUTIC CARE
FOR REFUGEES

Tavistock Clinic Series
Nick Temple, Margot Waddell (Series Editors)
Published and distributed by Karnac Books

Orders
Tel: +44 (0)20 8969 4454; Fax: +44 (0)20 8969 5585
Email: shop@karnacbooks.com
www.karnacbooks.com

THERAPEUTIC CARE
FOR REFUGEES

NO PLACE LIKE HOME

Edited by

Renos K. Papadopoulos

KARNAC

LONDON   NEW YORK

First published in 2002 by
H. Karnac (Books) Ltd.
6 Pembroke Buildings, London NW10 6RE

Reprinted 2003

A subsidiary of Other Press LLC, New York

British Library Cataloguing in Publication Data

A C.I.P. for this book is available from the British Library

ISBN 1 85575 283 2

Edited, designed, and produced by The Studio Publishing Services Ltd,
Exeter EX4 8JN

Printed in Great Britain by Biddles Ltd., Guildford and King's Lynn

10 9 8 7 6 5 4 3 2

www.karnacbooks.com

For Nina, Olga and Michelle

CONTENTS

SERIES EDITORS' PREFACE

Since it was founded in 1920, the Tavistock Clinic has developed a wide range of therapeutic approaches to mental health which have been strongly influenced by the ideas of psychoanalysis. It has also adopted systemic family therapy as a theoretical model and a clinical approach to family problems. The Clinic is now the largest training institution in Britain for mental health, providing post-graduate and qualifying courses in social work, psychology, psychiatry, child, adolescent and adult psychotherapy, as well as in nursing and primary care. It trains about 1,400 students each year in over 45 courses.

The Clinic's philosophy aims at promoting therapeutic methods in mental health. It's work is founded on the clinical expertise which is also the basis of its consultancy and research activities. This series aims to make available to the reading public the clinical, theoretical and research work that is most influential at the Tavistock Clinic. It sets out new approaches in the understanding and treatment of psychological disturbance in children, adolescents and adults, both as individuals and in families.

The plight of refugees stirs feelings of compassion and outrage in us all and raises fundamental issues for humanity. The rapid movement of refugees affects increasingly more people throughout the world. In Britain the debate about asylum seekers and refugees has reached a high profile and is at the centre of political concerns. It is important that all who are concerned with the refugee population in different capacities endeavour to deepen their understanding of the problems involved.

Therapeutic Care for Refugees: No place like home offers a comprehensive perspective on the issues of working with refugees. Renos Papadopoulos, with customary skill, has brought together a distinguished group of contributors with a wide knowledge of the field. The chapters cover research as well as psychotherapeutic practice. Although the book emphasizes the therapeutic care of refugees, it does not restrict itself to the psychotherapy of refugees alone, but approaches every facet of the refugee experience from a therapeutic perspective. The chapters introduce detailed discussion of the therapeutic dimension of work with refugees. The book describes innovative approaches to understanding refugees, and it is firmly based on the day-to-day reality of caring for refugees. It deals with the conceptual complexities and the dynamics of the therapeutic interaction from a systemic and psychodynamic perspective.

The book will be of interest to all those who work with refugees, even if they are not clinically involved in providing psychotherapy or counselling. It makes a new contribution to the field of knowledge about refugees.

Nicholas Temple and Margot Waddell
Series Editors

ACKNOWLEDGEMENTS

I wish to express my appreciation to:

1. Brunner/Routledge for granting permission to print in a modified form the chapter by Pamela Griffiths. Her chapter is based on her paper entitled "Counselling asylum seekers and refugees: a study of Kurds in early and later stages of exile" which appeared in the *European Journal of Psychotherapy, Counselling and Health*, Volume 4, Number 2, August, 2001, pp. 293–313. The publisher's website is: http://www.tandf.co.uk.

2. The Association for Family Therapy for granting permission to print in a substantially modified form parts of the paper by Renos K. Papadopoulos entitled "Refugees, therapists and trauma: systemic reflections" which appeared in *Context*, 2001, No. 54, April, pp. 5–8, special issue on Refugees which was edited by G. Gorell Barnes and R. K. Papadopoulos.

Warmest thanks to all the contributors to this book for their patience and collaborative spirit in responding to my editorial communications. I am grateful to all my colleagues at the Tavistock Clinic for their support, especially Emilia Dowling and Judith Bell, as well as our secretaries Judith Rogers and Alana Terry; also to my colleagues at the University of Essex, especially Andrew Samuels and Karl Figlio. The Series Editors, Nicholas Temple and Margot Waddell, offered useful suggestions and Eleanor Morgan was most helpful throughout this publishing project. Oliver Rathbone and Leena Häkkinen (from Karnac) were responsive to the various demands that emerged during the production of the book, and David Miller and Anita Mason from The Studio Publishing Services provided meticulous attention during the final stages. Special thanks to Aris Aristotelous, Lester Gilbert, Theodosios Lekkas, Noel Taylor and, of course, Evripides Zarifis for all their invaluable technical assistance.

I am particularly indebted to Andreas Coutas for the image on the book cover which is a computerized composition of two photographs which he took (in his capacity as photographer of the Public Information Office of the Republic of Cyprus) in July 1974. Following Turkey's invasion of Cyprus, nearly half the population of the island became refugees in their own country and Andreas documented most sensitively this human tragedy. This specific image encapsulates the refugee predicament and the central dilemma in responding to it: the first woman abandons herself to her pain and desolation whereas the second woman appears firm, dependable and resilient. Usually, therapeutic responses to refugees tend to either treat them as helpless victims or as self-reliant individuals, and this book addresses both the polarization of and interaction between these two perspectives. Andreas, who has received many international awards for both his news and advertising photography, succeeded in capturing this duality most movingly in this image.

This book could not have been completed without the unwavering support of my wife, Nina, and daughters, Olga and Michelle. Not only have they sustained me during my long hours of work on this book, but they have also actively assisted me with many tasks in its preparation and production.

Finally, I wish to express my deep gratitude to all the refugees I have worked with over many years, in different countries and in varied contexts. I have been humbled and enriched by their spirit and dignity in the face of adversity.

Renos K. Papadopoulos

FOREWORD

Celia Jaes Falicov

"Being away from my country is like a dream and nightmare come true at the same time. America is the beauty and the beast. Perhaps because my country has become in my mind, both heaven and hell."

A Chilean refugee in California

Human individuals and groups have always moved to other lands to seek safety, food, shelter for children, ideological or religious freedom or to escape wars, political persecution or torture. For the past two decades the world has been witnessing the largest and most diverse migrations ever recorded in history. It is estimated that 80 million people have left their countries in economic desperation. Today's migrants arrive after suffering significant stresses of poverty, extreme political and economic instability. They may have undergone fearful or traumatic passages as they migrate without proper legal documentation and may never obtain legal status and live under the threat of deportation. The tremendous influx of immigrants to the countries of the first world has challenged social and health services to create new programs, competencies and sensitivities. As a clinical psychologist and systemic therapist, I have dedicated my conceptual work, training and clinical activities to the development of mental health services attuned to the psychological, social and cultural issues of primarily economic immigrants.

If migration is as old as humankind, so is the violence of groups of people against one another. In 2002, according to the United Nations Commission of Refugees there are 33 million people worldwide that are designated as refugees. These include people that are placed in refugee camps temporarily or have been displaced within their own war ravaged countries and people who have fled to another country seeking a safe haven from massive killings of civilian populations, political incarceration or torture. What refugees have in common with all immigrants is the painful loss of home and separations from loved ones and the inevitable mixed emotions of sadness for what they have lost, as well as the elation for what they may have gained, the ambivalence of wanting to return and wanting to stay, along with the myriad ambiguities of living in two homes and two cultures. Both groups are engaged in creating a new life in the midst of experiencing multiple uncertainties and cultural dissonances while facing economic stresses and racist or prejudicial treatment in the host countries. What is of a patently different magnitude for refugees is the overwhelming assault to the individual human psyche, the losses of lives, the destruction of entire social communities, which are all devastating events that test the capacity to endure suffering, all happening in the premigration stage. Organized macrosocial violence often breeds excruciating and protracted internal violence and violence between intimates, thus adding, in Martin Luther King's words, "deeper darkness to a night already devoid of stars."

This extraordinarily timely and very important book addresses both issues masterfully: the refugees' experiences of uprooting and homelessness along with their attempts at recovering a sense of home *and* the refugees' personal experiences of either witnessing, suffering or being traumatized by physical and emotional violence. By drawing and deconstructing this distinction between the profound psychological meanings of home and homelessness *and* the profound individual and collective meanings of violence and trauma, this book contributes substantive scholarly insights to studies of migration and to studies of trauma, two issues that have been conceptually conflated and confused when treating immigrants, and particularly refugees.

The editor of this book, Professor Renos Papadopoulos, has gathered, along with his deep understanding of the subject matter, the thinking of a group of distinguished clinicians, researchers and academics from different disciplines and theoretical orientations (psychoanalytic, systemic, narrative) based at the Tavistock Clinic in London who work with refugees either in the country of resettlement or in the territory of origin. The challenges of this kind of work are formidable. To build bridges of human connectedness between strangers in language and in values about health and mental health, gender discourses, styles of emotional communication and other aspects of relational life, is the daunting task of all cross-cultural work. Imagine how much more so it is when therapists are visibly shaken by hearing the atrocities committed to the client and when they move in the unchartered nature of the work itself by being confronted constantly with multiple questions and difficult dilemmas. The array of dilemmas covered in these chapters include: how to incorporate an ethically necessary sociopolitical lens and still remain connected with the internal issues triggered for all involved; when to carefully help verbalize the horrific memories and when to help them to remain sealed off; how to fully recognize the suffering endured and yet not stereotype refugees as helpless victims, or reduce them to the diagnosis of post-traumatic stress; how to help effectively and not fall into the natural wish to rescue the clients and thus paradoxically block their natural self-healing; how to tap into the conational social networks that most immigrant groups can claim as their "social capital" when their internal "emotional capital" may interfere with the ability to reach out socially; how to help refugees adapt to their new surroundings and yet prepare to leave them if necessary.

The foregoing are just some of the many theoretical and clinical practice issues that are raised from multiple perspectives by this outstanding book. Several chapters also address the complexities of psychosocial work when therapists leave the parameters of their institutional settings to engage in projects to train and supervise the work of local mental health professionals in the countries where the refugees come from and to which many are returning to, in this case primarily Kosovo. As the writers explain, these local professionals are "insiders" that share with their clients a history of systematic violence. This commonality is an advantage, but their emotional resonance can narrow their responses. Although able to offer new alternatives, the well-intentioned outsiders, the international "experts", run the risk of unwittingly disturbing the local professional hierarchies and social ecologies by falling trap to cultural or professional colonizing roles. There are no easy answers to these inevitable problems but the honest and thoughtful revelations here offer valuable insights for similar international relief efforts in countries where large portions of the population have become refugees inside their own countries.

There is pragmatic quest at the center of this work: how can therapeutic care in its many forms (legal, educational, health and mental health care, public policy, volunteer, community organizing) expand refugees' opportunities to heal and learn to live with their incredible losses while restoring a sense of coherence and meaningfulness to their lives? This book is an essential resource for any professional or lay person interested in finding responses to this question. In a topic of wrenching dimensions, this comprehensive book explores incisively and compassionately the difficult dynamics of ethical intervention for everyone interested in helping to heal the deep wounds of individuals, families, communities and even countries in the aftermath of inhuman atrocities and subsequent massive dislocation.

Celia Jaes Falicov, Ph.D.
Clinical Professor, Department of Psychiatry, University of California, San Diego
Past President, American Family Therapy Academy
Visiting Scientist, Tavistock Clinic, London 2002

EDITOR'S FOREWORD

Renos K. Papadopoulos

Background

The world is intermittently stunned by images of human suffering following political upheavals and outbreaks of violence in various parts of the world. These spasmodic (but increasingly frequent) episodes stir feelings of compassion and outrage that usually get forgotten when new sound bites about other news dominate. However, for refugees and all the other affected people these feelings and their actual living predicament are not passing phenomena and they do not vary according to the political priorities of the day; this reality is also well known to all those who work with these groups of people. The debate about asylum seekers has recently acquired a high profile because of its political dimensions. However, the issue itself is not just political. The movement of refugees affects increasingly more people in increasingly more countries in the world today. Therefore, it is imperative that all who work with this population in different capacities endeavour to expand and deepen their understanding of the complexities involved.

Scope

It is in the context of this background that this book addresses some of the central issues pertaining to the mental health dimensions of asylum seekers and refugees. The book has been planned to be authoritative and yet accessible. The authors are experienced clinicians, academics and researchers, all associated with the Tavistock Clinic, in London.

The Tavistock Clinic is an international centre of excellence in mental health training, research, scholarship and, of course, clinical practice. More specifically, since 1920, when it was founded, the Clinic has been pioneering the application of psychotherapeutic methods which can be used as the basis for research into the social prevention and treatment of mental health problems and the teaching of these emerging skills to other professionals. Today, the Clinic has an interdisciplinary group of one hundred and twenty members of staff and it trains about one thousand two hundred professionals every year.

This book is unique in offering a comprehensive and wide perspective on the central issues of working with refugees. There are fifteen chapters covering theory, research, field applications, as well as psychotherapeutic practice. A second unique characteristic of this book is the emphasis on the therapeutic care of this group of people. This means that the book is not limited to the actual psychotherapy work (with individuals, families and groups) but it approaches every facet of the refugee experience from a therapeutic perspective. Therefore, it is intended that the book introduces new insights into ways of increasing the therapeutic dimension of any work with refugees. In this way, the book would be of benefit to all those who work with refugees, even if they are not engaged in formal psychotherapy as such. Of particular interest are three chapters exploring facets of a collaborative project the Tavistock Clinic has been engaging in with the International Organisation for Migration in offering a therapeutic response in Kosovo after the recent war.

Apart from offering an up-to-date review of the relevant literature, this book provides creative and innovative approaches to its subject matter. Although it is firmly based in the pragmatic realities of this work, it also deals with the conceptual complexities as well as the dynamics of the therapeutic interactions as they are affected by wider socio–political parameters. In terms of theoretical orientation, the book focuses on psychoanalytic/psychodynamic and systemic approaches for which the Tavistock Clinic is renowned.

In the specialist literature there is relatively little about the therapeutic care perspective on refugees and this book is intended to fill this gap, especially at this time when the subject matter is particularly topical.

Readership

Thus, the book will be suitable to all those who work with refugees, in various capacities, and all those who wish to develop an in-depth understanding of refugee issues. This means that the book would be a useful resource for specialist practitioners, supervisors, trainees, researchers and students, as well as for all who are involved in managerial, legal, administrative, and voluntary capacity with this group of people. More specifically, the scope and authoritativeness of this book could make it a textbook for specialist courses and a guidebook for therapists and students of related subjects. Moreover, this book aspires to contribute considerably to the wider debate in society on asylum seekers and refugees and, therefore, it would be of relevance also to policy makers and staff of international organizations as well as NGOs.

The specific socio–political and historical dimensions of our times make refugeedom an issue that no longer belongs to a narrow speciality because it increasingly affects not only our lives and work as professionals but also our very identity as citizens. Therefore, this book has been designed to assist both the specialist professionals as well as the wider public who wish to obtain a more thorough understanding of these issues in our societies today.

Renos K. Papadopoulos

CONTRIBUTORS

Majlinda Angoli is a counsellor and heads the Counselling Centre for Women and Girls, Shkodera, with responsibility for both the running of the organization, and training. She is a member of the Albanian Women's Network, played an important part in raising awareness of family violence within the country, and is a mentor to the Kosovar project reported in this book.

Jenny Altschuler is a consultant clinical psychologist, and systemic psychotherapist, based at the Tavistock Clinic in London, working with people facing major life transitions, including serious physical illness and migration. She is the author of *Working with Chronic Illness: a family approach* and the consultant and trainer to the project reported in this book. She has also contributed to the IOM-Tavistock Clinic training of counsellors in Kosovo.

Andrew Cooper is Professor of Social Work at the Tavistock Clinic and University of East London, and an associate member of the British Association of Psychotherapists. He has undertaken cross-national comparative research in child welfare over many years, and is interested in promoting and developing anti-racist mental health and therapeutic services.

Judith Farbey was trained as a barrister and has specialized in immigration and asylum law. She is currently at Tooks Court Chambers in London. She has been a member of the Executive Committee of the Immigration Law Practitioners' Association and a member of the Advisory Panel of the Immigration Services Commissioner. She has been acting as a consultant and has taught for a number of human rights and refugee organisations. She has been a visiting lecturer to the course "Working with Refugee Families" at the Tavistock Clinic since its inception in 1995.

Maureen Fox is a consultant clinical psychologist in the Child and Family Department at the Tavistock Clinic where she is a clinician and teacher. She is Convenor of the Refugee Workshop, working with refugee children and families and is currently engaged in setting up an Outreach Mental Health Service for Somali children and families in the London Borough of Camden. She is a practising adult psychoanalytic psychotherapist and a member of the British Association of Psychotherapists.

Caroline Garland is a consultant clinical psychologist and a psychoanalyst. She works in the Adult Department of the Tavistock Clinic where she is a clinician, teacher and trainer. She has a particular interest in the psychoanalytic understanding and treatment of traumatized states of mind. Fifteen years ago, she founded and now heads the Tavistock's Unit for the Study of Trauma and Its Aftermath which has seen and treated a wide variety of patients. The Unit's most recent work contains several chapters by Caroline Garland, and is published in *Understanding Trauma* (edited by C. Garland), London: Karnac.

Chris Glenn is a Senior Lecturer in the School of Health and Social Care at the University of Greenwich and a member of a child and adolescent mental health family therapy team. He trained at the Tavistock Clinic as a family therapist, and for his dissertation he researched the systemic connections between Somali refugee families and the school system in a London borough. He is a member of the editorial committee of *Context*, the bimonthly publication of the Association of Family Therapy, and an active trade unionist and socialist.

Pamela Griffiths is a physiotherapist, counsellor, and psychotherapist. She runs the MSc in Counselling in Health-Care and Rehabilitation at Brunel University and has a private practice in London. She has worked in Southern Africa and the USA. Her current research: "Holocaust Testimony as a Form of Remembrance" is part of a Clinical PhD in Child and Family Psychology based at the Tavistock Clinic and Birkbeck College, University of London. She has completed the Tavistock training course on "Working with Refugee Families".

Merita Halitaj is a counsellor and the manager of the Prizrin centre of the "One to One" Counselling Centre, in Kosovo. For the past three years, she has been running the centre, working clinically with refugees who have experienced extreme levels of violence, as well as playing an active role in the Kosovar Women's Network and several other Kosovar NGOs.

Violeta Hulme was born in the former Yugoslavia of fixed nationality. She has a degree in Albanian and English languages from the University of Belgrade and has completed the Tavistock training course on "Working with Refugee Families". She has worked with refugees since 1988 with various organizations, including the UNHCR in Belgrade, the British Refugee Council in London, and with various organizations as freelance interpreters. Now she is consultant for Eastern European Refugee Issues for the Islington Council and also for various other aid agencies and charities.

Francesca Hume worked as a forensic clinical psychologist before training as a psychoanalytic psychotherapist at the Tavistock Clinic. She now works at the Tavistock where she runs a service for adults abused as children in care. She is in her final year of training at the Institute of Psycho-Analysis.

Ifakete Jaseke is a counsellor and the manager of the Peya centre of the "One to One" Counselling Centre, in Kosovo. For the past three years, she has been running the centre, working clinically with refugees who have experienced extreme levels of violence, as well as playing an active role in the Kosovar Women's Network and several other Kosovar NGOs.

M. Kemal Kuşçu completed his medical training in Istanbul University, Turkey. After training in psychiatry at Marmara Medical School, he continued his studies in medical anthropology (M.Sc.) in University College of London and also obtained a Pg.Dipl. M.A. in Applied Systemic Theory at the Tavistock Clinic. He is Assistant Professor of Psychiatry at Marmara Medical School, Istanbul and Project Officer for Psychosocial Mobile Teams of the International Organization for Migration, in Kosovo.

Peter Loizos has taught Social Anthropology at the London School of Economics since 1969. For his doctoral research, he studied a village in Cyprus with mixed (Greek and Turkish) population before and after the Turkish invasion in 1974. He studied the Greek Cypriot inhabitants of this village, after they were forced to leave the village and has followed them up from the early months of their dislocation until now. Currently, he is interested in the long-term physical health of Greek Cypriot refugees. He has been a visiting lecturer to the course "Working with Refugee Families" at the Tavistock Clinic. He is an Emeritus Professor.

Natale Losi, PhD, sociologist, medical anthropologist, and family psychotherapist has been working in Africa (Mali, Ethiopia) and in Europe (Switzerland, ex Yugoslavia and Italy). He is currently the Head of the Psychosocial and Cultural Integration Unit of the International Organization for Migration (IOM), Regional Office for the Mediterranean and the Balkans. Until the end of 2000 he covered the same position in Geneva at the IOM headquarters, where he was also Maitre d'Enseignement et de Recherche at the University of Geneva. He currently collaborates with many groups of psychotherapists, including the School of Family Therapy of Milan founded by Mara Selvini Palazzoli and the Centre Devereux at the University Paris VIII on the "Ethnopsychiatric approach with migrants". His publications in Italian include: *The Friends of Water: doctors, patients and alternative medicines*, Milan, 1990; *The Mirror of Mali*, Rome, 1991 (also in English) and *Lives Otherwise, Migration and Psychic Suffering*, Milan 2000.

Sarah Majid is a specialist registrar in psychoanalytic psychotherapy at the Tavistock Clinic with a particular interest in working psychotherapeutically with refugees who have experienced trauma. She previously completed a MA in Social Anthropology at the School of Oriental and African Studies, London. She qualified as a Member of the Royal College of Psychiatrists while at the Maudsley Hospital where she had the opportunity to work with refugees from a variety of backgrounds living in deprived inner city areas in South London.

Renos K. Papadopoulos, PhD, is consultant clinical psychologist at the Tavistock Clinic, Professor at the University of Essex, systemic family psychotherapist, and training and supervising Jungian psychoanalyst. At the Tavistock, he has been involved with refugee work for many years working clinically with families and individuals, teaching specialist courses, and offering supervision and consultation to practitioners and services. As consultant to the United Nations and other organizations, he has worked with refugees and other survivors of political violence in several countries.

Sue Rendall, PhD, is a consultant child and educational psychologist in the Child and Family Department at the Tavistock Clinic, where she is also Vice Dean of Post-Graduate Studies. She is Course Director for Masters and Doctorate level training for educational psychologists at the Tavistock, and is Co-Chair of the National Educational Psychology Course Directors' Group and a member of the Training Committee of the Division of Educational and Child Psychology of the British Psychological Society. She is a Fellow of the University of Essex.

Valerie Sinason is a poet, writer, child psychotherapist, and adult psychoanalyst. She is a consultant research psychotherapist at St George's Hospital Medical School (Department of Disability, in Psychiatry) and Director of the Clinic for Dissociative Studies. She specialises in trauma and abuse in children and adults with or without a learning disability. She has published eleven books including: *Mental Handicap and the Human Condition* (Free Association) and most recently *Attachment, Trauma and Multiplicity, Working with Dissociative Identity Disorder* (Routledge 2002). She is a Consultant Psychotherapist at the University of Cape Town Child Guidance Clinic, and worked at the Tavistock Clinic from 1979 to 1999.

Dr Judith Trowell is a consultant child and adolescent psychiatrist with the Child and Family Department at the Tavistock Clinic. She is co-convenor of the Tavistock Legal Workshop. She has considerable experience in the field of child protection and is Vice Chair of Camden Child Protection Committee. Part of her large caseload of court work includes refugee children and families and unaccompanied minors.

Introduction

Renos K. Papadopoulos

Whilst completing this book, I read a striking report about an important but less known facet of the refugee experience. Under the title "Bosnian refugees returning home", the CNN.com website on December 3rd, 2001 gave an account of one instance of this return. Usually, we read about the difficulties refugees experience whilst away from home, but this was one of the few moving descriptions of recent returns. I was particularly interested to read this because I had been working with Bosnian refugees of all ethnic backgrounds both in parts of the former and present Yugoslavia as well as in the UK since the war broke out in that region. Here are some relevant excerpts from this report:

> DZEVAR, Bosnia-Herzegovina—It is freezing outside, but it warms Rade Kragulj's heart just to be able to fix the leaky roof on the house he left behind during Bosnia's war.
>
> At 62, after six years as a refugee, he is finally home, even if he is a Serb and his home is in territory now under Muslim control.
>
> With the return home of Kragulj and thousands of other Bosnian Serbs, U.N. officials feel they have turned a corner in efforts to undo

1

the human tragedy of a three-and-a-half-year war that uprooted 1.8 million people.

"Finally this year, we're seeing real results for all of our work since 1996", Aida Feraget, the U.N. refugee agency's Bosnia spokeswoman, told The Associated Press.

Persuading Serbs, Muslims and Croats to return to the homes they abandoned during the war remains Bosnia's biggest challenge.

Many feel they can never live together again because of the ethnic hatred stirred up in a war that killed at least 200,000 people.

. . .

But in the first nine months of 2001, these so-called minority returns were up by 65 percent to 56,683, according to the United Nations.

. . .

The Kragulj family came back from 20 miles away to find that their house in Dzevar, 110 miles northwest of Sarajevo, had been shelled during the 1992–1995 war, then blown up by vengeful Muslims.

. . .

"They looked sick all the time for six years when they were refugees", said the couple's 25-year-old son, Nenad. "As soon as they came back to their ruins, my parents suddenly looked alive again."

"There's no place like home."

The son's comments that after returning home his parents "looked alive again", and the reporter's observation that despite the cold weather it was heart-warming for the ex-refugee to repair the leaky roof of his ruined home, demonstrate the well-known healing effect of homecoming. Without ignoring the distinct types of difficulties refugees face when they return home, there is no doubt that the undeniable sense of settledness that returnees experience contributes substantially to their well-being both physically and psychologically.

However, alas, as we know, proportionally to the increasing number of refugees world-wide, these returnees are the exception. The great majority of refugees are destined to remain away from their homelands, struggling to make the best of their predicament.

Those who are lucky to end up in countries with specialist services which attend to more than their basic living needs (for food, shelter, medical attention etc) are likely to afford themselves the opportunity, eventually, to get in touch with their own psychological needs. It is impossible to replicate the healing effects described in this CNN report in any country outside the refugees' own homeland, where they end up as exiles. Yet, wittingly but mostly unwittingly, both the refugees and mental health professionals are likely to attempt to achieve this illusory goal or at least some variation of it. Exposed to the acuteness of the pain of dislocation, along with the host of all other disturbing accompanying memories, feelings and reactions, refugees and their helpers find it difficult to bear and digest the enormity of this psychological disruption. Inevitably, they are tempted by the seductive promise of this nostalgic (literally, in its original meaning of aching to return home) and heart-warming feeling of our returnee roof fixer.

If the main problem with refugees is their loss of home, why do they need psychotherapy? Is psychotherapy a replacement of home or should it be so? Needless to say, there are many forms of homecoming, apart from the literal one and some are more appropriate than others.

Human nature tends to reach out impulsively to ease pain, and aid workers find it difficult to bear the refugees' pain as well as that of their own. Thus, aid workers tend to create a warm sense of homely familiarity with refugees. However, as we know, this impulsive way of attempting to soften pain often pulls workers and refugees into collusive and indeed illusionary modes of interacting. Most certainly, this is not the appropriate way of working therapeutically with refugees. Not that refugees do not require ordinary human compassion and support; they certainly do and the provision of this kind of assistance should be part of any overall care plan for them, as long as it is carefully designed. However, psychotherapy should be reserved for something much more than that; psychotherapy has the potentiality of addressing the fundamental dynamics that are behind the expressed difficulties and symptoms that refugees experience, and this kind of deceptive recreation of homely warmth is not what psychotherapy should be offering.

Then again, traditional psychotherapy in its fuller form may not always be available to or, dare I say, appropriate for the majority of refugees who may not have either the right motivation or symptomatology for this kind of specialist work. However, I would strongly argue that *therapeutic considerations* can always be useful and should be included in any kind of care plan refugees are offered. This means that regardless of their suitability for or availability of psychotherapy proper, refugees will always benefit from appropriately adjusted forms of "therapeutic care". This is the reason that the title of this book refers to *therapeutic care* rather than to psychotherapy, as such. *Therapeutic care* refers to the wider application of psychotherapeutic principles to any form of assistance to refugees. This means that elements of *therapeutic care* can be included in all types of work with refugees, be it with reference to their housing, educational, medical or financial needs. It is this extensive application of therapeutic principles to refugees that this book covers without, of course, excluding important insights into the actual psychotherapy proper with refugees.

The following chapters address a variety of issues pertaining to the therapeutic care of refugees including theoretical, clinical, research, as well as applications of therapeutic principles in actual field projects. The book offers an opportunity to specialist and non-specialist readers to acquaint themselves with the broad spectrum and rich variety of this kind of therapeutic work that is done at the Tavistock Clinic. All the authors are either members of staff of the Clinic or they are associated with it in various ways. The Tavistock Clinic is an international centre of excellence in mental health training, research and scholarship, all based on clinical practice. More specifically, since 1920, when it was founded, the Clinic has been pioneering the application of psychotherapeutic methods in research into the social prevention and treatment of mental health problems and the teaching of these emerging skills to other professionals. The Clinic was founded in the aftermath of the Great War and it has retained its commitment to addressing social issues utilizing sound psychotherapeutic principles. This tradition continues today and the Clinic (in addition to its diverse range of other activities) has been working with refugees and other traumatized people from political violence, from all over the world in many different ways—offering direct psychotherapy to individuals, families and groups, supervizing and consulting to individuals and organizations who are engaged in this kind of work, conducting research, teaching specialist courses, organizing international conferences, contributing to the specialist professional literature as well as advizing relevant national and international policy-making bodies.

This book offers a sample of these activities and it introduces new and valuable insights into many aspects of conceptualizing and working with refugees in different contexts. The chapters are divided into four sections. In the first section, "Delineating the context", there are three chapters which address general issues of locating the refugee experience in the context of theoretical, anthropological and legal perspectives. In the second section, five chapters deal with specific issues pertaining to psychotherapy with refugees. In the third section, two chapters present and discuss relevant research projects and in the final, fourth section, there are four chapters which investigate facets of field projects.

Returning to the idea of home, everybody knows that home is more than the concrete physical house which provides shelter and (hopefully) human warmth and nourishment to all family members. Home can also be seen as a psychological category which combines the basic psychological processes which facilitate early human development. Once approached from this perspective, it could be argued that therapeutic care with refugees has the possibility of restoring some of the important processes that are associated with home and thus providing an invaluable boost for refugees that can activate their own resilience. Thus, although most refugees who end up in exile in other countries may never return to their geographical homeland, this does not necessarily prevent them from recovering from all adversity and being enabled to lead full and creative lives. We are often reminded that many famous people who have contributed substantially to humankind throughout history have been refugees.

Therefore, the returnee roof fixer's son dictum, that "there is no place like home" can be understood in many ways. Can the positive effects of home be recreated (not that the home itself can be replaced) through other means? Can therapeutic care for refugees, understood in a broader and creative manner, be one of them? This book attempts to contribute modestly to this debate.

Important clarifications

It is important to clarify that

— the term "refugee" is used here as a generic term and, therefore, is intended to subsume the differentiated category of "asylum seeker". This means that the two terms are used synonymously in this book, unless specific difference is indicated.

— the ideas and opinions expressed in the following chapters represent those of the authors, and do not necessarily represent the views of the editor, the Series Editors or those of the Tavistock Clinic.

DELINEATING THE CONTEXT

CHAPTER ONE

Refugees, home and trauma[1]

Renos K. Papadopoulos

I t is rather remarkable that with all the intensity and breadth of the debate on refugee issues and the extensive psychological work with them there is no substantial examination of the idea of home and its implications for refugees and their workers. Instead, what is more readily available is the plethora of theories on trauma and their applications. Whenever one thinks of refugees, from a psychological perspective, the first association is to trauma rather than to home. Home, after all, is not a psychological concept, as such. Yet, loss of home is the only condition that all refugees share, not trauma. Refugees are defined not as a group of people exhibiting any specific psychological condition but merely as people who have lost their homes. Their primary common characteristic is their lack of home. But what is home and what does it mean for refugees? How does home affect the therapeutic care and its interactive process?

In this chapter, I shall endeavour to explore the significance of home in understanding the refugee situation as well as the impact such exploration can have on our psychological approach to and work with refugees. Moreover, the development of an understanding of home in the context of refugees will provide a new perspective within which to locate the debate on refugee trauma and other related issues, thus arriving at an enriched comprehension of the complexities involved in the therapeutic care for refugees.

Home and Homer

Home is one of the most fundamental notions of humanity. Regardless of the shape or style of home, all human beings have a sense of home (if not an actual experience of, at least, one home) which often evokes powerful feelings, be they positive or negative. Home constitutes one of the central realities that humans share with animals. The whole dynamic of territoriality is directly connected with the locality and feeling of home.

If we were to examine the dictionary meanings of home, we would be reminded that home is "a village, a town, a collection of dwellings" (The Oxford English Dictionary). Etymologically, home is connected with the old English word "ham" (as in "hamlet" or "Eastham"). This means that one of the first characteristics of home is that it is not restricted to a personal home of one person or one family but it also has a collective connotation. The same dictionary further defines home as "the seat of domestic life", as well as "the place of one's dwelling or nurturing, with conditions, circumstances, and feelings which naturally and properly attach to it, and are associated with it". Therefore, "home is not only the place but also the cluster of feelings associated with it". This aspect is emphasized in additional definitions: "A place, region or state to which one properly belongs, in which one's affections centre, or where one finds refuge, rest or satisfaction". In games, we are reminded, "home is the place in which one is free from attack, [as well as] the point which one tries to reach; the goal". This teleological definition of home should not surprise us, as "in various connections", home also refers to the "grave, or future state; the 'long' or 'last home' ". Finally, home has a rich metaphorical range of meanings. "To be at home with" a subject or somebody means to be conversant and at ease with them; "to make oneself at home" has a similar meaning, i.e. of being at ease and being comfortable with something; and, finally, expressions such as "it struck home" or "bring a point/argument home" refer to home as "the very heart or root of a matter".

Although this is, by no means, an exhaustive investigation of the semantic and linguistic dimensions of home, it, nevertheless, reminds us of the wide spectrum of meanings that it conveys—"from a physical and geographical community, to a psychological locus of relatedness and communion; from a seat of origins, to the ultimate goal, the place of rest, beyond conflict" (Papadopoulos, 1987, p. 7). Thus, the notion of home, *per se*, includes "a polarity of seemingly opposite experiences, i.e. those pertaining both to beginning and end" (Papadopoulos, 1987, p. 8). The very idea of home includes in itself origins as well as aspired goals. "Home is both the perceived locus of origin as well as the desired destination, the goal, the end, the telos" (Papadopoulos, 1987, p. 8). Yet, the usual way we tend to comprehend the idea of reaching home is in terms of one direction only—the regression, the return to the home of origin (physically, geographically or metaphorically), to the location or cultural milieu or psychological space where we were born or grew up. Thus, when refugees yearn for home, it is important to keep in mind this inherent dichotomous direction that is engendered in their longing and which is likely to be subjugated by the dominant direction of regression.

Home and homecoming is such a basic concern of the human experience and history that it has been the theme of many artistic creations—from literature and film, to art and theatre. Homer's *The Odyssey* seems to have captured some of the key elements and nuances of the home-leaving and homecoming experience in a particularly apposite way. Written nearly three thousand years ago, this epic poem still touches people deeply and its title has become synonymous with the predicament of all those who endeavour to find a home for themselves and, by extension, to any arduous and long pursuit of a goal.

Homer inserts his famous image about home, when Odysseus yearns to see the smoke from his homeland and then die, right at the beginning of the poem, thus setting the theme and the tone. In this way, Homer indicates that *The Odyssey* is about the struggle to get home, or, to use a colloquial expression, it is about Odysseus dying to return home. More specifically, (only fifty-eight verses into the very first chapter of *The Odyssey*), Homer says "Odysseus is so sick with longing to see, if it were, but the smoke of his home spiring up, that he prays for death". But is this really what Homer said? This particular phrase comes from the translation by T. E. Lawrence (the famous Lawrence of Arabia).

It is important to note that Homer is not using the word "home", as it does not, in fact, exist in Greek. The closest equivalent word in Greek is *ecos* (*oikos*), the root of ecology and economics. *Ecos* refers more to the house, dwelling, abode as well as to household affairs and housewifery. Out of *ecos* comes the Latin *vicus* (quarter or district of a town, hamlet, an estate) which is the root of the English wick (as in Norwich). Homer uses the word *gaia* (γαῖα) which simply means earth, soil, land. It is the same word that Lovelock (2000) chose for his theory that our planet earth functions in remarkably inter-regulated ways, as if it was a single organism. So, whereas *ecos* emphasizes the inhabited space, *gaia* refers more to the land itself. However, both address the relational aspects of the inhabited and uninhabited spaces and certainly both highlight the collective dimensions of home rather than a definition of home as an excluded and isolated space. Thus, the specific Homeric home (*gaia*) accentuates the concreteness of the collective and relational nature of space and it refers to the actual soil, one's own land in a sense of inclusion rather than exclusion.

Returning to T. E. Lawrence, we may wonder whether his own turbulent and homeless life was connected with his choice of the word "home" instead of "land". Lawrence had no land of his own—either in terms of owning a house (at the time of writing this translation) or in terms of feeling strongly connected with one country. Born in Ireland, grown up in England and committed to Arabia, he did not have any land but, evidently, had a strong yearning for a home. It may be more of a passing interest to note that T. E. Lawrence (then called T. E. Shaw [1932]) began translating *The Odyssey* while in military service in Afghanistan in 1928.

Taking this theme further, we note that Alexander Pope (1688—1744) renders the same verses as follows:

> To see the smoke from his loved palace rise,
> While the dear isle in distant prospect rise,
> With what contentment could he close his eyes!

Pope, settled in his genteel villa in Twickenham, understands *gaia* as palace and gives the yearning for home a distinct romantic character, inventing even a "contentment" in Odysseus. Evidently, for Pope, the pursuit of home could not have had the dramatic and gutsy feel that T. E. Lawrence gave it.

It is interesting to consider three additional translations which are closer to the original Greek with reference to their rendering of *gaia*. Rieu (1946) renders these verses as

> and Odysseus, who would give anything for the mere sight of the smoke rising up from his own land, can only yearn for death,

Fagles (1996) as

> But he, straining for no more than a glimpse
> of hearth-smoke drifting up from his own land,
> Odysseus longs to die ...

and Lombardo (2000) as

> But Odysseus,
> Longing to see even the smoke curling up
> From his land, simply wants to die.

Although all three translations are closer to the Homeric original in so far as they all use "land" for *gaia*, still they differ in the overall feel they give to this important passage. These discrepancies and idiosyncratic renderings of home reflect the inevitably unique, distinctive and personal approach to the nostalgic yearning for home that the refugees have. Each person experiences and expresses his or her state of homelessness in a highly personalized way which then is understood and rendered differently and equally idiosyn-cratically (i.e. closely related to their own personal, professional, socio–economic and historico–cultural contexts) by all those who attempt to understand the needs of that particular refugee.

Moreover, using this Homeric passage, it could be said that home is constituted by two opposites: a most tangible and grounded element, the earth, the land, and the most tangible image of an intangible form of home—smoke. This powerful combination of the tangible and intangible, concrete and ethereal, physical and imaginary, inflexible/immovable and flexible/mobile, substantial and indefinable make the image of home a most potent and resilient cluster of psychological dynamics.

Staying with *The Odyssey*, it is worth making another relevant observation (Papadopoulos, 1987). The logical sequence of the poem would be that Odysseus arrives home, to the island of Ithaca, at the end of the poem. Yet there is something very curious in the structure of the poem which consists of twenty-four chapters (called "books"). Homer has Odysseus arriving in Ithaca right in the centre of the epic. At the very beginning of book thirteen Odysseus finally arrives home. Or does he? He certainly arrives on the shores of Ithaca but he is not even aware where he is. He does not recognize his "home" to begin with. So, whereas objectively, he had reached home, in effect he was not yet at home. This magnificent irony should not be forgotten. It is as if Homer keeps pressing us with painful questions as to how to define home.

What then happens in the second half of *The Odyssey* if Odysseus is already home? Evidently, his physical arrival in Ithaca does not end his odyssey, and does not amount to homecoming because not only does he not recognize his homeland but nobody recognizes him, either. Home, therefore, cannot be experienced without mutual recognition. Moreover, most importantly, once physically at home, Odysseus had to feel at home. Even after he understood that he had finally landed on his beloved homeland, he still did not arrive home. He had to re-encounter and re-connect with all members of his family, enter his palace, fight the suitors, and regain his royal position. "Homecoming is not only about external arrivals and the creation of established homes defined by legal contracts and delineated by geographical boundaries" (Papadopoulos, 1987, p. 15). Homecoming is also about the re-establishment of all meaningful connections within one's own family and own self. These re-connections cannot be taken for granted and are, by no means, easy. Homer makes this point very clearly in so far as it takes another odyssey for Odysseus to re-establish himself in his own home. Odysseus does not slip back into the position, place, role and identity he had left behind, but he has to fight ferociously if not even more so than when on his way to Ithaca. Homecoming is not just a retrospective exercise but also includes a prospective direction. Thus, Homer demonstrates most eloquently that the complete odyssey is not about regression, a passive return to the past, but it includes the totality of the duality of meanings of home—the return and a reintegration, the going back and arrival as well as the achievement of future goals. Moreover, he leads us to experience that the second phase of homecoming can be even more hazardous than the first one. Psychologically, it is subtler and trickier to re-connect with one's own family members and to risk losing everything, after all the heroic efforts to arrive home in the first place.

Following Homer, it could be argued that we could distinguish two kinds of successive moments in the homecoming process: the first is about external dimensions, about the physical arrival where navigation skills, diplomacy, strength, persistence are required to negotiate the external dangers and obstacles. The second moment is of a more internal and psychological nature, requiring more internal resources, stamina, containment, insightfulness and resilience. If the first is about arriving home, the second is about reconnecting with one's sense of self and accessing the dis-membered parts of one's personality.

"Nostalgic disorientation" and "mosaic substratum of identity"

Although refugees do not constitute any one coherent diagnostic category of psychological or psychopathological characteristics, the fact that they all have lost their homes makes them share a deep sense of nostalgic yearning for restoring that very specific type of loss. *Nostalgia* is the right word to describe this whole cluster of feelings, reactions, hopes, fears, etc. *Nostos* in classical Greek means "returning home" and *nostalgia* is the pain that accompanies the feeling of pining to return home. *Algos* is ache, pain and, therefore, *nostalgia* is the hurt, the pain, the sickness, the suffering that a person experiences in wanting to go home.

To understand this lack as a loss in the ordinary psychological sense is to miss the rich meaning and complexity that the loss of home entails. Papadopoulos (1997a) suggested the term "nostalgic disorientation" to refer to this uniqueness of the refugee predicament. The loss is not only about a concrete object or condition but it encapsulates the totality of all the dimensions of home, as discussed above. More specifically, this totality includes the three sets of binary dichotomous elements: i.e. (a) the two diametrical opposite directions of home which include both prospective and retrospective movements (towards the origins and the goals); (b) the double signification of home in terms of tangible and intangible entities (physical and imaginary); and (c) the two successive moments of the homecoming process (external and internal, physical and psychological, return and reintegration).

Refugees sense the impact of this multidimensional, deep and pervasive loss and they feel disoriented because it is difficult to pinpoint the clear source and precise nature of this loss, especially due to its complex and dichotomous nature. What is certain is that refugees have lost their homes; this is a tangible and precise concept and reality, whereas anything else becomes quite disorienting. The term "nostalgic disorientation" was advanced (Papadopoulos, 1997a) in order to clarify that this disorientation is enwrapped in a nostalgic sense of deep ache. Refugees never lose their awareness of the actual loss of home; however, what creates confusion and bewilderment is the intricate mixture of these other dimensions which get confused and which generate this feeling of "nostalgic disorientation".

However, human beings cannot tolerate ambiguity and tend to create certainty regardless of the amount of distortion involved in doing so. Thus, under the painful influence of this kind of loss, refugees tend to single out specific complaints as the sole source of their unhappiness. Often, these complaints are legitimate but they seem to acquire extraordinary and excessive significance, and they are evidently overcharged with feeling in a disproportional way. These may be focused on insufficiently attended needs connected with housing, schools, benefits, but mostly—physical medical symptoms.

It is as if the absence of home creates a gap in refugees which makes them feel uncontained and they then look around to fill the gap, to make up for that loss, to re-create the protective and containing membrane of home. Indeed, home provides such a protective and holding enwrapment. This is so because, *de facto*, most homes provide some kind of continuity that enables co-existence between many opposites: love and discord, distance and proximity, joys and sorrows, hopes and disappointments, flexibility and obstinacy, envy and magnanimity, rivalry and collaboration, loyalty and betrayal, enmity and friendship, similarities and differences, to name but a few. Within the context and relative permanence of home, one can experience the co-existence of seemingly irreconcilable opposites and this experience creates a special feel of containment that is not usually consciously appreciated. Regardless of how "dysfunctional" families may be, homes can provide that deep and fundamental sense of space where all these opposites and contradictions can be contained and held together. Inevitably, this develops a sense of security, regardless of whatever other traumatic experiences family members may also have as a result of their family interactions. This function of home is most important in minimizing or even avoiding archaic and fundamental forms of splitting.

It would be reasonable to assume that there is a basic and primary layer, which mostly is not visible or felt, that forms what could be called a substratum of human experience on top of which all other tangible and visible experiences and characteristics are grafted (Papadopoulos, 1997b). The very fact that one has experience of a home (regardless of how good or bad, long or brief, it may be) forms part of this substratum that contributes to the establishment of a foundation to being human. Ordinarily, this layer, being so basic and fundamental, is outside the reach of our awareness unless it is disturbed. This is precisely what happens when people lose their homes and become refugees. A primary and fundamental lack develops which imperceptibly takes hold of refugees, in addition to whatever other tangible losses they are aware of and they consciously mourn for.

The fundamental sense of home forms part of the core "substratum of identity" which is structured as a "mosaic" and "consists of a great number of smaller elements which together form a coherent whole" (Papadopoulos, 1997b, p. 14). Other elements of this mosaic substratum, in addition to the sense of home, are:

> the fact that we belong to a country, that our country exists, that we belong to a certain language group and we are used to certain sounds, that we belong to a certain geographical landscape and milieu, that we are surrounded by particular types of architectural designs [Papadopoulos, 1997b, p. 14],

and that we live within a space permeated by certain smells and tastes, etc. All these form part of a primary sense of human life and can be considered as a fundamental given. Although this mosaic substratum is mostly unnoticeable, it forms the essence of being human and its function consists of providing us with a primary sense of our humanity and a sense of predictability in the course of our lives. In other words, an intact mosaic substratum creates the conditions to develop the ability and confidence to get on with our lives, with the "sense of predictability of how human beings behave, of what to expect of life, i.e. how to 'read life', . . . [as well as an] awareness that certain human values identify us as humans and govern our interactions" (Papadopoulos, 1997b, p. 14).

Conversely, when this mosaic substratum is disturbed, e.g. when people lose their homes and become refugees, there is bewilderment, a sense of unreality and of an inexplicable gap because people lose something they were not aware they had, in the first place. This bewilderment which, in the context of refugees, is what the "nostalgic disorientation" is about, can create different kinds of reactions (e.g. panic, depression, apathy, suspiciousness, splitting) that can easily be misunderstood and often pathologized not only by the support workers but also by the refugees themselves. It is important to appreciate that disturbance of the mosaic substratum creates a kind of loss that could be characterized as primary, as opposed to all other secondary losses which are of a tangible nature and of which the person is aware.

Thus, the main argument here is that loss of home is not just about the conscious loss of the family home with all its material, sentimental and psychological values, but it is of a much more funda-mental and primary kind and it creates a disturbance (called here "nostalgic disorientation") which is closer to what has been referred to as "ontological insecurity", "existential anxiety" (Giddens, 1991; Laing, 1960), "existential angst", or "dread" (Kierkegaard, 1957; Sartre, 1948). The shared themes of these conditions are a deep sense of a gap, a fissure, a hole, an absence, a lack of confidence in one's own existence and consequently in "reading life" which leads to a particular kind of frozenness (Papadopoulos, 1997b). This frozenness is often erroneously diagnozed as traumatic dissociation (see below). Thus, the primary loss of home creates the overall syndrome of homelessness as opposed to the security of homeness.

The inter-related realms

Additional characteristics of home are connected with its multi-dimensionality. The containing capacity of home is the result of the stability that it provides in terms of continuity within a physical and emotional space where intimate relationships develop (regardless of whether they are positive or negative). The fact that these experiences are held within the context of a home creates a sense of constancy and stability. Conversely, what constitutes home is the space which holds these experiences and the positive sense that is derived from them. The feeling of safety may or may not be added to the primary sense of stability; whether a person experiences home as a safe place is different from the primary experience of stability that a home exists. This means that the continuity itself within a certain felt space contributes to the development of a deep sense of reliability about life. Thus, home is the locus where the physical and metaphorical meanings of containment are closely interlinked to a degree that they become inseparable dimensions of the same entity.

As such, the home, understood as this particular kind of container, impacts on at least three levels: (a) it can enable the growth and development of individuals within the family, (b) it can regulate the network of inter-relationships within its members as well as their conflicts and disturbances, and (c) it can mediate between these two levels and the outer world, the society, the culture, and the socio–political and economic realities. Thus, we could appreciate home as a key construct which interconnects three overlapping realms—the intrapsychic, the interpersonal and the socio–political.

It is within the context of the primary sense of home (not necessarily the actual conscious and ongoing experience of one) as a proto-space that these three realms can inter-relate in a meaningful way. Home, as the physical and psychological locus of the family, represents the most tangible systemic expression of the family interconnections among its members and the society at large. Moreover, it constitutes a primary locus where boundaries and limits are experienced and negotiated. External and internal, public and private, social and personal/family, family and individual, me and you, us and them, familiar and the other, all are dichotomies that the home addresses, thus providing a primary experience of how these are construed and negotiated. Again, the point is that home offers the proto-experience or even more precisely, the proto-sense of these crucial dichotomies and the ways that these can be negotiated, regardless of how successfully this negotiation happens in an individual's life history and experience. The very experience/sense of the existence of these dichotomies matters a great deal, and home is the locus where these are first sensed/experienced. Undoubtedly, the particular way they are experienced will certainly affect the psychological make up of the individual and it will either facilitate a positive personality development or it will leave a negative effect that will mark the individual, possibly for life. However, the fact that the individual had the sense of them within the context of home will form part of that mosaic substratum of one's identity and one's own sense of self.

Although discussing in any detail the theoretical premises of these ideas goes beyond the scope of this chapter, it would suffice to outline some of the basic principles:

1. Bowlby's theory of a "secure base" (1988a,b) provides the foundations for understanding that the continuity of secure bonds between an infant and the parent/s is essential in enabling the child to feel secure and to maintain a balance between seeking proximity and venturing into the unknown outside. The emphasis of this concept, as part of Bowlby's attachment theory, is on the early interpersonal relationships but one has to accept that home is the primary condition which provides the space for such relationships. Moreover, Bowlby referred to concepts very related to home when he argued that "there is a marked tendency for humans, like animals of other species, to remain in a particular and familiar locale and in the company of particular and familiar people" (1973, p. 176). Also, he referred to the idea of "home range" in animals, i.e. the tendency to "spend the whole of their lives within an extremely restricted segment" of "earth's surface" which is "ecologically suitable to them" (1973, p. 177). Finally, Bowlby made the clear distinction between security and safety: "a secure base, however much it may lead someone to feel secure, is no guarantee of safety" (1973, p. 216). In other words, the division between the primary sense of security of home and the secondary sense of safety of home is supported by the Bowlbian theories.

2. Donald Winnicott's ideas on "transitional space" (1982, 1989, 1992) suggest that there is a psychological space in between the

infant and the others which enables the development of intersubjectivity and entrance into the symbolic world. This is a potential space that he referred to as a "third area" which is in between the subject and the object, the inner and the outer, the physical and the psychological, the experiential and symbolic. As such, this idea has attracted attention even by geographers who are interested in the cultural and psychological potentialities of space (Aitken & Herman, 1997). One of Winnicott's posthumous collection of essays was even entitled *Home Is Where We Start From* (1986). Therefore, Winnicott's approach lends support to the importance of home with its double signification which includes the physical and psychological dimensions.

3. Wilfred Bion is particularly known for his astute examination of the very early matrix upon which human experiences are built. It is important to note that at that very early stage of human development, "the proto-mental system ... [is] one [in] which physical and psychological or mental are undifferentiated" (1961, p. 102). It is this proto-fusion that can be usefully applied to the understanding of home as both a physical and psychological entity. For Bion, the group, as an extension of the family and the place where early experiences with mother are contained and repeated, provides the ground and continuity for intense connections (i.e. pairing, dependence, fight–flight). Therefore, it could be argued that the proto-locus of the group (and by extension of all human) experiences is the home. Moreover, Bion's original contributions about the nature of space, place, position in relation to constancy and their role in the origin of the early sense of mind, thought, thinking and feeling (e.g. Bion, 1965) are highly relevant to the idea of home as, what could be called, a proto-space.

4. Daniel Stern's researches into the early infancy processes have suggested that a core sense of self is established as a result of separate networks of repeated experiences becoming integrated. These networks can only take place within a space that ensures that they are indeed repeated. Although he does not refer directly to home or the dimension of space as such, Stern offers a clear account of the early substratum when he clarifies that this "core sense of self" is "normally taken completely for granted

and operates outside of awareness. A crucial term here is "sense of", as distinct from "concept of" or "knowledge of" or "awareness of" a self or other. The emphasis is on the palpable experiential realities of substance, action, sensation, affect, and time. Sense of self is not a cognitive construct. It is an experiential integration" (Stern, 1985, p. 71).

5. Jung's theories of archetypes can provide a useful understanding to the importance of home. Theodore Abt (1983) examined the archetypal roots of man's relation to his milieu and discussed the idea of the archetype of home, equating it to the "archetype of ordered wholeness" (p. 135) which unites both the father and mother archetypes. James Hillman reminded us that for the Romans "*familia* ... meant primarily 'a house and all belonging to it'" (Moore, 1989, p. 202) and thus home and family are inexorably interlinked. The Jungian (and post-Jungian) contribution to our understanding of home emphasizes the ways that the psychological and physical dimensions of the archetype (Jung referred to this as the "psychoid" nature of the archetype) can enable the differentiation of personality from that early archaic potentiality; more specifically, this potentiality can be fostered in the psychological and spatial environment of home. Jung's insights into the inter-definition between intrapsychic and collective dimensions can throw much light onto our understanding of home.

6. Gaston Bachelard's "poetics of space" offers a series of elegiac insights into the meaning of house as a home. Choosing detailed facets and images of the house, he notes that these "house images move in both directions: they are in us as much as we are in them" (Bachelard, 1958, p. xxxvii). This interchange between us, our inner world, our imagination and the house as home and as intimate space is developed most aptly by Bachelard. Home belongs to us and we belong to home. Home creates us and we create home. Approaching space in an imagistic way, which reminds us of Jung, Bachelard shows how the setting is not a passive background but an integral part of the picture and of our own formation.

7. Gedo & Goldberg (1973) provided a hierarchical model of therapeutic interventions which they connected with a model of "progressive and regressive modes of functioning" (p. 73).

Instead of assuming a fixed and static developmental hierarchy, their model was based on the principle that "every individual can traverse the whole gamut of development" (p. 158). For the first two lowest modes of functioning, Gedo & Goldberg proposed that what is required is not the use of interpretation but "the utilization of extensive parametric techniques" (p. 161) which included "the regularity of therapeutic sessions" (p. 161) and "the continued availability of a reliable object, that is, the presence of a real person or even of a reliable setting" (p. 162). This means that the most basic form of therapy for individuals who are functioning at a very basic level (at a given period in their life) is the provision of a safe and reliable environment which is what home represents.

8. The French psychoanalyst Didier Houzel (1996) introduced the term *psychic envelope*

> to denote any structure that performs a boundary function between an inside and an outside and thereby allows the elements contained within it to be included in one and the same whole. The concepts of container, psychic skin, skin ego and psychic envelope are in my view equivalent. Each stresses a different aspect of one and the same entity. [p. 903]

Then, more specifically, Houzel developed the concept of a *family envelope* by which he meant:

> a group structure common to all members of a family, which provides for the succession and differentiation of generations, permits the complementarily of the maternal and paternal roles, guarantees the constitution of the basic and sexual identity of each child and, finally, contains all the members of the family in a single filiation and causes them to share one and the same sense of belonging. [p. 905]

For Houzel, "Belonging and connectedness are properties common to the individual psychic envelope and the family envelope. The kind of belonging concerned here is the belonging to the family group, which may be seen as a space delimited by its envelope" (p. 906). Houzel's ideas about "family envelope" are most relevant in understanding the concept of home as a psychological and psychotherapeutic structure.

This is a sample of theories that can assist in providing a connection between relevant psychological theories and the ideas presented here. In addition to the psychological theories, there is a host of philosophical contributions that can throw illuminating clarity on the development of a wider understanding of home. For example, Sartre distinguished "consciousness of self" as an earlier form of "knowledge of self" (1948) and argued that "distance" created consciousness; although he did not emphasize the spatial dimensions of this distance, it could be argued that it plays a central role. Heidegger's key notion of "heimat" (home, homeness) addresses home in a very similar way as it is done in this chapter. More specifically, Heidegger has the notion of "taken-for-granted-at-homeness" which is destroyed by the "dread" as a condition when we lose the familiarity the world has for us. This dread creates the state of "not-at-home" which he qualifies as "The not-at-home must be grasped as the more original phenomenon in the existential–ontological sense" (Heidegger, 1962, p. 189). This means that without the primary "taken-for-granted-at-homeness" state, a serious disorientation takes place which is of a fundamental existential and ontological nature.

Once we accept that home occupies a pivotal position in our approach to psychological development, then a new epistemology emerges where the sharp boundaries between inner and outer, physical and psychological, individual and collective lose their impermeability. This perspective is strikingly similar to the very dynamics of most therapeutic processes.

Home and stories

Whenever the home is lost, all the organizing and containing functions break wide open and there is a possibility of disintegration at all these three levels: at the individual–personal level; at the family–marital; and at the socio–economic/cultural–political levels. Seen in this context, the homecoming nostalgia acquires additional dimensions and refers to the yearning not only for a return to a physical house but also for a psychological need to re-establish that unique container within which all opposites of all these three levels can be held together.

Thus, thinking about families outside the context of their own home or their condition of homelessness is like thinking of a disembodied principle. Families and homes are inseparable entities. That is why considering the predicament of refugees in the light of their condition of homelessness is central to our understanding of families as potentially containing units. Homelessness is a state that encompasses not only physical and material dimensions but it contains psychological and existential characteristics, as well.

An additional important characteristic of home is that it grounds and provides coherence to the story of families. Each family has a story, its own story which does not necessarily coincide with an external historical account one may give of it. Like all stories, it consists of many more smaller stories of specific facets of the family. This big family narrative accounts for the most important milestones in the history of that particular family and amounts to being the connecting tissue among the various perceptions and feelings family members have about themselves and each other in the context of their history and home space. In Greek *istoria* means both history and story. *Istoria* comes from the verb *istoro* which simply means to tell, to narrate what one has learnt. Thus, the Greek language implies that history is nothing but one narrative, one story as told by a group of people; no illusions of any official objectivity in this definition. History is just another story, another narrative. Nevertheless, the stories families tell about themselves and their tribulations provide them with a sense of coherence and continuity, a way of containing good and bad times, heroes and villains. A coherent story enables family members to make intelligible their own experiences of themselves and of others, it facilitates the negotiation of changes and makes predictable the behaviour and moods of family members. Inevitably, family stories are anchored around the home. Conversely, when the home is taken away from the family, the very condition of homelessness needs to be included in their story and this is not always an easy task.

Therefore, family stories express the interconnection between the personal, family and wider parameters within the context of a sense of home that enables the holding and containing of all opposite and contradictory elements that threaten to disrupt the sense of continuity and predictability. It is this very continuity that is disrupted when people lose their homes and become refugees and it is precisely this dimension that therapeutic care for refugees should foster.

Refugee trauma

Undoubtedly, the predominant way that refugees are viewed today is in terms of the trauma theories. Although there are numerous and varied theories about the related themes of conflict, violence, power, identity, ethnicity, trauma, etc, it seems that there is unanimity about one prevailing belief according to which almost everybody affected by war experiences and political oppression is "traumatized". The term "trauma" has lost its specific psychological meanings and has become synonymous with painful experience; there is a widespread tendency to call "traumatic" most of the disrupting, distressing, disturbing, unsettling, tragic and hurting experiences. Whatever sharpness its psychological definitions were attempting to provide has been lost since the word "trauma" has been appropriated by journalists, politicians, social commentators, and demagogues who have been using it indiscriminately to render respectability to their claims. It sounds more authoritative, respectable and convincing when one says that a person had been "traumatized" by an event, rather than saying that the person had been "shaken" by it. The power of the word "trauma" lies in its widespread (and seeming) intelligibility which, of course, is deceptive because if pressed, those who use it would find it difficult to define what precisely they mean by it.

This means that there is a prevalent and indeed dominant discourse in society which makes people hold the conviction that when a person is exposed to adversity automatically he or she is traumatized. Inevitably, refugees have not escaped this indiscriminate precept and hence there is a particularly strong belief that most refugees have been traumatized.

Moreover, the "refugee trauma" discourse tends to be restrictive because it emphasizes only one segment of the wide spectrum of the refugee experiences. This spectrum could be divided into at least four phases which have been identified as:

— "Anticipation': when people sense the impending danger and try to decide how best to avoid it;

— "Devastating Events': this is the phase of actual violence, when the enemy attacks and destroys, and the refugees flee;
— "Survival': when refugees are safe from danger but live in temporary accommodation and uncertainty; and
— "Adjustment': when refugees try to adjust to a new life in the receiving country (Papadopoulos, 2000b, 2001a,b).

Unmistakably, the "refugee trauma" discourse privileges the phase of "devastating events" and blatantly downplays or even ignores the consequences of the adverse nature of the other phases. For example, Edith Montgomery (1998) in a large study with refugee children from the Middle East found that the most frequent specific types of violence-related events or circumstances were "lived in a refugee camp outside the home country" (92%) and the most important risk indicators for anxiety were again "lived in a refugee camp outside home country". This means that the worst experiences these children had were during the phase of Survival and not during that of Devastating Events. As we know, a large number of refugees may not have even experienced that phase at all, fleeing without having any direct violent contact with the enemy. Yet, the tyrannical nature of the "refugee trauma" discourse induces both refugees and workers to veer towards that direction, masking the painful impact of all the other phases.

Trauma

The literature on the nature, aetiology, diagnosis, socio–political parameters of trauma, especially with reference to refugee trauma, is enormous and the debates endless (e.g. Abramson, 2000; Ager, 1999; Arroyo & Eth, 1996; Bagilishya, 2000; Bentovim, 1992; Bertrand, 1998; Bloom, 1997; Bracken & Petty, 1998; Brunner, 2000; Caruth, 1996; De Jong & Clarke, 1996; Eisenbruch, 1991; Friedman & Jaranson, 1992; Gorman, 2000; Herman, 1992; Joseph & Yule, 1997; Kalsched, 1996; Klain, 1992; Kristal-Andersson, 2000; LaCapra, 2000; Lebowitz & Newman, 1996; Marsella, 1992; Marsella et al., 1996; J. R. Montgomery, 1998; Muecke, 1992; O'Brien, 1998; Papadopoulos, 2001a,b; Rechtman, 2000; Shephard, 2000; Summerfield, 1999a, 2001; Tedeschi & Calhoun, 1995; van der Veer, 1994;

Woodcock, 1994, 2001; Yehuda & McFarlane; Young, 1997; Yule, 1999; Zarowsky, 2000; Zarowsky & Pedersen, 2000; Zur, 1996). Is it then at all possible to attempt to address anything about truama afresh? What is trauma and how can we understand its connection with refugees? First of all, trauma, in Greek, means wound, injury and it comes from the verb *titrosko*—to pierce. However, in a recent etymological investigation (Papadopoulos, 2000b, 2001a,b) it was found that the root verb is *teiro* "to rub" and, in this context, in ancient Greek it has two meanings: to rub in and to rub off, to rub away. Thus, according to the original definition, trauma is the mark left on a person as a result of something being rubbed onto him or her. Then, depending on the way that the rubbing took place there are two different outcomes. More specifically, when a powerful and intense experience is rubbed in or onto a person, the "trauma" could be either an injury (rubbed in) or a new life, where the person can start with a clean slate and with the previous priorities erased (rubbed off).

The first meaning of trauma is well known and it is the one privileged by the "refugee trauma" discourse; although *prima faciae* the second one may appear puzzling, it is not unfamiliar to those who work with refugees. The "rubbing off, away" meaning of trauma refers to the not uncommon reaction people also have following a difficult and intense experience, when they realize that, despite the excruciating pain, disorientation, disruption, etc, their lives were also marked by a renewed sense of priorities and meaning. Needless to say, the "refugee trauma" discourse creates no space for any indication of the second meaning to emerge. Perforce, this imperceptible skewing leaves trauma firmly located within pathological parameters.

Left within an exclusively pathological context, trauma creates further concerns. Essentially, trauma, according to the "refugee trauma" discourse, is a linear concept which implies a clear causal–reductive relationship between external events and intrapsychic consequences. As such, it ignores systemic complexities such as the relational nature of the events' impact among family, community and ethnic group members, as well as the effects of the wider societal discourses which colour the meaning, emphasis and quality of events and experiences. Ironically, as trauma tends to polarize positions and reduce complexities to simplistic formulae within individuals and groups, so does the refugee-trauma discourse impose a simplistic connection between the events and psychological experience.

This is an important consideration which should mobilize our epistemological awareness to discern the various discourses that get intermingled around this most delicate issue. As argued elsewhere (Papadopoulos, 1998; Papadopoulos & Hildebrand, 1997), under the pressure of the unbearable pain and multiplicity of losses in these circumstances, we tend to confuse at least three sets of discourses: moral and ethical, clinical and pathological, with socio–political and historical ones. The usual result is that we tend to confuse the justified abhorrence of the atrocities (which are considered "the cause" of the trauma) by pathologizing the very persons who survived them. However paradoxical this may be, this is usually the case. In our effort to express our justified condemnation of the individuals, groups and policies that lead to political oppression and crimes against humanity, we offer as "proof" the fact that people have been "traumatized" by these despicable actions. In doing so, we ignore all psychological considerations of how people process experiences and, unwittingly, we end up doing violence to the very people we want to help. Thus, we tend to psychologise political dimensions and pathologize both evil actions as well as human suffering (Papadopoulos, 1997b, 1998, 2000a, in press, 2002c).

This argument should not give the erroneous impression that the refugee suffering is either ignored, underestimated or even idealized. On the contrary, once we locate it in the context of clearly delineated but interacting systems, we can proceed in a more prudent way to address the refugee predicament.

PTSD and "early aggressive phantasies"

The idea of refugee trauma is based on a relatively recent new understanding of trauma. Following its psychoanalytic debut in the psychological literature, trauma was losing the centrality of its importance when the American Psychiatric Association included the category of Post Traumatic Stress Disorder (PTSD) in its *Diagnostic and Statistical Manual* in 1980. It has been argued that the revival of trauma theory was due to three factors: (a) the aftermath of the Vietnam war; (b) the increasing awareness of the prevalence of child sexual abuse; and (c) the concurrent attack on Freud's abandonment of the seductive theory (Papadopoulos, 2002c). There is no doubt that the PTSD diagnostic category has enabled the identification of a distinct syndrome which was previously ignored. One of the main arguments for its introduction has been that had the knowledge of PTSD existed during the World War I, many soldiers who were executed for cowardice or desertion would have been spared and, moreover, helped with their traumatic reactions, instead.

Essentially, PTSD is a medical concept because it focuses on the symptoms of one individual; moreover, these symptoms are a mixture of psychological and somatic reactions. As such, PTSD neglects the collective parameters of the experience as well as the wider socio–political context within which the stressor factors have been produced. Much has been written about the advantages and disadvantages of this category as well as the limitations of its applicability cross-culturally (e.g. Bracken & Petty, 1998; Eisenbruch, 1991; Friedman & Jaranson, 1992; Marsella et al., 1996; Zarowsky & Pedersen, 2000). One of the main dilemmas facing clinicians working with traumatized individuals as a result of political oppression and violence is that the psychological reactions are part of a wider response to these socio–political events and taking the pathological-sounding symptoms out of their context we may distort the unique position individuals adopt in relation to these violations. Moreover, even from a solely psychological angle, traumatic responses do not always need to be classified as psychiatric "disorders" (which is what the PTSD stands for). For example, Joseph et al. (1997) developed a perspective within which they viewed the PTSD symptoms not as exclusively pathological but as covering a continuum ranging from normal adaptation to pathological conditions.

Regardless of its justified critiques, what should not be forgotten is that PTSD is a useful category and still serves a useful purpose in identifying acute reactions that require specialist attention. However, regardless of how PTSD is defined, it remains a psychiatric category based on the reactions to external events whose socio–political nature is ignored.

Moreover, by placing the emphasis on the external reality, PTSD fails to account for the intrapsychic factor. In other words, the field of psychological and psychiatric treatment to people suffering from political violence and oppression seems to be polarized between two extremes: on the one hand, there is the school of thought (where PTSD seems to belong) according to which the experienced trauma is considered to be a response to external events and, on the other hand, there is the (predominantly psychoanalytic) approach which emphasizes the intrapsychic dynamics and early personal history without having a coherent way of incorporating the external factors (e.g. the phases of the refugee trauma, outlined above) in their theory.

Martha Bragin has recently developed a new approach which attempts to combine both perspectives. In her doctoral dissertation at the University of New York (2001), she proposed that the persistence of traumatic reactions well after the external events occurred could be due to the fact that these events reactivate repressed early aggressive phantasies. Based on the Kleinian view of early aggressive phantasy, she argues that:

> Exposure to extreme violence, rather than feeling overwhelmingly foreign, feels frighteningly familiar to survivors. This sense of familiarity is the result of an unconscious awareness of similar material in phantasy early in life. Sights of death and dismemberment in particular, and scenarios of sadism and torture as well, represent enactments in the real world of the early aggressive phantasy that, according to Klein, is universal in human development (1927, 1928). It is repressed, however, by the end of the first year of life. [Bragin, 2001, p. 26]

By combining the early infantile phantasy with current external events, Bragin attempts to integrate both approaches. Moreover, according to the original Kleinian views, these phantasies are not necessarily pathological as such—they are part of normal human development and therefore, the traumatic reactions do not need to be pathologized.

Medical traumatology, frozenness and storied community

Returning to the idea of trauma as "wound", it may be useful to ponder on an important recent development in medical traumatology.

Medical specialists have become aware of the puzzle that if left unattended and in cold conditions, severely traumatized individuals did not bleed to death as previously expected. This phenomenon was particularly evident during the war in the Falkland islands when soldiers with multiple and severe wounds were left alone for a long time in the cold. Despite predictions, the death rate of these soldiers was unexpectedly low, and after much research it was found that the cold conditions enabled the body to develop its own self-healing mechanisms. This means that our impulse to wrap up a wounded person paradoxically prevents the body from attending to the trauma by activating its own self-healing mechanisms. This finding has radicalized the field of medical traumatology and the new approach attempts to facilitate rather than block the organism's response by, *inter alia*, introducing measured hypothermia.

This development should be most instructive and indeed inspirational for therapists dealing with psychological trauma, too. It could be argued that it is important to position ourselves as therapists in a specific way which enables us to be aware of both the pain, disorientation and vulnerability of refugees as well as of their inherent resilience as individuals, as families, as groups and as communities. It is only through this re-positioning that we can facilitate the activation of self-healing mechanisms. Thus, by containing both potentialities implied by the dual definition of trauma (as wound and as an opportunity for a fresh start in life) we can empower the survivors to facilitate their own healing. If we fail to do this, inevitably we will lock the refugees in pathological positions with dire consequences.

The hypothermia image could have additional meaning for and application in working with refugees. Under conditions of deprivation, and with a multiplicity of losses, individuals, families and communities seem to "freeze up" and the repertoire of their feeling, perceiving and functioning becomes restricted. This is the "frozenness" referred to in connection with the "nostalgic disorientation" above; externally, it could have all the symptoms of a dissociative state and, in a sense, it is one. However, on closer examination, it could be discerned that it is more the result of the primary loss of home rather than of the long list of the secondary ad tangible losses.

This state of frozenness (Papadopoulos, 1997a) can be understood either as a pathological condition and consequently treated as such, or it can be appreciated as a temporary, emergency and indeed an appropriate response that an individual, family or community resorts to in order to ensure survival. In other words, we can either perceive it as an abnormal reaction or as a normal reaction to abnormal circumstances. In the state of frozenness, an individual, family and community limit their activities to the bare essentials and conserve energy which helps them develop a reflective and meditative stance. Moreover, this psychological hypothermia can limit the damage done and also activate the self-healing mechanisms. This temporary withdrawal can provide unique vantage points from where to review and reassess their lives, their past, present and future; it may also assist them by allowing them to digest the impact of their losses, by creating the respectful stance to mourn the dead, by enabling them to regroup and direct their energy more appropriately. All this activity usually happens in an unnoticeable way, if the right conditions and circumstances can contain the disruptive potential of the primary loss of home. In effect, all this imperceptible work could be understood as a reworking of their own life and community stories. However, if support workers and other therapists (or the refugees themselves) were to panic and see this important phase only as an unhelpful and indeed pathological disorientation rather than an expression of the "nostalgic disorientation", the opportunity for re-orientation is then likely to be lost. Instead, everybody involved (refugees and helpers) would seek impulsively the comfort of covering the pain up with the blanket of active professional help, thus blocking the activation of self-healing processes.

Within the repertoire of every community there are narratives of how the sanctioned space for this kind of frozenness can be developed and maintained as well as how it can enable healing and further growth whilst minimizing damage. Therefore, therapists could have the additional task of enabling such stories to emerge and flourish instead of imposing our own psychological theories. Enabling the families and communities to re-member their dismembered stories could restore the self-healing of families and communities, thus transforming them from homeless communities to "storied communities" with all the resultant self-therapeutic dynamism (Papadopoulos, 1999b). Without masking the negative and disturbing consequences of homelessness, communities can also reconnect around stories and community narratives of overcoming adversity. Individuals, families and communities can restructure themselves and their inter-relationships, they can rebuild old and construct new relationships in sharing narratives of pain and resilience. In short, they can recreate the primary conditions of home.

All systems have a dual need for both *stability* and *change* and if therapists were to only keep attempting impulsively to change everything that does not conform to our own theoretical models of normality, we are likely to contribute to the further destabilization of the system. Respecting the positive potentiality of therapeutic frozenness can strengthen the stability of a system, thus balancing out and counteracting the enormity of changes that refugeedom has produced.

Frozenness does not imply pathological traumatic dissociation, although certain functions, feelings and connections may temporarily be suspended as part of the emergency phase that requires concentration on the maintenance of a limited range of vital functions. Conserving resources and lowering the level of overall functioning would indeed be an appropriate response. However, if the refugees themselves or their workers/therapists do not appreciate this positive function of frozenness, a pathological connotation will be offered instead. This specific kind of frozenness does not imply paralytic passivity, at least on the therapists' part. Instead, it can promote the stance of "therapeutic witnessing" (Papadopoulos, 1997b, 1998, 1999a), as opposed to the active attempt to change things. This stance has been found to be particularly valuable in these circumstances (Blackwell, 1997; Papadopoulos, 1997a,b) because it enables and empowers individuals, families and communities to re-story and restore themselves by reconnecting with their totality rather than focusing exclusively on the devastating impact of secondary losses.

Moreover, "therapeutic witnessing" can create the appropriate warmth that can rekindle the process of "thawing". "Thawing [in this context, as well as in general] is a delicate process which may damage the frozen item if not used appropriately" (Papadopoulos, 1997, p. 15). The mutuality of this kind of witnessing can re-member the images of home along with their complex multidimensional interconnections. This is a direct opposite process to the sterile polarization and oversimplification which is created by the condition of homelessness and the linearity of trauma. In the process of thawing, it is possible for refugees to acknowledge not only the regressive tendencies of nostalgic disorientation but also their progressive and prospective direction and value. Homecoming then is not only about the physical return back to their geographical homes but also the reconnection with all the complexity of the dimensions, layers, directions and everything else that home, in its primary sense, can provide. Thus, by respecting the positive potentiality of the temporary frozenness, through re-storying which is enabled by the therapeutic witnessing, refugees can reconnect with and develop further the richness that the entire ecology of the primary process of homeness can offer.

Other refugee perspectives

As emphasized repeatedly, the only criterion that defines refugees is the external fact that they have lost their homes. Therefore, their very identification and definition as refugees is an undeniable external and historical fact. However, the very term refugee has so many connotations (from psychological to political) that refugees inherit a host of other characteristics that they are not always aware of. This can be expressed succinctly in discerning two main perspectives (Papadopoulos, 2001a): the "essentialist" perspective reminds us that refugees have sustained a multiplicity of actual losses and they have been exposed to many painful situations; this perspective helps us realize the complexity and the multidimensional nature of the refugee situation—regardless of whether they have any psychological needs, refugees definitely have financial, medical, educational, social and numerous other concrete needs that should not be underestimated. In addition, a "constructivist" perspective focuses on the ways that refugees define themselves, their needs and their very own experiences in the context of the wider socio–political constructs. Moreover, the constructivist perspective assists us in appreciating the wide range of perceptions, feelings, attitudes that others (including aid and support workers, therapists and administrators) have about refugees. In addition, each group of refugees at each given time in each receiving country is faced with different sets of feelings by the local population depending on the wider socio–political contexts, interests, and media coverage. This perspective emphasizes the multifaceted influences that shape the refugee experience; how they feel they are experienced and how they experience themselves.

Against this background, it would be useful to keep in mind the following:

— As being a refugee is not a pathological condition, what is the therapists' *entitlement*? How should therapists position them- selves in relation to them, to their difficulties and to the network of other professionals? Can we intervene if not asked to do so? How can we respond to their undeniable suffering without pathologizing it? How can we appreciate their predicament without psychologizing its political dimensions? Although there are no clear and general recipes to these answers, bearing them in mind can allow us to create appropriate parameters for our work (Papadopoulos, 1999a).

— Relationships within refugee families undergo radical transfor- mation and role reversals are not uncommon. For example, as children usually assimilate faster than their parents, they acquire new responsibilities (even looking after their parents); mothers tend to attain new authority due to their involvement with their children (at school and in the neighbourhood) and fathers seem to become more isolated as they lose their traditional position— they become more vulnerable especially without the authority of the employment status they had in their home country (Papadopoulos, 1999a; Papadopoulos & Hildebrand, 1997). Therapists cannot afford to ignore these radical changes of roles and relationships in the families; these changes produce confused images of home and contribute to deepening the confusion of the primary loss of home.

— It is usually considered that refugee families are torn between two "oppositional discourses" with regard to their loyalty and overall orientation (Papadopoulos & Hildebrand, 1997). On the one hand, they wish to remain loyal to the culture, language, traditions of their home country and to honour the past but, on the other hand, they want to grasp the opportunities open to them in the receiving country and to build the best possible future in their new home. Moreover, this conflict is often perceived as being exhibited between the age divide in the family, with the older generation holding on to the past whilst the new generation races forth, accepting the new life and being scornful of the ways of the old country. Research has shown that this view is not entirely true and the situation is more complex than that: "far from having detrimental effects, the oppositional discourses may enrich and assist families to live more creatively" (Papadopoulos & Hildebrand, 1997, pp. 232–233). Also, the oppositionality does not follow rigidly the age divide. More specifically, it was found that the family as a system seems to assign roles to family members, almost arbitrarily, so that at every given time there is a relative balance between both sides. Thus, although grandparents by and large are the holders of the traditional values and customs of their home country at the same time they were found to do their utmost to assist their grandchildren to do well and make the best of the opportunities in their new country. "Grandchildren were also not exclusively oriented towards their new world in the UK but had moments when they privileged their pre-refugee world". For example, "a teenage girl, although she seemed preoccupied with fitting in with her school friends in appearance, mannerisms, music preferences etc, also spent time with her grandmother learning to cook ... specialities" from their home country (Papadopoulos & Hildebrand, 1997, p. 227). This means that it is possible to avoid following stereotyped perceptions and enable refugee families achieve creative ways of interacting.

— One of the most difficult dynamics in working with refugees is the closed system of victim–saviour that refugees and therapists can easily co-construct. Essentially, if the refugee is pathologized and seen exclusively as just a victim, invariably the therapist is likely to occupy the saviour role. However, this system is not limited to the dyad of victim–saviour because saviours do not save victims without an attempt to protect them from their violators. Thus, the triangle of victim–saviour–violator tends to keep perpetuating itself creating endless variations with different people in the same roles. The most common variation is for the:

> victim–saviour couple to keep on producing increasingly more enemies that they will need to defend themselves against, such

as the managers of the therapists' services and other individuals and bodies that do not offer the kind of unconditional support that the couple expects and demands. [Papadopoulos, 2001, p. 8]

"Something you somehow haven't to deserve"

In his poem *The death of the hired man* Robert Frost has a character asking for a definition of "what you mean by home". The answer comes as follows:

Home is the place where, when you have to go there,
They have to take you in.

I should have called it
Something you somehow haven't to deserve. [Frost, 1955, p. 38]

This awkward sounding sentence conveys most expressively and movingly the essence of home as a primary condition where one's presence and entitlement are taken for granted. Unquestionably, one does not have to earn the right to be at home. One should not be required to achieve anything to gain the right to be at home. Home is where one is.

Yet, refugees have to struggle to regain their homes. Their struggle is arduous and lengthy at many levels: at a political level with various governments and organizations to enable their repatriation, administratively and legally in the receiving country with various authorities in order to gain their rights, psychologically with themselves to keep in a fit state to make sound decisions and choices. The pain and nostalgic disorientation are considerable and the resultant confusion creates pressure on refugees and on all those who work with them to simplify the multifaceted and multidimensional complexity of being a refugee and to focus on tangible goals. This is a necessity and it needs to be done; however, if this is all that is done and if the pain and complexity are abandoned then there is a danger that the primary level of disorientation is not addressed. Any intervention which does not take on board the positive potentiality of the frozenness of the nostalgic disorientation is likely to adversely affect the activation of resilience and self-healing mechanisms in individuals, families and communities.

Trauma is not just an intrapsychic condition which is created in a linear and causal-reductive way by external violent events. It is also a social construction and it fits within wider social constructs which also permeate the function and structures of our mental health services that are set to address the refugee difficulties. This means that certain types of service provision and referring networks may also perpetuate pathologized versions of the refugee trauma discourse. Unless the primary and indeed archetypal nature of the homecoming process is included in the conceptualization, planning and implementation of such interventions, the service provision is likely to be skewed towards pathologizing models of trauma. In other words, what is important to emphasize is the inclusion of home as an important psychological and psychotherapeutic category (and not just as an epiphenomenon) in our therapeutic care for refugees. There is plenty of evidence in the existing psychological theories to enable us to develop this idea further.

Ultimately, human suffering is not always synonymous with psychological trauma and discerning the delicate balance between therapeutic intervention and therapeutic witnessing is not easy. If the homecoming pursuit is not only retrospective but also prospective, then therapeutic care for refugees has the potentiality of helping them to gain much more than they already deserve.

Note

1. This chapter includes modified sections from the article "Refugees, therapists and trauma: systemic reflections" by Renos K. Papadopoulos which was published in the special issue on "Refugees" (edited by Gill Gorell Barnes and Renos Papadopoulos) of the "CONTEXT" (the publication of the British Association for Family Therapy), Number 54, April 2001.

CHAPTER TWO

Misconceiving refugees?

Peter Loizos

Introduction

Serious students of refugees have warned us of the difficulties which attach to the very word "refugee". Zetter (1991) discussed several problems. First, that refugee is not a simple universal idea (such as, a one-legged man), but the outcome of sometimes arbitrary political or administrative decisions. Secondly, refugees often resist and resent the labels and policies of those who seek to help them. Thirdly, there are too many variations in "types" of forced migrants for the term refugee to be more than suggestive: some are displaced within the state where they are citizens but are not granted the status of refugees in international law, no matter how much they have suffered; others are forced out of their state of origin and are dependent on international quotas to find a new state to live in. The degrees of compulsion are elastic, from the economically discontented to those who fled in fear of their lives. Zetter's last point is that because there is a highly developed world of public policy with NGOs, governments, and intergovernmental agencies all involved, the question of who is and who is not defined—bureaucratically "labelled"—as a refugee is a matter of entitlements, or their denial; this is one reason for the "ambivalent and disjunctive responses which refugees frequently display towards assistance programmes" (Zetter, 1991, p. 41).

More recently, a philosopher used the example of "a woman refugee" to illustrate difficulties which arise when we slip without awareness from one kind of statement to another. That a woman had been forced to migrate from a war zone in fear of her life or assault would be a straightforward fact about a person, as objective as her height, or the colour of her eyes, and it would be straightforward to say that she had become a refugee. But there is also the social classification of a kind or category of people as "women refugees" which

> is the product of social events, of legislation, of social workers, of activists, of lawyers and the activities of the women involved. This kind of person, as a specific **kind** of person, is socially constructed. Or simply: the **idea** of the woman refugee is constructed. [Hacking, 1999, pp. 9–10]

It is this constructed image which may also lead to a stereotype of the refugee, and one which this essay is concerned to question.

I am approaching the understanding of refugees from the perspective of social anthropology, a discipline which seeks to see the individual as part of an encompassing social system which operates through institutional sub-systems such as kinship and marriage, religion, politics, and economics.

While the classical emphases of anthropology were upon the social system as a steady-state "going concern", more recent approaches have looked at change, conflict, upheaval, and disruption, as normal rather than exceptional, and have shifted from viewing individuals not as passive recipients of "socialization" but as active creators of ideas and practices which may exceptionally contribute to major changes in encompassing systems; these often contribute to smaller changes which on a daily basis may be seen as acts of resistance to the pressures of dominant systems. Where the therapist may encounter people who have been brought to a halt by crushing pressures, the anthropologist more often encounters people struggling to make their way through, or around structural constraints. The desperate but determined people who try at great risk to themselves to enter Britain by jumping aboard trains at the entry to the Channel Tunnel are one kind of example.

In a recent paper I argued that refugees may be helpfully understood through the framework of "social capital theory" (Loizos, 2000). In briefest outline, social theorists have long argued that the human infant's long dependency period requires forms of social support, from its birth mother or any appropriate and committed carer, female or male. Speech is learned from others, and the range of skills needed for economic survival are also learned, either in families, peer groups or schools. Social life, and the understanding of reciprocity and exchange as essential features of small group living means that humans are highly adapted as *social* creatures; although individuals can survive alone in extreme situations, few would question the rewards of successful social relationships.

Social capital theory builds upon these assumptions, but takes them further, to argue that there are benefits to having strong social networks, shared values, trust and a commitment to trustworthiness, and access to reliable information. I traced the fortunes of several sets of long-term refugees, arguing that the initial disruption of previous social relations had to be compensated for in two ways—by conserving those long-standing-relations which remained, and by judiciously developing new ones. These findings form the intellectual background to this chapter, as well as insights derived from the study of a community of 1500 people who became refugees in Cyprus in 1974, and whose adaptation to this dislocation has been monitored at intervals since then (Loizos, 1981, 2001).

This chapter discusses five common assumptions about refugees, which could make an appropriate professional relationship with a particular person more difficult. These are that a refugee is usually or necessarily traumatized by the experience of forced migration; that a refugee is a helpless and dependent person; that a refugee is socially isolated; that a refugee will have difficulty in adjusting to life in a new country because of "cultural differences"; and that a refugee needs across-the-board support.

The fallacy of inevitable trauma

Common sense and empathy suggest that to leave home, livelihood, familiar places and persons at short notice in fear of one's life is deeply upsetting, and initially disorienting. A temporary state of shock is likely, and depending on many other circumstances, people may remain distressed and incapacitated by these experiences and their implications for months, and even years. But such experiences do not necessarily make a person profoundly incapacitated, psychologically deeply wounded, because the person in question may have felt in conscious control of the way they escaped from a threatening situation. They may have planned their exit slowly and thoughtfully. Some of the people who have been accepted into Britain as refugees or asylum seekers may have decided to leave their country of origin deliberately, over a period of months, in the face of mounting political difficulties. Had they remained where they were they might have suffered physical danger, imprisonment or loss of livelihood, so there is no need to doubt the legitimacy of their claims to have been *forced* to migrate. Some of the Kurdish refugees in Britain may have left Turkey, where a fifteen year civil war raged in the South East of the country, in such a deliberate state of mind. Certainly, many "Boat People" left Vietnam after much careful planning (Knudsen, 1988).

There are many accounts of people escaping from conflict zones experiencing great deprivation and fear on their way to safer places, and some will have witnessed or experienced violence. But people have capacities to put such experiences into a framework of meaning in their attempts to move forward in life, and only a minority of people who have had experiences of forced migration will be psychologically disabled by them. Only this minority will definitely need specialist assistance (Summerfield, 1999b). However, to assume that all or most refugees are suffering from a "wound which will not heal" and that they need specialist support, is to underestimate the capacity of people to successfully heal themselves, or to gain the support they need from those who lived through similar events. I would *not* include in this category of self-healing in a social context those who have experienced rape, or who have had their loved ones killed or maimed. Mazower (1993) described a woman who had survived a massacre in the Greek civil war, in which a number of her children were killed. What could self-healing, social consolation or, indeed, therapy offer in the face of such losses? Garland (1998) suggested that in such cases people cannot be expected to "get over" such profound damage. At most, they may manage to get on with their lives. We may note here that in recent years individuals who have lost a loved person have made the main theme of the rest of their lives a project in the name and memory of the lost person, which aims to prevent such harm befalling others. The Suzy Lamplugh Trust, named after a young woman who was abducted while showing a property to an apparently *bone fide* client, was founded by her mother in order to improve the safety of other young people in similar professional fields, exposed to similar risks. It is an ability to take and make meaning from an unbearable loss which has been noted by Summerfield (1999) as a protective factor which sustains refugees who are also political activists.

To say that an assumption of "trauma" may be an inappropriate lens through which to view a refugee is not to suggest that a person can walk free and unaffected from an experience of forced migration. The memories of flight, the nostalgia for familiar places no longer accessible, and a sense of injustice because such an exit became necessary will in all probability remain with a refugee for many years, perhaps for life. But such memories and attitudes do not add up to trauma or functional incapacity, and it is unhelpful to a refugee to be handicapped with such an assumption: it foregrounds an assumed disability, and puts into the background, the capacities and abilities the individual refugee may possess (Papadopoulos, 1999b, 2001a).

For a number of reasons, it is not possible to say what proportion of refugees have, or have not, been exposed to decisively traumatic events. The crucial theoretical point is this: flight from danger does not in itself traumatize. It is additional experiences—suffering violence and/or witnessing violence—which do the lasting damage. If there is room for doubt, it is better to keep an open mind than to assume "trauma".

The helpless refugee?

When television and news photographers show images of refugees, they are very often of people in flight, or huddled in a state of terror, clinging to each other, dirty, unkempt, tired, probably hungry and thirsty. The long columns of refugees who walked out of Kosovo will still be present in the memories of many of us from television news broadcasts. Almost identical images exist from columns of refugees during World War Two. The reasons media use these stereotypes are beyond the scope of this article (Wright, 2000; Papadopoulos & Hildebrand, 1997) but may as Wright has suggested be partly rooted in the familiar symbols of Christian religious paintings, Biblical stories of Jewish exile and wanderings, and such images as Mary and Joseph seeking shelter in Bethlehem, or fleeing with infant Jesus from Herod's persecution. Wright shows how images from Renaissance painting have been re-packed by modern poster designers, as have powerful "original" images of distress first captured by realist photographers. Once a powerful image has been discovered it is frequently re-used so that it may become persuasive. If we have been deeply but unconsciously influenced by such imaging traditions, we may not be fully in control of our "default" assumptions about the refugee as a *helpless* person. To need to flee implies a temporary lack of power to resist the forces of destruction or persecution. To become a refugee is very often to be temporarily destitute by loss of property, income and the opportunity to earn. But there is no need for a short-term disadvantage to be translated into a loss of a more destructive kind. It is said that Mao Tse-Tung, the Chinese communist leader was once asked why he was not worried about the Chinese birth rate, and the problem of "millions of extra mouths to feed". He replied, "Fortunately, every mouth comes with a pair of hands". This applies to refugees too.

The key point is this: refugees will have skills and capacities from their pre-flight lives, and the experience of flight does not normally extinguish these. Flight does not de-skill people, and exile does not entail a memory-wipe. Nor does temporary disorientation remove the power to analyse a new situation, and make relevant decisions about it. The move from the pre-flight situation to a new one may involve all kinds of difficulties, such as periods in detention or reception centres, or waiting for the outcome of immigration decisions and rights to benefits. Such a transitional period may well be confusing and difficult for the new refugee, particularly if they lack appropriate language skills, or have come from a secluded life, or a rural community. But temporary confusion or upset does not to render a person helpless in the medium- to long-term.

A key question to ask when trying to assess a person w
taken refuge is this: is this person temporarily unable to us
varied skills, because of the constraints they are currently forc
live under? The truly helpless and necessarily dependent persc
rare, and is usually the result of old age, physical illness and severe
mental incapacity. Refugees are not usually helpless. Knudsen
describes refugees from Vietnam interned in a transit camp in
Bataan, Philippines. After dramatic, difficult and dangerous sea-
voyages, within a few weeks of arrival and confinement in the
camp, one family had taken over a small bakery business from other
refugees who were about to leave the camp (Knudsen, 1988, pp. 54–
55) and another family took over a small food and drinks shop.
They simply could not wait to start earning their own livings.

There is clearly a character difference which helps make one
person size up a situation very quickly, and act decisively, where
another will adopt a more "wait-and-see" approach. When study-
ing people in Cyprus who had recently been forcibly dislocated, I
noted a few who decided within a few weeks of initial expulsion
that they would not be returning to their houses, farms and shops,
and started trading, or wage-working straight away, while others
waited twelve months or more before being emotionally prepared
to commit their energies to "something new". So, in an early period
of transition, and major uncertainty, a normally active and decisive
person may temporarily be restless, indecisive, and apathetic. But
during such a phase of *coming to terms* with the reality of
dislocation, there may be a good deal of active mental work going
on, in which issues are thought through, capacities and goals re-
assessed, and plans made to start towards economic activity.
Ordinarily, active people become frustrated by waiting too long
without being engaged in rewarding work.

The procedures for assessing the claims of persons seeking to
remain in Britain as refugees or asylum-seekers are often protracted,
resulting in months in detention or reception centres, without
employment. The experience of being unable to work often leads to
depression. In this way, then, a person with no history of depression
may be made depressed by the steps required to make an important
life change. But it is more an outcome of an administrative process
than an incapacity rooted in the experience of flight. In countries
and contexts where refugees are allowed to start quickly on self-

sustaining work—agriculture or trading for rural African refugees —people seem to be too busy for depression to take hold of them (De Berry, 2000; Bowen, 2000; Kaiser, 1999).

The isolated refugee?

There are people who, by a variety of misfortunes, end up in a strange country where they know no-one, are in contact with no friends, relatives or co-ethnics—in short they embody the proverbial expression "fish out of water". A survivor of a massacre may be in such a plight, as may a labour migrant or asylum seeker, who may have left all friends and relatives a long way away. But many refugees arrive in another country as part of a larger movement of people, and they may have brought family members with them, or may have teamed up with others to make their escape. Labour migrants often arrive following links in a chain of people from their home community who have already migrated, and being assisted by them through guarantees, invitations, job offers or other forms of sponsorship. Refugees may use similar social networks to conventional labour migrants.

It is important to get a sense of the social networks, if any, to which refugees have recourse and to consider the social context they now live in, and how all this relates to the recent past. If a person's previous life has been in a socially rich and dense rural community of plentiful kin and in-laws, then to live on a suburban council estate, among strangers, may be experienced as deprivation. But the situation may also be reversed: refugees from urban contexts, who had been living alone as young professionals, or in small nuclear families, might find the social atmosphere of a reception centre or a council estate oppressive.

In thinking about the social context in which particular refugees find themselves, we must keep in mind modern technological communications media, and their importance in offsetting physical separation. There was a memorable moment during the Kosovo refugee exodus when a man stepped forward to a television journalist, asked if he had a mobile, and on being given it, swiftly punched in a few numbers. Moments later, he handed it back, smiling "I have just learned that my sister is safe in Canada, and she now knows we are safe, too" he announced. The telephone (and the internet) has now been added to letter writing as ways by which people keep in touch in spite of involuntary separation. Additionally, through satellite TV broadcasts downloadable by "dishes" a person in London can watch the evening news broadcast in Ankara, or Kabul. "Isolation" is an idea which needs to be re-examined, handled with care, thought through, and checked against the refugee's actual social reality—their social connectedness to significant others, by virtual as well as face-to-face communication. A person who has no-one to care about *anywhere* is in a profoundly isolated condition. But a person whose loved ones are in another town or another country may be missing these people, but in communication with them, and may be otherwise be socially robust, with local links to other valued people. To think of such a person as "isolated" might be to misunderstand their situation.

Refugee adjustment: a problem of "cultural differences"?

It is easy to assume that because a refugee comes from another country, there will necessarily be what might be termed "difficulties adjusting to British culture". The word "culture" now slips so lightly off our lips that its fuzziness is not readily appreciated. (Bauman, 1996) But "culture" is a loose descriptive word which doesn't *explain* anything.

Consider a small British town with, as yet, few immigrants in it. We cannot easily talk about the "culture" of the town without noting that, whatever it is, culture has to cover: differences of social class; differences of generation—from infants to the elderly; differences of gender; differences of religious affiliation. So, the "culture" of Dorchester would turn out, on close inspection to be a fuzzy phrase which would have to cover a lot of different sub-groups with different, specific outlooks, interests, and life-styles. How much more fuzzy would the phrase "British culture" be? And such distinctions might be equally true of the society from which our sample refugee has come. "Cultural differences" is not a very helpful way of thinking about the difficulties a refugee may be having because the phrase is too vague to tell us very much.

But there are, of course specific language problems, and mismatches between central ideas of incomers as they encounter the dominant society, and such matters are suggested by the term "acculturation" which means "the process by which migrant groups adjust to being in contact with different cultures" (Dona & Berry, 1999, p. 171). This breaks down into issues concerning possible responses to contact with the dominant system (culture, society) which might include assimilation, integration, marginalization, or reactive separation. These authors further argue that such processes are multidimensional, complex, non-linear, and may involve inconsistencies within individuals, and within groups. Too much coherence in the process should not be expected. "Acculturation then becomes a process of negotiation between two systems of belief and behaviour" (Palinkas & Pickwell, 1995, quoted in Dona & Berry, 1999, p. 171).

Let me give an example of the need to get down to something more basic than "cultural differences". A refugee in Britain who has lived here for many years but does not have a good grasp of English can be viewed as experiencing a "cultural" problem. Such a perception is not very helpful. It is better to see language skills as a technical problem, with generational and social class components. English can be learned. Teaching is usually available. But who will find such learning difficult, and who will find it easy? Perhaps, there is an obstacle: Is the refugee in question of an age to learn and motivated to do so? In the early 1950s I worked in the school holidays at a biscuit factory in South London. On the night shift many of my fellow workers were Poles in their fifties and sixties who had come to England during or just after the second world war. They often had professional backgrounds, but Britain had no particular use for Polish generals, Polish lawyers or Polish literature teachers. So these men had taken the only jobs which were available, and did not require proficiency in English. They were not strongly motivated to learn English well. It was "too late" to train for a new career, and who would have paid for this? They felt they had come down in the world, and were doing work which was "beneath them". But their lives and their difficulties are only superficially understandable as "cultural adjustment" problems. In each case, the problems were much more specific to their age, class, and pre-arrival professions (Littlewood & Lipsedge, 1997, p. 65). Younger Poles from humbler origins took jobs as coal miners, or studied and learned more English and made better adjustments. They did not stop being Polish in various respects and being bearers of "Polish culture", but it is easier to become bi-cultural if you are younger. And, while we are thinking about language and culture, Polish and English, there is also the example of Joseph Conrad, a Pole who did not start writing in English until he was forty, and went on to become one of the most distinguished English-language authors of his day. Conrad was not, in any simple sense a refugee, but he was a political exile, and certainly, a labour migrant.

Suppose a woman is a refugee from a rather patriarchal society, where men value themselves more highly than women, and also restrict the social and sexual freedom of their wives, sisters, daughters. Such patriarchal values may be imposed on women by the dominance of men. In such a case, the refugee woman may well not be committed to such values, even though she is influenced by them, and may be seeking a greater personal freedom in Britain than would be open to her living in her father's house in her original home. The point is, that if this woman is socially supported in other ways, her "new life" in England may involve fewer cultural adjustment difficulties, and it may be more a matter of taking advantage of her greater room for manoeuvre as a woman in a more gender-egalitarian society.

To summarize this section, a culture, if it means anything at all, should not be thought of as a kind of straightjacket, something tight and encompassing which limits movements. It wasn't because the Polish generals and lawyers were Poles that they didn't want to learn English. It was because they saw themselves as exiled, and "too late" for a fresh start. If any clothing analogy makes sense, it would be better to think of culture as a cloak, which could be worn in many ways, even taken off when not needed, or pulled tightly around the body when it's cold. It is a cloak of many patches: language, food habits, artistic traditions, bodily modifications and adornments, moral rules, religious allegiances—the list is potentially open to many more additions. Many of these features are adopted or manipulated by individuals, or, to keep the cloak analogy, sit lightly on them, and can be set aside at will. So, refugees are not "prisoners" of their cultural differences, or ours. In comparison with the unclarity implied by "cultural differences", if we say a person is suffering from racist attacks on a sink estate, we say something precise.

Refugees: in need of long-term support?

If someone arrives after a frightening journey, an unsettling period awaiting immigration status decisions from the Home Secretary, an enforced sojourn in a designated town, or a period of enforced residence in a Reception Centre, they may be in need of many kinds of support in order to become economically active and socially independent Shelter, income, job-training, or job-placement, health, schooling for children: "We know that many refugees find jobs in the labour market which do not use their skills and capacities to the full, and which reward them poorly" (Bloch, 1999). There are benefit entitlements, training schemes, and various kinds of social work support available to the refugee with a legal status who makes contact with the right agencies. In additional to what British state and society may offer, there are voluntary sector agencies and groups, and there are ethnic self-help associations for many refugees who enter the UK.

One of the difficulties of bureaucratic systems is their tendency to make very definite rules about what they will offer and to whom and how they will offer it. One example has been the tendency recently for refugees to be given food vouchers for use in shops. The visible use of vouchers means that the refugees are easily identifiable to the sort of people who might harass them, so this system has been widely criticized, and is about to be dropped. It is possible, however, to take a view of refugee needs which allows the refugee himself or herself to have a stronger voice in specifying what forms of assistance they would prefer. It may be that a given refugee needs a less costly assistance package than planners might suppose, but that they need more freedom of action about what kinds of support they can opt for. Perhaps the relationship between society and the new refugee should shift from "Here's how we can help you" to "How would you like us to help you?".

Because of the backwash effects of recent conservative critiques of the welfare state, there is a widespread idea that support to people in need is likely to create "dependence". Therefore, there has been a tendency to keep support to a minimum, both in quantity and duration. Such an approach fails to take note of the fact that most people in most societies wish to make their own way economically, and that self-respect involves being active, earning and doing. New refugees may need major support but usually for a short period of time, only. The likelihood of long-term support is small, and dependence on such support is not for most refugees an attractive option.

Three-dimensional histories?

Among the most appropriate ways to avoid seeing a refugee through the stereotypes just discussed would be to get a good account of their life from the person in question. But here there are difficulties. History, as used in medicine, concentrates on very specific details of illness. Busy General Practitioners and consultants are often concerned to get what they see as the essential facts as quickly as possible, and they have very definite criteria for what is and is not relevant information. This clinical "history" moves at the doctor's pace, on the doctor's terms. But because of the constraints, and the doctor's motives and criteria, it is inevitably a reduction of the patient to the dimensions of age, sex, marital status, occupation, illnesses and treatments (Perring, 1992; Sinclair, 1997). A recent study of mentally ill patients who had been in hospital for many years found that their clinical case-histories described them simply as persons with some symptoms, and detailed the medical treatment that was offered to them. The medical case-histories were highly reductive—they reduced people to "smaller than life" persons, patients-with-problems. The researcher then attempted to build up much more rounded accounts of the person's pre-hospital life, their social networks, skills, interests, hobbies, and to "re-constitute" them from one-dimension flatlander "case-histories" to three-dimensional named people, more complex, more capable, more fully human than hospital records had ever suggested. However, of course, this took many visits, and open-ended exploratory conversations without a clinical agenda.

Psychotherapists believe that they do not operate in this reductive way. However, they too have time-constraints, criteria of relevance, and a clinical focus. If a refugee has reached a therapist because of very real difficulties of an incapacitating nature, such as depressive illness, then the therapist's wish to engage with the factors which have brought the refugee low will be compelling. But if the point of contact is less clinically urgent and severe, and aspects of the case-notes suggest more uncertainty as to the problems the refugee faces, it could be beneficial to adopt a more exploratory approach, which allows the refugee more space to give a more fully rounded account of themselves and their previous life.

It has also been noted (Ager, 1992; Dona & Berry, 1999, pp. 190–191) that some refugees come from backgrounds in which direct question-and-answer procedures are not common, or carry the unwelcome implications of an interrogation by distant authorities; they may be more articulate in situations where they are invited to "tell stories" about themselves at their own speed.

The family cycle

Most people grow up in some form of family, and at some point in life start one of their own. They may in time become grandparents. In many societies, young people are more free to live their own lives, but in many other societies they have major obligations to support younger siblings, or their parents, before thinking much about their own needs. Because having dependants usually gives people a sense of purpose, it is important when thinking about an individual refugee to understand where he or she is at, in terms of obligations to others. Being a parent, having brothers and sisters, having parents, having grandparents are all likely to affect the way a persons thinks about themselves, their life-goals. Those with fewest attachments or obligations may be most vulnerable to transitions from a more rooted life, before flight, to the new as-yet unrooted or uprooted life. And much depends on where the important people are, and what conditions they are living under. If a man or a woman has arrived with young children to care for, their priorities will be apparent to them. If they are regarded as key bread-winners by people far away, the same thing applies, although it might be easier to start drifting in a strange and difficult environment if one does not actually have one's dependants to go home to at the end of the day. Older people, those who have themselves raised families, may feel that they have "done their bit" and be disinclined to become economically active again, particularly if this involves learning a new language, or taking a job which is

beneath one. Gold (1992) described a Soviet Jewish woma
about her mother's frustrations when the three generati
tried to settle in the USA. The grandmother was upset bec
grandchildren were speaking English, not Russian, and she c
communicate with them. But in addition:

> Back home, she was a doctor, she had a career. Here she is just
> another old woman who doesn't know English and she is not ready
> for this role at all. And nobody really needs her right now. [Gold,
> 1992, p. 86]

The same author describes adolescents from refugee families
seeming to develop no social life outside of their families, who tend
to over-protect them in America, just as they did in the rather
different context of the USSR. This over-protection resulted in the
young person being intensely lonely.

To sum up, on the Family Cycle issue, then: to get a proper sense
of who a refugee is and where they are in dealing with their new
situation, it is important to have an informed sense of where they
are in the bio-social cycle of growth, maturation, personal freedom,
courtship, and parenthood, which shapes the lives of most people. If
the individual's sexual preferences mean that parenthood will not
be an easy option, there may nevertheless be other important
constraining obligations, to siblings, parents or grandparents, to
friends and former partners.

Diaspora associations

Immigrants often form associations based on common origins in
villages or towns, in their new country of residence. This is usually
an urban phenomenon. Ethnic minorities may also gather at
particular places of religious worship in a major city, and word
spreads among more scattered members. Such religious rituals
become social gatherings, where information is exchanged, new
relationships formed, and old ones reconfirmed. Political groupings
may also have offices or cafes where members meet, or from where
a newsletter is edited and circulated, notices of forthcoming
meetings posted out. Knowing that these meeting places exist can
be a valuable support for a newly arrived and disoriented person;

and the realization by a reception worker that refugees, like classical immigrants, have the capacity to support each other, is one step towards a more realistic appreciation of their social character. The church, the mosque, the synagogue, the temple are, then, institutions serving several purposes: apart from the comforts of religion, they may act to focus charity for the needy, to provide visits and sympathy to the sick, company for the lonely, and their wider social events may assist young people to meet companions and life partners (Boyarin, 1991; Loizos, 2000; Pattie, 1997).

If the arguments of this article are accepted, it is reasonable to expect a refugee to be a person like one's self, until other evidence appears. That is, a person with a full range of skills, energies, ambitions, a social network, and personal life-goals. Dona & Berry (1999) cite a longtitudinal study by Beiser (1994) of Vietnamese refugees in Canada, and their health problems. After the Vietnamese had spent ten years in Canada, their unemployment levels were below the national average and education achievement was at or above the national norms, and health indicators (anxiety, psychosomatic symptoms, depression) did not reveal heightened problems.

People can always surprise us, confounding our most careful assessments and proposals.

Acknowledgements

I am grateful to the Economic and Social Research Council for funding which supported my earlier research on refugees in Cyprus.

I am grateful to the following colleagues for comments on earlier drafts of this paper, but they do not share responsibility for any errors: Caroline Garland; Renos Papadopoulos.

CHAPTER THREE

The refugee condition: legal and therapeutic dimensions

Judith Farbey

W ho is a refugee? What is the essence of refugee status? In this chapter, I argue that these questions must be answered by reference to legal and not psychological criteria. I am aware that this chapter is in a book addressing the psychotherapeutic care of refugees. However, I believe that analysis of the refugee condition remains incomplete without reference to the legal framework which determines who is and who is not to be recognized as a refugee. Moreover, it is important to examine the role of psychotherapeutic dimensions in the process of determining this status.

Refugees are a disparate group, with multiple forms of past experience and multiple causes of exile from their home communities. They are united only in so far as they have all undergone a legal process and have satisfied certain legal criteria in the United Kingdom. Consequently, refugee status is externally bestowed by the State and does not reflect any shared psychological characteristics or internal pathology. In order to make good this thesis, I begin by considering the legal criteria for establishing refugee status.

Refugee definition

The foundation of modern refugee law is the 1951 Convention relating to the Status of Refugees as amended by the 1967 Protocol relating to the Status of Refugees.[1] The United Kingdom is a signatory to the Convention and, through the Home Office's application of domestic Immigration Rules, must assess all asylum applications according to its provisions.[2] Under Article 1A(2) of the Convention, a refugee is essentially a person who has "well-founded fear of being persecuted for reasons of race, religion, nationality, membership of a particular social group or political opinion".[3] Unless an asylum claimant satisfies each of these elements, she will not be entitled to refugee status.

The first element is a subjective one: "fear". It is subjective because it is assessed by reference to an individual's state of mind. This does not mean that an asylum claimant must demonstrate any particular psychological reaction or syndrome.[4] Rather, it means that she must demonstrate a personal alienation from her country of origin. This personal alienation may be glossed by reference to both prospective and retrospective elements. James Hathaway (whose work has been regularly cited and approved in English courts) highlights the prospective aspect. He casts subjective fear as a refugee's own assessment of future harm:

> In a linguistic context, it is understandable that the reference to "fear" in the Convention definition has led many commentators to assume the relevance of a psychological assessment of the claimant's reaction to conditions in her state of origin. While the word "fear" may imply a form of emotional response, it may also be used to signal an anticipatory appraisal of risk. That is, a person may fear a particular event in the sense that she apprehends that it may occur, yet she may or may not (depending on her personality and emotional makeup) stand in trepidation of it actually taking place. It is clear from an examination of the drafting history of the Convention that the term "fear" was employed to mandate a forward-looking assessment of risk, not to require an examination of the emotional reaction of the claimant. [Hathaway, 1991, p. 66]

This clarification is interesting and most instructive to psycho-therapists. It is an important example of how a term such as fear, which is ordinarily considered to be of psychological nature, does not have psychological import in the legal context.

In addition, alienation may be subject to retrospective assessment because a refugee has already suffered a breakdown of relations between her and her own State. She has fled from her own State as a person who "has been cast adrift" because of her aspirations, beliefs or alliances (Vernant, 1953, p. 5). The motivation for seeking international protection lies in this pre-existing alienation, which triggers departure from country of origin.

In practical terms (and always within the UK context), the Home Office assesses an applicant's subjective fear by evaluating her own statements about her past experiences. The asylum claimant must prove that her motives for leaving her country are grounded in actual experiences generating alienation. If the Home Office does not believe that an asylum claimant is telling the truth about her past experiences, refugee status may be denied on the basis that subjective fear is not established.

The subjective fear must be "well-founded" in that it must be "supported by an objective situation" (UNHCR, 1979, para. 38) in an asylum claimant's home State. Thus, the claimant's own, internal anticipation of risk must be rooted in evidence suggesting that the risk may eventuate. The Home Office will consider whether conditions in the country of origin provide objective justification for an asylum claimant's subjective fear. The question is whether persecution is reasonably likely to materialize. In UNHCR's words:

> The competent authorities that are called upon to determine refugee status are not required to pass judgment on conditions in the applicant's country of origin. The applicant's statements cannot, however, be considered in the abstract, and must be viewed in the context of the relevant background situation ... In general, the applicant's fear should be considered well-founded if he can establish, to a reasonable degree, that his continued stay in his country of origin has become intolerable to him ... or would ... be intolerable if he returned there. [1979, para. 42]

In this respect, the assessment must be wholly prospective. If a person has suffered persecution in the past, but cannot demonstrate that she will suffer persecution in the future, her fear will not be well-founded and she will not be recognized as a refugee. Conversely, a person who has never suffered persecution may be recognized as a refugee because she can demonstrate that she will suffer persecution in the future.

An asylum claimant's fear must be a fear of "persecution". What is persecution? The UNHCR Handbook highlights that there is "no universally accepted definition" (1979, para. 51). A general humanitarian approach requires that the meaning be kept broad and flexible. This approach is well encapsulated by Professor Goodwin-Gill:

> There being no limits to the perverse side of human imagination, little purpose is served by attempting to list all known measures of persecution. Assessments must be made from case to case by taking account, on the one hand, of the notion of individual integrity and human dignity and, on the other hand, of the manner and degree to which they stand to be injured. [Goodwin-Gill, 1996, p. 69]

The English courts, while retaining a high threshold, have been slow to circumscribe the definition. The Court of Appeal has held that persecution "must be at least persistent and serious ill-treatment".[5] As UNHCR and others recognize, threats to life and liberty, as well as other serious violations of human rights, will be treated as persecution (UNHCR, 1979, para. 51). Fear of natural disasters, economic collapse, prosecution and even civil war do not amount to a fear of persecution. Thus, the popular use of the word "refugee" to describe groups of persons displaced as a result of generalized misfortune fails to reflect the impetus of the refugee definition. Refugees are those who are at risk of individualized harm. This does not mean that an entire ethnic or racial group cannot be persecuted. It does mean that a member of the group must demonstrate that she is a member of a targeted group, rather than simply a person caught up in general misfortune by the exigencies of place and time.[6]

Hathaway (1991) regards persecution as the "key definitional criterion in the Convention" (p. 99). The concept of persecution takes us to the heart of the refugee definition, which concerns the relation between individual and State. Persecution is "most appropriately defined as the sustained or systemic failure of state protection in relation to one of the core entitlements which has been recognized by the international community" (p. 112). International human rights norms are a cornerstone of the relationship between individual and State, in that an individual is entitled to look to her own State for protection against human rights violations. If the State is unwilling or unable to bestow this protection, the relationship breaks down and the individual is forced to seek "surrogate protection" (p. 135) in another State. A persecuted individual becomes alienated from her own State: she loses her stake in the community, the stake by which she exercises and vindicates her human rights.

The well-founded fear of persecution must arise from one of the five grounds set down in the Convention: race, religion, nationality, membership of a particular social group or political opinion. Unless an asylum claimant fears persecution "for reasons of" one or more of these Convention grounds, the asylum claim must fail.[7]

The five Convention grounds are widely interpreted so as to include in the class of refugees those who are persecuted because of their civil or political status. Refugees are persons who are persecuted on account of essential characteristics which relate to who an individual is or what she thinks. This approach has recently been adopted by the House of Lords in *Islam v Secretary of State for the Home Department*[8] which approved a passage from the United States' case of *Re Acosta*:[9]

> Each of these grounds describes persecution aimed at an immutable characteristic: a characteristic that either is beyond the power of an individual to change or is so fundamental to individual identity or conscience that it ought not be required to be changed ...

> Refuge is restricted to individuals who are either unable by their own actions, or as a matter of conscience should not be required, to avoid persecution.

In this way, the meaning of a "particular social group" is fleshed out. It is a:

> group of persons all of whom share a common, immutable characteristic. The shared characteristic might be an innate one such as sex, color, or kinship ties, or in some circumstances it might be a shared past experience such as former military leadership or land ownership. The particular kind of group characteristic that will qualify under this construction remains to be determined on a case-by-case basis.[10]

When the State fails to protect against assaults on an individual's immutable characteristics, the relationship between individual and State breaks down, forcing the individual to seek surrogate international protection.

The Convention grounds suggest that the purpose of the Refugee Convention is to grant protection to those who suffer discrimination in the sphere of human rights. The Refugee Convention:

> is concerned not with all cases of persecution, even if they involve denials of human rights, but with persecution which is based on discrimination. And in the context of a human rights instrument, discrimination means making distinctions which principles of fundamental human rights regard as inconsistent with the right of every human being to equal treatment and respect.[11]

The Convention grounds are markers of human dignity: discrimination on a Convention ground is an attack on the dignity which defines us all as human beings.

Thus, a refugee is a person whose essential dignity stands to be harmed by a continued stay in her own State. The essential duty of a State is to foster, not to denigrate, the dignity of individuals within it. Hence, loss of dignity is characteristic of loss of protection owed by the State to an individual. The unprotected individual is forced to re-establish herself in an asylum State.

Determining refugee status

In the United Kingdom, the task of determining whether a person is a refugee lies with the Home Office. Reflecting international best practice, the Home Office determines refugee applications on an individual basis. Each application for refugee status is determined on its own merits according to principles of refugee law. Although Home Office procedures have been subject to several revisions over the past few years, an asylum claimant will in essence submit a written application and also undergo interview by a Home Office official. The asylum claimant has an opportunity to submit supporting documentation, such as medical evidence of past torture or documentation showing past political activity, before a decision is taken on her claim. If a claimant is unsuccessful, she can appeal to an immigration adjudicator who will determine the case afresh. The asylum claimant is free to adduce oral and written evidence. Subject to a number of exceptions, further appeal lies to the Immigration Appeal Tribunal and then, on points of law only, to the Court of Appeal and House of Lords. Under current Home Office practice, if a person is recognized as a refugee, she will be granted indefinite leave to remain in the UK.[12]

As set out above, those recognized as refugees in the UK have undergone an individualized status determination procedure. The determination of refugee status is a "process of ascertaining and evaluating the facts" (UNHCR, 1979, para. 205) within the framework of refugee law. The process triggers duties in both the asylum claimant and the decision-maker. The asylum claimant must co-operate with the fact-finding process and must supply as much information as she can. In return, the decision-maker must ensure that the asylum claimant has an opportunity to present the facts of her case fully and must evaluate both the claimant's subjective fear and the objective elements of the case (UNHCR, 1979, para. 205). When the Home Office determines that a claimant fulfils the criteria for refugee status, it recognizes the claimant as a refugee and grants her leave to remain in the UK. The outcome is recognition, not bestowal, of a status. Refugee status is inherent in those who fulfil the elements of the refugee definition and the decision-maker merely determines and declares that a person has that pre-existing status. As UNHCR (1979, para. 28) puts it, "He does not become a refugee because of recognition, but is recognized because he is a refugee".

Nevertheless, this pre-existing status does not suggest a concomitant pathology. It is a status defined and granted by the process of law. It amounts to a legal classification, not a pathology. It implies no particular way of looking at the world and no particular social or cultural allegiances. Whereas refugees may share certain psychological and psychiatric traits, these arise empirically from factors such as past trauma and loss of homeland, rather than as a result of anything inherent in having the status of refugee. It is society, through its government and law-makers, which classifies a person as a refugee or not—depending on its interpretation of the Refugee Convention.

Forced status

On this basis, I suggest that refugee status is both a forced and an externally defined status. First, a refugee is a person who has departed involuntarily from her country of origin as a result of a breakdown of relations with her State. As elucidated above, she is in effect forced to adopt surrogate relations with a new, asylum State. It is not a matter of choosing a new identity or choosing a new lifestyle in a new society. The desire for a more prosperous or personally rewarding lifestyle is irrelevant. Refugees are forced to accept surrogate protection as a last resort—as the sole way of preserving their dignity as human beings. The condition of refugee is thrust upon them.

Secondly, refugees have submitted to status determination processes and have been deemed to fulfil the refugee definition under the 1951 Refugee Convention. They become subject to a legal classification as a result of which they become eligible to live in the UK. On the one hand, the Refugee Convention is a dynamic instrument—it can be interpreted in an evolutionary way, so as to reflect evolving moral and political values. On the other hand, the criteria set down in the Convention have purely legal meanings and there is no underlying psychological theme. Refugee status is not assumed by any form of identity with a particular condition of exile. It is not assumed by attitude, sentiment or beliefs about exile. It is an unchosen status, bestowed by external application of settled, legal criteria. By providing surrogate protection, an asylum State reaffirms the inherent dignity of an individual whose dignity was previously eroded by her own State. Beyond this general reaffirmation, refugee status says little about an individual's personal identity or her psychological state, whether past, present or future.

Refugees are persons who have suffered from the evil ways of humankind and who are buffeted into seeking international protection. I would thus caution against any framework within which refugees are characterized as anything but ordinary people who have acquired this status involuntarily.

The role of mental health professionals in refugee status determination procedures

The UNHCR Handbook suggests that techniques for examining

refugee claims should be modified in cases where a claimant suffers from "mental or emotional disturbances that impede a normal examination of his case" (1979, para. 207). The Handbook suggests that medical evidence be obtained which should "provide information on the nature and degree of mental illness and should assess the applicant's ability to fulfil the requirements normally expected of an applicant in presenting his case" (1979, para. 208). Immigration adjudicators, as well as the Home Office, are frequently swayed by medical reports which, properly formulated by someone with appropriate expertise, can assist an asylum claimant in proving her case. The main emphasis here is on *psychiatric* reports, because a psychiatrist can express a medical conclusion whether an asylum claimant's current psychiatric symptoms are consistent with her account of the past trauma which caused her to flee her country. Medical conclusions are regarded as more objective and more useful than general psychotherapeutic discourse.

A report from a psychiatrist may function as a "sword" in proving an asylum claimant's case. Psychiatric evidence may corroborate a claimant's testimony, in that a psychiatrist may diagnoze a medical disorder, such as post traumatic stress disorder (PTSD) or depression, and conclude that the particular disorder is consistent with the cause specified by the claimant. Established legal principle is to the effect that psychiatric evidence should not be rejected solely for the reason that it is based on what was related to the psychiatrist by the claimant but may be discounted if the court or decision-maker has other good reason not to believe the underlying facts of the asylum claim.

Psychiatric evidence may also function as a "shield" in rebutting Home Office challenges to an asylum claimant's credibility. It may explain apparent weaknesses in a claimant's testimony, such as inability to give a rational account of past events, inconsistencies in testimony or delay in disclosing material facts. Psychological evidence (as opposed to psychotherapeutic evidence) may also act as a shield—for example in cases where a claimant's asylum testimony appears weak because she suffers from difficulty in concentrating, inability to attend to questions, poor memory or cognitive disability. Thus, there may be circumstances when psychological evidence is appropriate.

There are few circumstances where a psychotherapeutic report is appropriate, save that a psychotherapist or counsellor can testify to the fact that an asylum claimant has undergone counselling and can give some account of whether counselling has led to improvement in the asylum claimant's mental state. Combined with a psychiatric report, this will give the Home Office or the courts a full picture of an asylum claimant's treatment for PTSD or other disorders. Asylum claimants are badly served by counsellors and others who seek to do more and who write reports to the effect that an asylum claimant's current psychological state indicates past trauma connected with the events that led her to become a refugee. These reports will carry little weight with the Home Office or courts and in my view ought to be avoided.

In order for psychiatric or psychological evidence to be useful, the expert must be informed about, and adhere to, her role. The role may be presented to the expert as assisting an asylum claimant to convince the Home Office or a court that an asylum claim is true. It is a well established legal principle that experts give evidence and do not decide the overall issues in a case. A particular expert's opinion on whether a patient is telling the truth remains a personal opinion. It is a matter for the court to decide whether the asylum claimant is telling the truth, using all the tools of the law of evidence and having regard to all the evidence in the case. My experience is that asylum claimants are let down if experts start from the premise that the asylum claimant is telling the truth, rather than assisting the decision-maker to assess credibility (if this is the issue). The Immigration Appeal Tribunal and the higher courts have criticized mental health professionals who purport to comment on whether an asylum claimant is telling the truth. This is a most important point that needs to be remembered by mental health professionals in this field whenever they are involved in writing reports which will be used by the courts. It is also imperative for those who write reports for court proceedings to set out their credentials as fully as possible. In the absence of a full statement of credentials, a court may well refuse to accept that the writer of a report has sufficient expertise to comment.

Ultimately, psychiatric or psychological evidence will be one of several strands in evidence which may cumulatively persuade the Home Office or the courts that a person has well-founded fear of persecution. Different pieces of evidence form different building blocks which form an overall evidential structure. As expressed by the Court of Appeal, the issue whether someone has well-founded fear of persecution on a Convention ground "raises a single composite question" which "should be looked at in the round and all relevant circumstances brought into account" (see note 5, 105). It is an exercise in speculation about future risk to the asylum claimant, but speculation is conditioned by legal principle and legal argument. In this way, the refugee definition has a "content verifiable according to principles of general international law" (Goodwin-Gill, 1996, p. 3) and also our own, domestic body of law as applied and developed in our courts on a continuous basis.

Professor Ronald Dworkin has written that law "aims ... to lay principle over practice to show the best route to a better future, keeping the right faith with the past" (Dworkin, 1986, p. 413). This is vitally true of refugee law. By defining and giving content to the refugee concept, refugee law not only describes who deserves protection but also prescribes that the signatories to the Refugee Convention take principled decisions about the infliction of intolerable suffering on one human being by another.

Notes

1. For the Convention, see United Nations, Treaty Series, vol. 189, p. 137; adopted by a Conference of Plenipotentiaries of the United Nations on 28 July 1951; entered into force on 21 April 1954. For the Protocol, see United Nations, Treaty Series, vol. 606, p. 267; entered into force on 4 October 1967. A useful commentary is contained in UNHCR's Handbook, 1979. The Handbook does not have the status of law, but passages are often cited with approval by the English courts.
2. See especially the Asylum and Immigration Appeals Act 1993, section 2: "Nothing in the immigration rules ... shall lay down any practice which would be contrary to the Convention".
3. Other aspects of Article 1A(2) are beyond the scope of this chapter.
4. It is recognized that "psychological reactions of different individuals may not be the same in identical conditions" (UNHCR, 1979, para. 40).
5. *Ravichandran v Secretary of State for the Home Department* [1996] Imm AR 97, 114.
6. See, for example, the House of Lords' decision in *Adan v Secretary of State for the Home Department* [1998] INLR 325.

7. In the UK there is a parallel regime for dealing with those who cannot fulfil the refugee criteria but who claim that expulsion from the UK would breach their rights under the European Convention on Human Rights. The paradigm case is a person who will face torture on expulsion but who cannot prove that the torture will take place on a Convention ground. If a person cannot be expelled without breach of the European Convention, the Home Office will grant exceptional leave to remain for a period which may vary with the circumstances of the case but is usually four years under current Home Office practice.

8. [1999] INLR 144, 152C ff.

9. (1985) 19 I&N 211.

10. *Islam*, supra, at 152D-E.

11. Ibid, at 161G.

12. There is no duty in international law to grant permanent residence in this way. Previous governments granted four years' stay.

CLINICAL

Remaking connections: refugees and the development of "emotional capital" in therapy groups

Caroline Garland, Francesca Hume and Sarah Majid

Introduction

When refugees are referred for psychological help to the Adult Department of the Tavistock Clinic it is not primarily because of their status as refugees. Nevertheless the *fact* that they are refugees, or asylum seekers (as opposed to economic migrants) is often crucial to the understanding of the nature and degree of the difficulties they are struggling to manage. As well as the need for housing, medical care, work and a living wage on the way to economic, social and political integration into the host culture, there are the social and psychological factors that will determine the ability to make use of whatever help may be offered, as well as to deal with local hostility or opposition to their presence. Whether or not the refugee succeeds in managing these burdens and these tasks in the long run may well depend upon the presence or absence of potential "social capital". Social capital refers to those factors promoting social coherence and integration inherent in social systems, such as kinship and the family, marriage, friendship, and mutual support in local social, religious or political groups (Putnam, 2000). Loizos (2000) has argued persuasively that refugees' capacity to tap into, develop and make use of these is as relevant to the success or failure of an immigrant population as is the degree and kind of the support they receive from the host culture.

Although refugees very often lose their economic and material capital, they rarely lose nearly as much of their human and social capital. Even when their stocks of both are greatly reduced, or devalued by dramatic changes in contexts where they could be applied, the refugees may with time, determination and support, replenish them. It is, I argue, their characteristics as "social capitalists" which assist significantly in the issue of their longer-term adjustment ... and government policies which ignore or disrupt such processes inflict additional penalties upon them. [Loizos, 2000, p. 126]

However, not all refugees who arrive in this country are able to find and connect with their own (or for that matter new) ethnic or cultural groups. This may be because they do not exist—there are simply too few members of that group in the country or they are too widely dispersed to know of each other. And it may also be because they are already psychologically damaged and do not have the internal resources to make the emotional connections that are the basis of the capacity to profit from social capital. Such damage may of course derive from either their early developmental history or from the extreme circumstances that have led to their arrival in this country as asylum seekers. Most often it is both. To emphasize an early deficit is presumptuous in the face of the devastating events that many asylum seekers have endured in the months or years before their arrival in this country. At the same time to ignore the nature of the internal world that informs and often determines the capacity to form crucial emotional connections is to miss what may be absolutely necessary for survival—although not always suffi-cient. This is the point of psychoanalytically-informed treatment. It can offer the chance to get to grips with those internal factors that prevent or inhibit the capacity to make use of whatever is available as potential for the rebuilding of social capital.

Group treatment

The majority of refugees referred to the Adult Department will be offered treatment in out-patient psychotherapy groups. These are heterogeneous groups. Their populations vary widely in terms of presenting problem, psychopathology, demographic status and ethnicity. In fact, although this is not an inevitable outcome of the theory lying behind the composition of therapy groups, such groups therefore often come to represent a cross-section of the local population—in this case, London. Therapy groups, in which seven or eight patients meet together for one and a half hours on a weekly basis with a single therapist, are sometimes regarded as cut-price, economy class treatment, less valuable and less effective than first-class travel with an individual therapist. We would argue strongly against this point of view. Not only is group treatment the treatment of choice for a great many patients, it is particularly so for patients who also happen to be refugees.

This is for two reasons. The first is that many referred to us are *traumatized* as well as being dislocated in terms of culture and ethnicity. They have suffered events of an extreme and destructive nature, and have fled to this country. For many of them, the psychological damage is such that it leaves permanent marks on their capacity to live their lives in an ordinary and relatively unpersecuted way. Traumatic events tend to take up a central position in the mind of the survivor and consequently to serve as "organizers" not only of post-trauma experience but in retrospect of the pre-trauma life as well. As well, the traumatized individual tends to withdraw his emotional connections with the world around him and reinforce his own boundaries against penetration by the world. These two factors taken together add up to a tendency (expressed simply) for the survivor to become more "self" centred. Group treatment operates against the hardening-up of these tendencies, and the redefining of a post-traumatic personality around the central position of *"I am a survivor of such and such"*. Groups offer the opportunity to become involved in others' lives and difficulties, within a safe setting. This keeps personal boundaries open, and fosters a sense of psychological agency, crucial for those in whom a prolonged sense of helplessness has crushed initiative and fostered an unhelpful dependence.

We therefore offer a short series of individual consultations (usually between two and six sessions) which set the framework of treatment. In these consultations the traumatic experiences are addressed and acknowledged but within a context of the life and personality of that individual. The aim of subsequent group treatment with a heterogeneous population, who often have widely differing kinds of background and experience, is to help with the process of *integrating* the experience into the life and personality as a part rather than as the whole of it. It is the person that becomes the focus of treatment, rather than the trauma.

The second reason concerns the way in which the individual's internal world becomes visibly manifested in the group as external relations with others in the room. The explicit nature of the group's negotiations over their relations with each other forms part of the psychological "work" that is the basis of the modification of the projections and introjections that take place in all groupings, and in inter-group relations. At the end of a period of successful group treatment, individuals are more autonomous and more self-aware, more at home with the recognition of self in all its strengths and vulnerabilities—and correspondingly more aware of and capable of concern for others as separate beings. In one sense the therapy group enables a shift from a position in which narcissism dominates functioning (whether it derives from recent trauma, appearing as post-traumatic "self" centredness; or from early psychopathology) to a position in which object relations, or emotional connections with others, are more possible and more based on reality. There will accordingly be a greater capacity for functioning in a way that recognizes others' needs, vulnerabilities and difficulties, and the ambivalence felt for these others who may be competitors for valuable and scarce resources, or for those who may be perceived as inadequate providers.

This move, which is also a move away from a paranoid view of the world in which others are felt only to be dangerous and untrustworthy, may be slow and exceedingly painful when it involves, as it does for the dislocated, the deprived, the damaged and the unwelcome (characteristic of many of the refugees we see) the recognition of the reality of their lives post "Year Zero", the enforced start of a new life. The nature and degree of the losses that have to be faced involve real mourning. This is probably the most profound of the psychological tasks facing the refugee or asylum seeker. Mourning is always intensely difficult work even for the most psychologically intact. It may feel like an impossible task when the personality is damaged and disabled by traumatic events, and personal resources are at their lowest ebb (Garland, 1998). When mourning breaks down or is impossible, the personality can become dominated by melancholia (Freud, 1915), by manic denial (Klein, 1940) or by grievance (see Gibb & Young, 1998). In these kinds of cases the individual can remain stuck in a position in which the potential for finding and attaching to groupings and social institutions, whether old or new, formal or informal, is limited or missing altogether.

The work of becoming a member of a therapy group reflects in microcosm the work that faces the dislocated individual within the macro-culture. Within the therapy group the task is largely emotional and psychological. In the external world, it may be largely practical, but the extent to which that external functioning is possible or successful will be based upon the individual's emotional and psychological functioning. We propose the notion of *emotional capital* to encompass the body of internal resources an individual requires in order to function in a social world. No-one can capitalize on social resources, in whatever form they may be available, when he or she does not have the internal resources, the *emotional capital*, to do this work. This is the point of an intensive experience in a small group. The internal damage and deficiencies are identified and addressed within a framework that is manageable for the individual. The innate sociality of the human creature is mobilized, and the capacity for emotional and psychological growth and integration within the small group may in time be exported into the larger society.

1. The "refugees' group"—
the resurgence of emotional potential

In spite of our conviction that mixed groups were the treatment of choice, we came to recognize that, for some, placement in an English-speaking heterogeneous grouping was not possible at the point of referral. This was particularly so for those most recently arrived and most traumatized by the experiences that had brought them to this country. We offered these individuals a three-stage treatment: the one-to-one consultations already described; a shorter-term specialist group for asylum seekers whose English was limited; and eventually dispersal to the heterogeneous groups already discussed. The short-term specialist group was designed to offer an extended period of settling-in, the opportunity to speak English (the variety of nationalities present made this inevitable) and the opportunity for members to begin to feel that however isolated they might be in practical terms, there is potential for social capital to be drawn on in terms of *connections and relations with other human beings regardless of culture or ethnicity*. This does not mean that culture and ethnicity are left outside the door. However it does mean that the overarching concept of "human being" is crucial in a group for refugees, disparate as the membership is likely to be, just as it is in a less obvious way in a group largely composed of nationals. It is the capacity to recognize, value, help and be helped by those perceived as "other" that we mean by *emotional capital*. We as staff within a predominantly white profession are of course clearly "other", but so too is each member of the Refugees' Group for every other.

Supporting framework

We recognized that the kind of work we had in mind could only be done within a context where practical needs and support had already been acknowledged and addressed. Often this involved the two therapists in much work outside the group. Each member needed to have in place a medical General Practitioner or other medical consultant (for example the Medical Foundation for the Care of Victims of Torture) to whom the asylum seeker was already known; an official recognition of his or her legality in London; plus referral to Community Mental Health Teams and Social Services where necessary. As well, in some cases voluntary support agencies were involved, which included translators who provided invaluable care and assistance. Although the negotiation of such arrangements could occupy group time, the fact that group members could see we knew these matters were vitally important gave a basis of confidence in therapists who had got their priorities in order. The frightened, the severely traumatized and the emotionally starving are not yet in a position to hear interpretations about their relations with relative strangers.

The patients

We describe three typical patients in the Refugees' Group as representing different aspects of the emotional problems inherent in dislocation and resettlement in a strange country. Each had asked for an interpreter during the consultation process. The request was not refused, but in each case the interpreter (in C's case her own sixteen-year old son) was asked to leave the meeting after the first fifteen minutes or so. This was because we were clear that although language might be limited, meaningful emotional contact could only be made when the interpreter was not interposed between the two main parties at the meeting.

Z was a forty-one-year old Romany man from Eastern Europe, who had fled from persistent persecution in his own country, including beatings by the police. He had been unable to find work because of his Roma status. The referrer was acutely anxious that he was about to kill himself after thirteen months in a detention centre and a further ten months in a hostel during the endless wait before his case was heard. However during the consultation Z was found to have more internal resources than it had seemed from the referral letters. Although he spoke minimal English, he had linked up with other European Roma in London and had a social life that seemed to involve much smoking and beer-drinking. He had also managed to put together from the charity clothes shop a coherent and quite dashing appearance, in spite of his beer belly. He had a sense of humour behind the passive and hang-dog manner with which he had originally presented. He had rapidly learned to find his way around London. He attended the first session of the group, but then became unwell and stayed away for four weeks, only returning for the fifth session. Chronic physical symptomatology (headaches, joint aches, coughs and colds) was common in our patients in the early stages of the group, but Z may also have found it intolerable to be in the room with such damaged and sometimes desperately distressed women. He may also have felt that he was less damaged than they were (which was true) and that he could not face the depression in the room, the depression that lies in wait for all refugees as they face the need to mourn what it is they have lost. However, encouraged by his referrer, he returned and began to struggle to express himself with his very restricted vocabulary.

J was a 26-year old African girl, imprisoned, raped and horrifically tortured and mutilated by the prison guards for protesting about her father's political assassination. J had been helped to escape and had stowed away in the hold of a cargo ship for eight weeks before she arrived in England. She was acutely depressed at the separation from her large family, especially from her very young son, and at her own physical and mental condition. "I am ruined", she said repeatedly at consultation. "My body ruined, my head ruined". We felt she was a high suicide risk. In terms of social capital there was nothing available. Emotionally however matters seemed a little different as she began to make use of the consultations. There was some capacity left in her to fight for her own emotional survival, which is to say the survival of a belief that the important figures carried inside her (or the representation of those figures—her good internal objects) could help her to win through this exceptionally difficult part of her life and come to have a future once more—perhaps to see her family again, and to become once more a mother to her son. She had been a trained nurse in her home country and she wanted to retrain here, and then find her son and bring him over. This was clearly a daunting project, but she showed she still had the capacity for hope. In the second session of the group she had said in her very limited English that she had tried to get another young girl from her country, deeply in trouble, to come with her to the Tavistock, because "Is good to talk".

C was a young woman from Kosovo who had managed to flee to this country with her husband and two children. The family had witnessed many events of extreme violence and horror, in which many other family members had been slaughtered. They themselves had barely survived. C was now virtually unable to let her family out of her sight, which presented real problems for the children who were showing they could begin to make an adjustment by attending school and learning English. C's husband was a broken man, who felt shamed by having his wife need weekly treatment at a mental health clinic. She would not travel on her own, and he could not bear the shame of accompanying her. This took the adolescent son out of school on a regular basis. C's constant crying was also a product of helpless rage. Once she had started to speak in the Refugees' Group this rage could be addressed directly, which seemed to give her some relief. She stopped crying as she began to struggle to put her anger into words. The following week she came in with a new hair-cut, and her hair coloured. "My son did it, he say Mama you shouldn't have old face", she told us disarmingly.

The fourth session

We were struck by how quickly the basic elements of group life asserted themselves in this disparate group of damaged and deprived individuals. There was clear rivalry, not only for the attention of the two therapists, but also between each other as to who was the most troubled and needy. There was the search for similarities, always central in the early stages in any group, but with an added intensity since the similarities had nothing benign about them: torture, brutality, rape, imprisonment and flight, as opposed to ethnicity, culture, social groupings, kinship, religion, work, mutuality. Yet there was also the beginnings of one of the most powerful therapeutic processes in any therapy group, which is the regaining of *a sense of agency* through the capacity to extend understanding to others, and to think on their behalf. Freud (1926) makes explicit the way in which trauma is the outcome of a prolonged sense of helplessness. To offer emotional help to others calls upon one's own internal resources and begins to reduce the sense of helplessness. To help another, perhaps at first simply by listening, implies one has something to offer from within one's self, even when one did not know there was anything left ("I am ruined...")—and this in turn reduces the sense of helplessness. In a therapy group, what is therapeutic comes from other members (patients) quite as much as from the therapist. Thus in psycho-analytic terms, group treatment acts to reduce envy of the breast, that which is felt to possess all the resources necessary for life itself. When each group member can not only feel him or herself to be starving and helpless—the infant—but *also* a part of the resources (the breast) for others, then envy, which impedes internal growth and development, is mitigated.

CLINICAL MATERIAL

In this fourth session, there was a new member, A, from C's own country. The difficulty the two patients had in connecting with each other was at first about the potential political and social difficulties linked with co-ethnicity. Had they been on the same side? Would they gossip about each other to mutual acquaintances? Might they look down on each other? The fear of being shamed was very powerful. Yet they also illustrated something of the internal factors that can operate against making connections and rebuilding social capital.

The two women had come up in the lift together side by side, not speaking, and this continued as they sat looking straight ahead at the therapist. When she asked if they had already introduced themselves they shook their heads and remained silent. C sat sullenly back in her chair, turning away from A, who was perched anxious and expectant on the edge of hers. After further comments from the therapist on their difficulty in speaking and their lack of interest in each other, C eventually asked the therapist "Is she new?" shooting a look at A, but unable to address her directly and clearly fed up at the feeling she was expected to have anything to do with her.

In this fourth session, one of the group's two therapists was away, and C's sense of deprivation must have been acutely exacerbated by A's potential as a new member to steal what resources and nourishment might be left. C was the central figure in her own home. She felt she needed constant attention from both children and husband if she were not to break down altogether. Perhaps she wanted to recreate this situation in the group. She seemed unable to bear her envy and rivalry with someone else seemingly in this position, even briefly. Eventually C, speaking exclusively to the therapist, related a nightmare in which she had been hit by two men with a stick who were going to kill her. When she woke she found real bruises on her knee. What seemed terrifying was the confusion over what was real and what was nightmare, particularly when what are nightmares for most people had also for her been real events. A started to cry, clearly feeling a connection with something that C was saying, but too overwhelmed to put into words what was in her head. Then she said that she didn't like to think about these things. At the same time she agreed with the therapist's comment that though they *tried* not to think about their experiences, they kept coming back to them in flashbacks and nightmares.

At this point J arrived, about fifteen minutes late. With prompting from the therapist, she told her own nightmare of opening the front door to a man who had wanted to kill her. She had woken terrified and confused as to whether it had really happened, and had had to climb into the bed of another woman in the house because she was too terrified to sleep alone. All three woman could identify with the terror of being alone, and suffered the same sense of isolation from a world in which other people seemed to be able to tell the difference between what was real and what was not. Yet in spite of this they remained unable to relate directly to each other in the group. They connected only through a mutual agreement with the therapist's comment to any one of them. This seemed the safest way for them to be together, apparently the only alternative to desperate and hostile rivalry for the therapist's attention. The rivalry between A and C was perhaps composed of two elements: desperation about not getting enough *external* supplies to survive (food, shelter, therapy), as well as by the revival of profound *internal* anxieties deriving from infantile feelings of rage and frustration. These, when split off and projected into others in the room, become paranoid fears about incipient attack.

Whenever the therapist finished speaking the tense silence between the members resumed. The therapist commented on their wish to feel less alone, yet how difficult they found it to speak to each other—they still had not exchanged names with the new member. C said she was fed up, not interested in anyone else. She agreed with the suggestion that she wanted to be on her own with the therapist and was angry at the pressure to consider others. J said she wanted to talk but had always been shy. Her dream suggested that opening the door to anyone at all was very dangerous. A said she wanted to talk to people with similar experiences, but whenever she started to talk she began to weep and could not continue.

In the continuing tension and silence, the therapist commented that being from the same country didn't seem to make things any easier for them. A and C both agreed. A eventually explained that though it was easier to be with people from the same country who might have had similar experiences, she didn't like to be around people from Kosovo because she couldn't bear them to know what had happened to her. She felt she knew just what they would think—it would be too shameful. J agreed. They wanted to be able to talk about their experiences to complete strangers. In the group, not getting to know each other was perhaps a way of maintaining anonymity to preserve the session as a place where it might be possible to speak about things that otherwise seemed unspeakable. The terrible shame and the wish for anonymity inhibited any supportive or creative connections they might otherwise make socially, particularly in their own cultures.

J then started to talk about her guilt in relation to her son. She explained how after her first experience of torture which left her facially scarred he had begged her to stop her political activities. She had continued, driven to denounce publicly the injustices of the regime that had assassinated her father and stolen his property. Then one day she opened the door to a man who was supposed to take her to her party's political meeting. Instead he took her to prison where she was further tortured. She never saw her son again. She wept at the pain of missing him and at this terrible sense of his now being without a mother. A and C could both identify with the pain of being apart from their loved ones, unable to contact them or even to know if they were alive. They shared too the agony of having had to leave their parents behind to save their own lives. A and C began to talk as compatriots instead of rivals: "Yes, these bad things happen in our country. This is what it is like since the war".

C then asked A whether she was married and who she lived with, at last speaking directly to her with a more benign interest. J talked about the loss for ever of her everyday life and routine. A and C could identify with this. Neither had ever thought they would leave their home towns, let alone move to another country. Now all three felt completely disorientated. J said she looked in the mirror and did not recognize herself. She was no longer the young woman she had known. For the first time they seemed much more connected and spontaneous, relating shared experiences of disconnection from their loved ones, their sense of self, their previous existences. By the end of the session they seemed much more like a group. They could see for themselves the similarities and connections between them instead of being dependent on the therapist to point them out.

This session demonstrated some of the difficulties that severely curtailed the ability of its members to develop wider social relations in the world outside the group. C clung desperately and possessively to whatever she could acquire, and was aggressively rivalrous towards any competition. A was in a frozen state where any connections precipitated overwhelming feelings that she could not articulate. She seemed paralysed by shame and grief. J lived in a persecuted state of fear and suspicion, in which any contact was potentially very dangerous. For all of them any contact threatened what little internal and external resources they felt they possessed in a strange country, and provoked the fierce need to protect these resources. This of course aggravated their sense of being disorientated and alone, both internally and externally. Yet the experience of saying these things out loud, however disjointedly, exchanging glances from time to time, meant the tentative beginnings of connectedness. This growing recognition of commonality with other human beings is both cause and effect of a capacity to move outwards into a more social and sociable world.

> Three months later, a letter arrived at the Clinic from J's family in Africa, the first news of her family she had received for nearly two years. She tore it open hungrily in the room with the others and wept in relief and distress: in it there were photographs of the family, but she also learned her much loved grandmother had died. A while later, when the first intense emotion subsided a little, she passed the photographs around the group (five members by then), gravely labelling each member of her family. "This is my mother. This is my son. This is my sister. This my sister's husband. This my brother". Then she asked one of the therapists to read the letter aloud to the group. It was in French. There was a somewhat stumbling translation, but the group listened intently and with great emotion. In it her mother thanked God that after all her daughter was alive and in safe hands. The therapist commented, "Now you have two families, one at home and one in this country". C added, "All women in group is my sister". This was a silent reminder of the murder of her own biological sister, yet C was also showing her capacity for sympathy and empathy—a considerable move out of the entrenched and rivalrous position that she had so vigorously adopted at the beginning.

2. The long-term therapy group—
developing emotional potential

The patient

We now describe the treatment in a heterogeneous therapy group of a twenty-seven-year old African man. He was referred to the Trauma Unit in the Tavistock Clinic following a hit-and-run traffic accident, after which he had become increasingly depressed and anxious. At the time of referral he and a young woman from his own country were drifting from hostel to hostel, doing bits and pieces of work.

Q had come to England from the European country to which his parents had fled to escape from the war in their home country, leaving their new-born son behind in the care of the maternal grandparents. Q had nightmarish childhood memories of villagers being tied up and shot in front of him by troops from a neighbouring country.

Q had then been sent to join his parents at the age of eleven. His subsequent experience was of a father who had bullied and taunted him in order to "strengthen" him. Africans, he said, expect much of their only sons and his father found him to be a disappointment. His mother sided with his father. However the grandfather was remembered as a loving man. The Trauma team consultant felt during the assessment that the presence of this one good early figure in spite of Q's powerful sense of abandonment by his parents, and the subsequent violence and suffering, might mean he had sufficient internal resources to attach himself to and make use of longer-term psychotherapy.

In general however, Q exuded an air of hopelessness. He spoke vaguely of his lack of motivation and his difficulty in completing anything he started—even a game of pool—and his sense of belonging nowhere. Africans saw him as European and Europeans saw him as African. In Britain he was simply "black". He would daydream about being an important person such as a political leader, someone with a solid base at the social and political centre. Yet the picture that emerged was of a lost and rootless young man, confused about his identity, and homeless both geographically and psychologically. The consultant also noted how his passivity could provoke questions or directions which he would then experience as intrusive and abusive. In complaining about and opposing any questions, he seemed to rid himself of any sense of guilt or responsibility for his own contribution to his predicament. Yet he also seemed to have some moments of insight into his capacity for self-destructive behaviour and he was clearly relieved to be offered a place in a group.

The group

This consisted of eight men and women between the ages of twenty-five and forty. They were of mixed race and socio–economic status but there were no other refugees and no other Africans. Several had also had past traumatic experiences. Q was one of four who did not have English as a first language. He joined the group mid-way through its three-year course, reflecting his experience as the newcomer to his family, to Italy, and then to England. He would enter the room with his head bowed, sit with his coat on and look round the room apprehensively. Then he would stare at the therapist, trying to catch her eye in order to give her a timid smile. She began to feel that only when she met his gaze could he have any sense of owning any resources of his own. He could hardly be heard when invited to speak. From the beginning he was important to the other group members who felt envious of his obvious vulnerability and neediness, but also compassionate and interested in him. He himself had no sense that the others felt his presence was important. Yet he told the group that on starting therapy he had given up cannabis and this change endured. Over his first therapy break he went back onto an anti-depressant until therapy resumed three weeks later.

Very gradually he began to speak of his life and troubles. His lateness at work meant he was frequently sacked. He had feelings of angry inferiority. His life seemed to consist of a series of transient, disconnected and incomplete endeavours and engagements. However towards the end of his first year there were some changes: his appearance became more coherent and he began to listen and to take an interest in the other members. He had acquired a mobile phone and would make a point of showing it as he switched it off at the beginning of the session. It was not until the beginning of his second year however that he began to make his presence in the group apparent. His difficulties in the extra-group world now began to find expression in his relations with other group members and with the therapist, as happens when there is a real engagement with the therapeutic process.

Clinical material

Q returned from the Christmas break to tell the group that he had visited his family in Europe and had stood up to his father who had falsely accused him of taking some money from his sister. He felt pleased and strong—"more like a man"—but this was short-lived. The following week he came back depressed and despondent and did not know why. Gradually the group helped him to see how he no longer felt he had a place in the family. He had lost their approval and now he felt he was rejected by them for having stood up to them, daring to have a mind of his own.

In contrast to this felt loss, he started to be more a part of the group. He asked more questions of the others and seemed to hold on less to the therapist with his gaze and more with words. Often he would repeat things she had said, using her phrases and inflections, as though he were trying to establish her inside himself as a valuable emotional resource. Other patients began to notice the changes in him. However, at this point something happened within the group that enabled the other members to experience directly his extreme sensitivity to rejection and displacement. The week before this sequence of events he had been talking in the group to a young lesbian woman who was struggling with her own need for approval from her homophobic parents. He told her she must stand up for herself and not be so dependent on them. She had slightly disagreed with him, feeling more in touch with the sadness of having disappointed them and her feeling that she should respect their point of view.

The following week was important for all the patients. A long-standing female member of the group who had been absent while she gave birth turned up in the group with the baby. Sadly the baby had just been found to have a rare genetic disorder. She left the group early to attend to the baby and there was then much discussion about the baby and the group's mixed feelings about it. Q however was morose and silent. Suddenly he became upset, accusing the others of lacking generosity, failing to accept the baby's presence. He became more and more agitated until someone commented on how upset and cross he seemed. He said, "You all ignored me today after my row with Y last week. No-one looked at me when I came in—you all blanked me out". Someone suggested that perhaps he had after all felt pushed out by the baby, but he denied this strongly.

At first the group could not understand what he meant by "the row". When he explained that he was referring to his exchange with the lesbian patient, they were even more perplexed. Had he not been standing up for her and for gay rights? As they went on to remember Q's need for approval from *his* parents too, things became a little clearer. Someone suggested, "You needed our approval when you came in today after being braver in the group last week and then you saw our lack of eye contact as disapproval—but in fact we were just engaged with something else". However at this point Q could not feel helped by these comments.

The following week Q came back to the group quite paranoid. He felt the entire group was against him, attributing this to their racism—it was written all over them, in their body language, their comments and in their not looking at him. They hated him and wanted him out. Someone had even described him as "black". The young lesbian woman was singled out for attack. She became upset and did not attend the following week (though she subsequently returned). In the session in which she was absent, Q laid into another female member whom he called unthinking and stupid. She was very upset and protested that she was very aware of racial issues. She was married to an African and had mixed-race children.

At this point the therapist intervened. She pointed out that Q had been the last member to join (apart from one other who had dropped out). She interpreted that he felt like the unwanted bad black cuckoo with no nest of his own. He felt bad because he had invaded this nest and was now taking all the space (as he had done for the last two weeks), pecking at and wounding the others and even managing to evict them altogether. She added that it didn't matter what anyone said to him now, this was how he felt, hated for being an attacking cuckoo. This was how the others were now starting to see him. Q looked visibly relieved, and one or two others began to regain their own capacity to think about what was going on. The therapist then said that perhaps the group offered a chance to understand these awful, unwanted cuckoo feelings and that this might make it possible for them all to believe in a "mixed-race family"—a group where everyone could have a place.

It then became possible to move away from Q's individual problems and back to the issues that concerned them all: the impact of the Christmas break, and the arrival of the real "intruder", the damaged baby who had trumped them all for neediness and stirred up feelings of rivalry, pity and guilt. Perhaps some of the persecution in all of them had been generated by guilt over hatred of this mother–baby pair. They started to look at the destructive effect that their own feelings of exclusion and jealousy had had in their lives, and Q could at last acknowledge hating the sight of the pregnant patient's belly. It reminded him of his mother's pregnancies with his younger siblings, whom he felt "really belonged" inside the family group.

Q was now able to work more effectively in the group. His attendance and his punctuality improved and there was evidence that his life outside the group was better. He and the girl had become a couple, and they were given a council home of their own in which to live. The importance of this was very great. It signified his right to a home in this country but it also reflected his growing capacity to experience himself as a man with something to contribute to the world of the therapy group.

At this point he told the group a long-held "ugly secret" (his words) of which he was very ashamed. As a fifteen-year old boy he had interfered sexually with his much envied younger sister, fondling her genitals when they were obliged to share a bed. This confession revealed the depth of his self-loathing and aggression towards himself. He expected others to run away from him in disgust and fear and to see him only as a vile abuser. In fact, his self-loathing at that point had less to do with being black or being a refugee than with a more immediate feeling that in the group he was an unwanted, rejected outsider at every level. Q had looked at the other patients in the group as he had looked at his family, feeling *they are all right, they belong; I am bad and that is why I do not belong.*

Reviewing Q's treatment, the therapist felt that as he started to find something had changed, and that the group had become important to him, at first he found it difficult to believe. He searched for proof that he was still the hated unwanted outsider. He tried to get himself hated and rejected by treating the others badly. It is to the credit of the rest of the group that they could tolerate his behaviour and resist these attempts. This situation reflected his situation in the world at large. Being a refugee is to find oneself a dependent marginal in a host society that often has cultural norms very different from one's own. The refugee has been displaced and has lost his home, and his homeland. Psychologically, the experience entails the fear of exclusion, the sense of being an outsider or "alien", all of which may be reinforced by hostility and rejection within the host nation.

Yet Q experienced himself in the therapy group as more of an outsider at some times than at others. It was when he felt stressed, persecuted and insecure about his place in the group that he accused the other members of racism and rejection. At these times "racism" and "refugee status" were used defensively by him as a catch-all way of accounting for the many problems he had, many of which pre-dated his experience as a refugee. In the group he became gradually able to find words to describe his infantile terrors and his agony of feeling lost and without internal resources, and consequently able to unhook these emotions from the peg of being a victimized black refugee. In a similar way, his self-loathing had had no words. He just felt terrible. The word "black" had come to carry a sense of badness and of difference that had little to do with the colour of his skin, in that it had existed in his family of origin quite as much as it did in the group. The containment and the thinking available in a therapy group meant that these aspects of his defensiveness and the underlying anxieties could begin to be examined in a safe setting.

The group also showed Q that his feelings of not belonging and of being marginalized or rejected, pushed out, were not unique to him. Everyone in the group felt these things at certain times. At the end of the group itself, every member felt like a refugee, forced to leave what had come to feel like home. The knowledge of this in itself helped to reduce Q's sense of isolation. Q's career in his therapy group illustrates the interplay of phantasy and reality in his view of himself in the social world, and shows how the psychological work helped begin to make the crucial distinction between the two. Had this not happened, Q would have been condemned to a life of feeling himself to be an unwanted outsider, and inclined to attribute this to his refugee status. As it was, some mourning for the family he had not had could happen, his sense of grievance was reduced, and he began to make increasingly solid connections of his own—not only in the group but also in his personal life.

Summary and conclusions

Relationships internalized in early infancy do not belong to the past, but come to form the dynamic present of the individual's relations with his social world. When internal preoccupations (abandonment, cruelty, neglect, exclusion, unwantedness) coincide with external circumstances, as often happens in the case of refugees, it can be hard to distinguish fact from phantasy. Yet unless the work of sorting out what belongs to each is undertaken, the refugee's life can become dominated by a melancholic depression, by a defensive mania, or by an increasingly entrenched sense of grievance, all of which interfere with the necessary processes of mourning and recovery. When these sources of interference are profound, emotional capital is increasingly eroded and thus the opportunity to *capitalize on the social* is diminished.

The use of therapeutic groups as a treatment modality for refugees and asylum seekers can provide an experience that bridges in a very specific way the internal and the external worlds. The work of the therapy group consists of developing progressively deeper and more trusting relationships with others in the group, while at the same time—and with the help of the therapist—understanding and modifying the internal factors that help or hinder those relationships within the individual. Thus alongside the theory of "social capital" which "unites a term from sociology and anthropology with another from economics to produce a concept which seems to integrate two approaches traditionally treated as opposed" (Loizos, 2000, p. 124), we have proposed the notion of *emotional capital*.

Emotional capital refers to those internal resources that determine an individual's capacity to relate to and connect with *other human beings*, and thus ultimately to their capacity to contribute to and profit from the social capital generated by a particular group. The notion thus links sociology and anthropology, which deal with the *group*, to psychoanalytic theories of psychic development which concern the *individual's* psychological structure. Psychoanalytic theory differs from economic, rational and cognitive conceptions of human behaviour, in that it includes a recognition of unconscious mental processes which determine apparently irrational behaviour. In particular, it is concerned with the notion of an internal world populated by objects (figures, or aspects of figures) existing in dynamic relation to each other. We suggest that this notion is important for a full understanding of the failure or success of individual refugees in their post-relocation world. Therapeutic groups offer not only the chance to observe these psychological and social forces in action, but also of modifying their more toxic or less constructive manifestations in the individual. Individual growth in terms of autonomy, self-esteem and relatedness contributes not only to individual satisfaction and peace of mind, but also to the welfare and success of the group itself.

In the same way, a psychotherapy group mirrors the wider society within which it has been created. As Q was helped to become a valuable contributing member of his therapy group, so he became more capable of feeling he could take part in, even contribute to, society at large. The primitive fears and anxieties felt by any group as new members are introduced into it are reflected and magnified in society's response to the great influx of refugees and asylum seekers within recent years. The reality of the availability of national resources needs to be recognized fully, as of course does the reality of the varied nature of different immigrant groups. However, as well as an acknowledgement of a society's capacity to extend a tolerant and forbearing welcome, we would also hope for a parallel examination of the *irrational* sources of fear and hostility to strangers in society at large. The fact that there are destructive forces in the individual, in the small group and in the large group needs to be acknowledged and addressed if these are not to work against and even negate the creative and generous impulses that are also part of human nature.

CHAPTER FIVE

Refugee children and abuse

Judith A Trowell

Introduction

The increasing numbers of refugees in this country as single adults, families and children alone, have meant that Local Authorities and all Child Protection professionals have had to find suitable ways of working with this varied group of people. Investigating and assessing child abuse, both risk and then treatment, has always been a delicate and sensitive task. Parents are frequently hostile, alienated both by the implicit and explicit accusation and also by the process itself. With refugee families and children, there is the added complexity of language, communicating through an interpreter, and culture. Many refugee families can both speak and understand some English; often the children understand more but frequently even where the child appears fluent and articulate, an interpreter may be helpful. The apparent language skills often cover limited comprehension and the subtleties of the questions may be too sophisticated for a child to follow. Direct questioning is of course inadvizable if one is holding in mind the use of the interview for evidential purposes. As a last resort, direct questions may be useful in very limited circumstances, recognizing that they need to be asked in such a way as to leave the possible answer as wide open as one can.

The issue of culture can cause much confusion and concern. When is an action or a lack of an action, an attitude or expectation acceptable, even if markedly different from mainstream UK standards, and when does it cross the unacceptable bottom line for child care? Department of Health guidelines are not explicit and much is left to practitioners and the Courts. The Children Act (1991) puts emphasis on respecting ethnicity and culture and this is of course imperative but it leaves uncertainty. Cultural advisors are available, some Local Authorities have their own, others use specialist resources, the Medical Foundation for Victims of Torture can usually supply a person to consult, who will offer telephone advice and may be willing to come and meet the child and/or family. Professionals do not always find it easy undertaking joint interviews with interpreters or cultural advisors; it certainly changes the interview and requires time, before and after the interview to establish a working relationship and then talk over the interview. Where abuse has occurred, the emotional impact may be profound and the advisor or interpreter may need support to come to terms with what they have heard and not become over-involved, or lose their empathy and cut off.

Recent revised guidelines from the Department of Health, "Working together to Safeguard Children" (1999) and the "Framework for the Assessment of Children in Need and their Families" (2000) indicate increasing awareness of the need for thoughtful sensitive interventions whilst at the same time being aware of the legal framework of England and Wales and what is acceptable and what is not. There was a very strong reaction to Child Protection procedures exposed in "All Equal Under the Act" (1991) when it was pointed out very vividly that predominantly white middle class social workers, police and child and family mental health professionals were making biased judgments about child rearing practices, discipline, physical contact and sexuality and the emotional environment. This resulted in a change in response so that behaviours and child care were tolerated, excused, and accepted, that were damaging to the children even resulting in child deaths (Tyra Henry, 1987). Perhaps the situation has changed again, racism is less and professionals are much more aware. There are many more ethnic minority professionals so that families can have a more sensitive service even if the language and culture cannot always be matched. The *laisse faire* attitude has been reduced too, professionals are still wary of being seen as racists but they have more confidence in themselves and their professional groups with the ethnic diversity.

The impact and stress on the system created by the arrival of the refugee, asylum seeker community has been considerable. Compassion is very great for these people but the demand on resources, housing, schools, social security and all areas of health has been considerable. The outcome is ambivalence, compassion for the individual but resentment of the group. Politicians have responded similarly, the individual cases arouse concern, outrage, and a wish to provide asylum, but as the numbers have increased, the financial implications and awareness of the long-standing nature of the issue has meant that the response of the population has become more hostile. Politicians have become more concerned with repatriation, with the image of "fortress Britain", and tend to view refugees as economic migrants. The need to label asylum seekers as scroungers is growing. When some of these families are thought to be harming their children, the reaction is strong; it can be taken as confirmation that the refugees are here to grab as much as they can with no real concern for their families, that they are not decent hard working people who may have needed to escape persecution. The stress they may be or may have been under is ignored.

Clinical illustrations

This will be illustrated with four cases, a child from Sub-Saharan Africa, two children from the Middle East and a child from East Africa.

A young child of primary school age arrives on a plane alone. She is met by a parent she has not seen for several years, her "mother". The child only vaguely remembers this person, she has been living with her grandmother, she thinks; her father is dead—he was killed in front of her and a younger sibling has died of AIDS. She arrives with no knowledge of English and when "mother" enrols her in a school she has to try and learn to communicate very rapidly. "Mother" is very determined the child will work hard and do well in school. It is reported she constantly speaks severely to the child about her poor progress and mother complains about the teaching methods.

One day the child arrives at school with a large bruise saying mother has hit her and the child begs not to have to go home. Social Services are contacted, assess the situation and the child is placed in foster care. Physical evidence of the chastisement is clear, the argument begins to centre on what is reasonable chastisement in their culture and how to understand the emotional and psychological environment of this child. A prolonged assessment is begun, a number of questions arise immediately, such as, What is the legal status of this "family'? What is culturally acceptable? Why is mother here? Despite being reasonably fluent and articulate, how much is really understood by mother and by the girl.

Mother is insistent she is here because the situation is too dangerous back home, claiming that relatives have been killed, that they were a different tribe to the one in power and that she has escaped to safety. She has permission to stay in this country but has short-term permission. She sees how she disciplines her child as her decision and stresses her wish for the child to "receive a good education". She also says most of her family is dead back home and she is HIV positive and not too well. An intelligent woman, she has no remorse or guilt and is angry with her daughter for causing the trouble. She can say very little about her own background and her own experiences. There is something cut off, detached, cold about her. During this process she was granted asylum. The child is pretty and very chatty, she wants to see her "mother" but not live with her, she did not want to return to her country of origin, she gave graphic accounts of her "mother's" inadequacies, such as, no food available, "mother" often out so she was alone in the flat and "mother's" frequent rages and outbursts complaining about or attacking the child.

What slowly emerged was mother's dissociated state, her inability to be in touch emotionally with the child or to allow anyone, including herself, to understand and think about what had happened and the effects of this on the relationship between mother and child. A cultural advisor tried to assist but whilst this perspective assisted the professionals, it did not make sense to the mother who refused to be involved. Mother and child refused an interpreter but this perhaps should have been insisted upon to ensure there was real communication. As the girl was seen for longer, the extent of her disturbance became apparent, it was pretty clear she had witnessed brutal murders, that she had been sexually abused, both by strangers and carers and that she saw herself either as a sexual object for others or as a useless worthless individual, thus she could also be angry and destructive herself.

Mother increasingly withdrew, she became more unwell physically and found unbearable any discussions of her feelings and her experiences, and her numb cut-off state increased. The Court finally decided on permanent separation and attempts were to be made to find the child a long-term placement. The horror of the child's past and current experiences was very upsetting for all the lawyers; mother's cut-off, cold detached presentation left all the professionals distressed and angry, but also very concerned.

*   *   *

The next illustration is of a young girl who was brought to this country and placed with her sister, as her parents had been killed. They were from the Middle East and after a few weeks the "uncle" left the country.

The girl, aged eleven, was enrolled in a school by her nineteen year old sister who was here on a course. The sister was due to leave the country when the course finished, and the girl had applied for asylum. The assessment was requested when the girl alleged sexual abuse by her sister's boyfriend. By now she had been in the country three and a half years, spoke English well and saw England as home. She wanted to stay, if not for ever, at least until she had completed her education. Education for girls at home was a huge problem. This girl was functioning well at school, the relationship with her sister was strained. As the girl herself became more forthcoming the extent of her despair, the horror of what had happened to her parents and the worrying relationship with this "uncle" emerged. The girl had flashbacks when she saw the bodies of neighbours, smelt decaying bodies and relived the disappearance of her parents. She often became sexually excited and talked of violent and sexual activity in her family, or was it in her neighbourhood in London—it was not clear. The sister was ordered to leave the country and the Refugee Council took up the girl's case. A strong report was presented, the girl was not covered by the Children Act as she was not a UK citizen, so special grounds had to be made to stress the extent of her difficulties and her need for treatment alongside her anglicization and the danger she would be in if she returned. This girl clearly was depressed and was suffering from post traumatic stress disorder, but how much the Court process and the need to make a special case confirmed or exacerbated these problems was unclear. It certainly would have helped if she had been able to begin treatment.

*   *   *

A second girl, aged twelve years, came from the Middle East with her mother and father. They were granted asylum when she was ten years. At school she told a friend about her father physically abusing her and her mother, and that her father sexually interfered with her. Social Services investigated and the father was asked to leave the home. Mother was shocked and horrified by her daughter's consistent account and became more and more distraught. Mother confirmed father was physically violent but implied this was normal in her culture but she was sure he would not have sexually abused their daughter. Mother had problems with English and reluctantly agreed to an interpreter. The shame for herself and her husband became obvious as she became frantic, now that someone in their community (the interpreter) knew of the possibility of the sexual abuse. It was explained to us that if the abuse was proved the father could be killed. Cultural advice was very clear, there was no way abuse could be acknowledged and help sought. Father was a very forceful man insisting his daughter was tricky, that she had made it all up to cause trouble for him because he tried to impose controls and discipline and, yes, perhaps he did hit her and his wife. He deeply regretted this and planned to try and reduce this. He felt his daughter could not stand his relationship with his wife.

The girl, aged twelve, was a tall well developed child, articulate and rather street wise, clearly involved in London life. She talked about all they had seen and survived prior to arriving in this country, the violence, the fear, the friends and neighbours who disappeared but she went on to describe the fear and violence in the family particularly since coming to England. She was angry and distressed at what she saw as her rejection by mother, and very hostile to her father. She begged to remain in care. A bright, able girl she had quite severe post traumatic stress disorder but was also caught in a complex triangle with her parents at the time of assessment, desperate for an exclusive pairing with her mother. Her own violence and destructiveness has emerged whilst she has been in care as several foster placements broke down. She also became cause for concern as she dropped out of school and took up with various young men.

*   *   *

The final case is a boy from West Africa.

Father arrived here and was given permission to stay as a refugee. He was joined by his wife and two children. Both children were bright and settled quickly in school and could communicate in English. The parents, particularly mother had considerable problems both with the language and the life in England. She missed her extended family with the support and friendship it had provided. The boy, aged nine, came to our attention because he was picked up frequently quite late, having run away from home. When interviewed, the boy talked of father's violence and constant demands. He was doing reasonably well at school but father had very high expectations and was never satisfied. The boy did not talk of major difficulties for himself, his mother and sister in their home country, but of how he missed his extended family and friends.

In the family meetings father was both dominating, controlling the family and speaking for everyone, but also incredibly vulnerable. Not only had he been in great danger because of the political situation, but whilst in England he had been diagnozed with a life threatening illness. It was very difficult for him, for whom one felt considerable compassion. His wife, the boy's mother, was subdued and withdrawn, and using an interpreter did not help to understand or involve her. The daughter was articulate and charming and seemed able to charm father and so he was less confrontational. At all the family meetings father talked, mother was almost silent, the daughter smiling joined in and the boy became so angry that he walked out.

Seen alone, he was profoundly depressed and angry but also very confused by his father and mother and their attitudes and expectations. The boy and the family felt the situation was impossible and the boy after a violent assault by father was placed in a foster family. He settled and did well resuming his progress in school and visiting his family regularly. Sadly, father died a while later and mother, who continued to care for their daughter, refused to look after the boy.

The boy became profoundly depressed, the foster placement broke down, the new placement meant changing school and he could not re-engage in the work to make friends. He found it very hard to trust anyone or dare to make any attachment.

Discussion

The emotional impact on children of persecution, fear, disappearances, and the witnessing and experiencing of violence and fright are very great. Many children are left traumatized and present with panic attacks, flashbacks, re-experiencing and dissociation. In addition, there may be grief almost certainly when close loved ones will have disappeared or been obviously killed. The child is then displaced alone or with some other family members and arrives in a country with a different language and culture. They and their carers have to adjust to this whilst living with the uncertainty of their status. How can they invest in making friends at school and struggling to fit in and catch up with the school work?

The turmoil in their internal world is powerful, broken attachments, adults around who are often preoccupied if available, who have no resources to help a child make sense of their experiences, who may have never been able to provide the emotional environment to help the child feel contained secure and safe.

It is interesting that in all these abuse cases the children themselves seemed bright and cognitively capable. In reality it seemed that the need to be alert and monitor had led these children to rapidly acquire a new language and adjust to the new situation. What emerged was the lack of creativity, risk taking and poor memory, so that making sense of situations, giving a context and a history with emotionally appropriate actions was rare.

Assessing abuse (be it physical, sexual, or emotional) in these cases is complex. Traumatised individuals when re-traumatized develop more severe post-traumatic stress disorder quite frequently. For ordinary children, containment and good enough parenting detoxifies fear, envy, destructiveness, and sexuality. For these children, their societal environment used fear, envy, destructiveness, and sexuality to dominate and control. Any healing of the psychological unconscious split between hate, envy, and love, was impossible for these adults and children, on the contrary, it was constantly reinforced. In addition to these processes in society, the children presented here had to cope with these same behaviours in their family—the use of fear, envy, destructiveness, and sex to control and dominate. These children had no safe secure base within their families to provide a possibility of emotional and psychological growth and mental health.

The young East African girl superficially coping, charming, chatty, and delightful, internally was in a state of panic, confusion, distress and sexual excitement. The physical and emotional abuse by a detached and unavailable mother left her in a fragmented dissociated state. She had very little memory, little understanding and a terror of knowing. At the same time she exhibited sexualized behaviour and appeared to be very knowing.

The two Middle Eastern girls were at once more obviously deeply troubled. The first girl had, in addition to the abuse, no security. Her mental state was precarious, the flashbacks and re-experiencing of her early traumas were mixed in with her accounts of the more recent sexual abuse. It was hard to be confident about the current abuse; that she had been interfered with sexually was not in question, but it was not clear whether it was then or now. She felt her relationship with her sister was her lifeline and the sister's boyfriend threatened this. There was a strong resemblance to the oedipal triangle, but the sister herself also contributed, she resented the responsibility for her sister and also was desperate to stay in the UK and foresaw she would be told to go back, to a different less dangerous area of her country. Uncertainty seemed the pervading emotion for the girl and her sister and in the end for the professionals. But this girl's desperate wish to remain in what she felt to now be her home with no close relatives that wanted her (including her sister) was very painful.

The second Middle Eastern girl had almost certainly been sexually abused, her account was convincing and the family dynamics were powerful; Father's need to dominate and control, to feel a powerful man in the context of his wife and daughter was graphically obvious. The opportunity for abuse was not disputed, the marital perversity apparent. Mother's need to preserve her husband whatever the price and the rage with her daughter, the girl's distress and triumph were all painful to witness. The whole family were functioning with no containment, no capacity to metabolize love and hate, no way of appropriately managing violence and sexuality. They all seemed in a state of post-traumatic stress disorder with flashbacks and re-experiencing. The daughter herself did seem able to distinguish then from now and it later emerged that the maternal grandmother had been her main carer until she was six years old. When with her parents, she struggled to have an exclusive relationship with each, but then felt betrayed by them both.

The West African boy was so sad and so infuriating. There had been hope, a fresh start in the UK, but the war in their country continued to be waged in their home, in their family, and the boy could not find any safety, any containment. Death and violence from before appeared to follow them and the boy was left re-traumatized by the physical abuse, and then felt guilty that he had contributed to his father's death. The rejection by his mother led to his psychological death with no wish for relationships, no hope for the future and an inability to use new relationships that reached out to him. His depressed dissociated state left him cut off, isolated and desolate.

The emotional pain of these children and families is over-whelming. When the violence, cruelty and sexual violation comes inside the family should it be surprising? Sadly, given the events they have endured, there seems an inevitability that family boundaries will be crossed if the adults have not had sufficient good enough early experiences of their own.

The power of post-traumatic stress disorder cannot be under-estimated. Dissociation leaves individuals detached and cut off so that the consequences of their actions are not held in mind. Flashbacks and re-experiencing phenomena lead to confusion about who is who and what is happening now in reality and the memory and emotional distortions contribute to the confusion and inability to think. In these circumstances the intergenerational and societal transmission of abuse must be anticipated and help should be offered as early as possible to prevent the abuse recurring. When it has occurred, all involved need help and need to struggle with the confusion about violent and sexual behaviour.

CHAPTER SIX

Finding a way through: from mindlessness to minding

Maureen Fox

"Thus the legacy of the abandoned child is usually not only the burden of being abandoned but of being left with extremely inadequate mental resources to cope with a degree of pain which would overwhelm the most favourably brought up child"

Boston & Szur, 1983, p. 78

Introduction

Unlike economic migrants, asylum seekers and refugees come to the UK not from choice but from necessity as a consequence of the accumulated persecution and intimidation they have experienced. They have suffered unimaginable loss of family, friends, home, community, country and language. Once here, they find themselves subjected to poverty and discrimination as well as a loss of self-esteem, status and identity. Some demonstrate remarkable resilience and fortitude in facing psychological pain, dislocation and hardship. In spite of having been abandoned by the protective authority who now threatens their safety and security, they remain in contact with a life force, a good internal object, that enables them to tolerate and endure these privations and losses without becoming overwhelmed by them. As a consequence, they are enabled to make the best of the situation in which they find themselves, using whatever help is available to rebuild their lives.

What I want to explore in this chapter are the ways in which, for some asylum seekers who are less resilient, it is the loss of contact with a supportive internal relationship that depletes their capacity for resilience, leaving them inadequately resourced to face and endure the realities of their situation. Instead, their resources are employed in trying to avoid knowing, in one part of their mind, what it is that another part of them knows to be only too true about the painfulness of their predicament. The absence of significant contact with an internal figure that can know about and support them in their state of turmoil results in a range of defensive manoeuvres which, whilst calculated to circumvent suffering, actually leaves them locked into the world of pain that they are seeking to avoid. These manoeuvres involve the use of primitive defences such as splitting—whereby people or events come to be experienced as either all good or all bad; projection—whereby undesirable or unbearable aspects of the self are attributed to others; and disavowal—whereby feelings, that would normally accompany understanding, are negated. In this way, what is felt to be tolerable is separated out from what is felt to be intolerable and the latter is prepared for evacuation into whatever receptacle makes itself available, be it their children, the professional agencies they encounter or parts of their own body. Fundamental to their predicament is an inability to mourn the loss of attachments and relationships that have been left behind, to let go of them externally whilst continuing to feel supported and nurtured by them internally, leaving the self free to make new connections.

Freud (1917) described how in the early phases of mourning there is an attempt to deny the loss of the object by trying to preserve it through an identification with the lost loved one. Because of this identification the mourner believes that if his object dies then he must die too, and conversely, that if he is to survive, it is the reality of his loss that has to be denied. If mourning is to be worked through successfully, the mourner has to let go of his object, even though he is convinced that he himself will not survive its loss, and face the despair engendered by this paradox (Steiner, 1993). The difficulty in letting go of an attachment to a lost object is exacerbated when the feelings towards the person or country in question are predominately ambivalent or hostile. It is so much easier to relinquish contact with an object when there is confidence that love endures. A failure to work through mourning results in melancholia, a persecutory state of mind in which the hostile feelings directed towards the lost loved one are turned back upon the self. In this situation, the identification is with a dead or damaged object, creating a feeling of internal deadness. For those refugees who have difficulty in letting go of ambivalent attachments to friends, family or a country torn apart by civil war, mourning may be replaced by melancholia and they may become a melancholic community in exile.

Using clinical material from two cases, I will illustrate how psychoanalytically informed therapeutic work can help asylum seekers re-establish a connection with an object that can support them in tolerating the painful realities of their situation and in using whatever help may be available in establishing a new life for themselves. Sustained contact with a good internal figure acts as a container for mental pain and anxiety in much the same way as a responsive mother attends to the anxiety and stress of her new baby through her capacity to endure and meaningfully engage with his suffering without herself becoming overwhelmed by it. Whilst not taking away the infant's very real experience of fear, anxiety, hunger or colic, it is the infant's gradual introjection of mother's capacity to know about and survive his distress that enables him, in time, to know about and survive his own anxieties.

I will draw on my experience of working with asylum seekers and refugees, over a number of years, at the Tavistock Clinic as well as in community settings such as schools. Whilst some of this work has taken place within the traditional therapeutic setting, much of it has been less intensive in terms of frequency and duration although certainly not in depth of contact. It has been my experience that a slow and steady pace of work has been helpful, sometimes on a fortnightly basis, which allows time and space for the seemingly unending range of meetings and appointments that these families are required to attend, whilst simultaneously creating a mental space that is containing without being intrusive, where psychic reality can gradually be encountered and metabolized. Some refugee individuals and families may opt to terminate treatment once they begin to feel better, often returning at various stages over the years when they experience the need for further help. For others, the continuity of the work may be determined by relocation either through dispersal or the re-allocation of housing or through the outcome of their application for asylum. A further consideration with regards to the structure of the work has been the limitation of staff resources and a concern to use these resources to greatest effect.

Mind and body

Asylum seekers arrive in the UK from different countries having had a wide range of experiences that affect their health. These experiences differ greatly depending on where they come from, on what they have experienced prior to leaving home, on their personal circumstances and on their quality of life (Kings Fund Publication, 1999). Once here, they face the effects of poverty, dependency on the state, and the lack of a coherent support system, all factors that undermine health, physically and mentally. A small number may suffer from serious conditions such as TB or diabetes, which an inadequate healthcare system in their country of origin has been unable to address. Headaches, backaches and non-specific body pains are common and may be a consequence of trauma, tension or emotional distress (Burnett & Peel, 2001). For some, these symptoms are a natural and temporary response to a situation which is experienced as overwhelming, becoming the embodiment of feelings of loss of family, friends and home, of the experienced fears, dangers and violence that precipitated their flight, the terrors and anxieties of the journey during which they may have been deprived of food and sleep and the arrival in a host country where they find they are not welcome. Remarkably, many demonstrate a resilience that enables them to re-establish a sense of equilibrium, calling upon inner resources to engage with the world in which they find themselves despite all adversity. An instinct for life and relationship and a curiosity about the world around them provides them with the strength and courage they need. In spite of the loss of self esteem, exacerbated by being refused permission to work, by the minimum benefits they receive and the allocation of temporary, rundown accommodation, they still manage to survive.

Many express disappointment at the absence of a kindly welcome holding an idealized view of the generosity that awaits them in Britain, a fantasy soon dispelled in the face of reality. Yet, this sense of let down needs to be considered within a context in which the UK remains a highly sought after destination, however basic the provision available. Through the support of friends and community groups, many endure these privations with courage and they are able to confront the anxiety generated by a cumbersome application procedure which most often results in a refusal of asylum; this refusal necessitates a series of appeal hearings incurring additional delay and stress. Throughout these years, consolation for some may be derived from the relief from imminent danger, the education of their children and their aspirations for their future. But for others, the physical pain, nightmares and sense of hopelessness are not temporary and for them depression continues unabated. Their inner resources have been insufficient to enable them to re-establish a sense of self beyond their experience of suffering. Even the most resilient asylum seekers may develop complex health problems as a consequence of their upheavals, family separations, traumas, and social difficulties. Recognizing the additional support they need, the British Medical Association has argued for additional payments to be available for those doctors offering an extended range of services to asylum seekers (BMA, 2001). Many of the health problems associated with refugees are related to poverty, homelessness and social exclusion. Their most distinctive health problems are psychological and these may be linked to trauma, isolation from friends, family and community or to racism and discrimination. Problems of adjustment are most common although a significant minority may experience persistent mental health difficulties (The Health of Londoners Project, 1999).

The concept of mental illness varies from culture to culture. Traditional African culture emphasizes worship of the ancestors and this gives rise to the idea that mental and physical afflictions are caused by a failure to propitiate these spirits. Amongst Somalis the concept of mental illness is limited to severe mental disorders and does not include stress or depression. A person is either seen as "sane" or "mad" with no gradations of difficulty in between. Physical symptoms of stress, such as headaches and sleep difficulties, will be recognized but not identified as stress related. Thus, to view all refugees as victims or as mental health patients is to ignore the resources implicit in the human capacity to survive (Papadopoulos, 2001a) and the substantial contribution and enrichment they have made to our culture over the years. Positive mental health flows from inner resources (CVS Consultants, 1999) and it is the way in which inner resources or emotional capital (Garland *et al.*, 2002) can become undermined by the upheavals of seeking asylum that I intend to explore. Some, like Mrs B, have difficulties that predate their flight but these difficulties have been considerably exacerbated by it.

Case study: Mrs B

An unusually detailed referral letter to the Child and Family department at the Tavistock Clinic from a helpful community worker stated that Mrs B and her three young children, boys of six, four and two years of age, came to the UK from their home in Africa, less than a year ago. On arrival, they had been taken by the agent and escorted to a community centre and left there; this is not an unusual occurrence. Over the next six months, the family was allocated accommodation in five different Hotels and Bed and Breakfasts located in three separate London boroughs. Their next move was to a predominantly adult homeless persons' hostel where the noisy liveliness of the children became a focus of discontent for a number of the other residents.

The letter described Mrs B as suffering from depression, despair and hopelessness, frequently breaking into tears. She complains of severe pain in her head and in other parts of her body but hospital investigations have found no physical cause. At times she becomes disoriented, losing her sense of time and place and her children regularly call her back to "reality". She had entered into a violent marriage against her family's wishes and, as a consequence, contact between them had been severed for a number of years although there had been a reconciliation prior to her departure. She had separated from her husband who belonged to a different tribal group but as tribal conflict increased, the authorities decreed that all mixed blood children were to be removed from the community and transported to the border. In order to protect her children, Mrs B had decided to leave and seek asylum in the UK.

Adjusting to becoming a sole carer was enormously problematic for her and she was struggling to cope with the children's demands and unruliness. Back home, she had been economically secure and had been used to help and support with child care. For their part, the children were described as insecure, anxious, difficult to manage and preoccupied by worries about mother's health. Mrs B had difficulty in understanding their behaviour and in relating it to the upheavals they have experienced. The referral requested that she was considered for therapy to address her emotional difficulties and suggested that some assessment of the children's needs was also indicated.

In thinking about this referral within the clinical team, we experienced a daunting and overwhelming feeling that resonated with the description of Mrs B's own feelings of despair and hopelessness. There seemed to be so many issues to consider relating to mental and physical health, the needs of the children, housing and the uncertainty of the outcome for their application for asylum, which although not mentioned in the letter, was assumed to be in progress. In addition, the family lived some way from the clinic and there were anxieties about whether they would manage the journey and be able to keep appointments. The longstanding nature of mother's problems, her difficult relationship with her own family, her violent marriage and her wish to save her children were all reflected upon. Other ideas were expressed in relation to our own resources: would our way of working hold any meaning for them, would we be able to work with them across our cultural differences of language, traditions, value systems, and social and religious structures, would we require the support of an interpreter, would their needs and pain be too much for us to bear and, on a practical front, did we have the staff resources to provide what might be required.

At a meeting with the referrer to explore some of these issues, we learned that Mrs B's health was continuing to deteriorate. Nevertheless, she was keen to come to the clinic and she had been enquiring about how the referral was progressing. Their conversations together were now being conducted in English, although much checking out of each other's understanding continued to be necessary. The community worker felt under considerable pressure in her work with this family and was most keen to have the support of another agency. It was her belief that Mrs B would engage in work with us and she firmly pressed her case. We agreed to offer Mrs B an initial exploratory appointment together with the community worker. It was decided not to involve the children at this point as we wanted to assess mother's state and capacity to work with us before inviting them to participate.

On first meeting, I was profoundly struck by the fragility of her appearance, in particular, by the way her whole body conveyed a sense of suffering. I noticed that her eyes seemed to be constantly on the verge of closing and that she was making an enormous effort to keep them open. As the work progressed, I came to understand this as an eloquent communication of the ambivalence of her contact with me. There was a limit to how much looking at her situation she believed she could tolerate. She spoke slowly and with considerable effort about their recent move into a flat where they could finally establish some semblance of family life and she was pleased about this. She went on to tell me about her pains and her various hospital visits as a result of which she had received medication; however, this produced no end to her suffering. She needed help but had great difficulty in elaborating what she meant by this. In response to my explorations, she invited me to ask her questions as she did not know what more to say.

I suggested that she wanted me to know just how much pain she was suffering in her mind and in her body and that it was very difficult for her to think about it far less put it into words. I went on to say that I was interested in finding out more about her pain but I was also interested in getting to know her and learning about her life before coming to this country. Briefly, she became a little more animated and talked about the difficulties in her marriage, her husband's disappearance and the fact that because her children are mixed blood, they would be taken away from her if she had remained living in her own country. The affect she conveyed was despair and hopelessness. At times she would turn to the community worker for support in finding an English word or in making sense of what I had said. We were both aware of Mrs B using the worker as a kind of transitional object, as a source of ego support whilst she explored the possibility of establishing a new relationship with me. I was acutely aware of her despair and its impact on me, but I felt that at some level I was being tested to see if I would join her in closing off and turning a blind eye. As we approached the end of the session, I asked if she would like to come again and suggested that we could continue to think together about her difficulties. She agreed immediately to this invitation and, making eye contact for the first time, said she would come but she could not bear to start again with someone else. I assured her that I would be the person she would see each time and she began to cry.

Following this initial meeting, I arranged to meet with her fortnightly, by herself, and over the coming months came to understand more about her history and the meaning of her physical pain which at times led to acute hospital admission. It is not within the scope of this chapter to explore this case in detail but I would like to make a few points in relation what has been said about the ways in which, for those asylum seekers who are less resilient, it is the loss of contact with a sustaining, life enhancing internal voice that leaves them inadequately resourced for the challenges they face.

During our first and subsequent sessions I felt that Mrs B was letting me know that there was something that she felt was too unbearable to be looked at, something that filled her with despair, that was causing her great pain and making her ill, something that had become located in her body and that had to be got rid of, preferably through some prescription that would require minimum involvement from herself. Internally, she felt depleted and tortured, and I began to have some understanding of her need to disorient herself from the feelings and thoughts she feared would overwhelm her, should she dare allow their entry into her mind. Indeed, it was from the content of her mind that she was retreating and I was reminded of the description, in the referral letter, of the way her children would regularly call her back to "reality". McDougall (1989) suggests that:

> such people had in fact experienced overwhelming emotion that
> threatened to attack their sense of integrity and identity ... They
> were not suffering from an inability to experience or express

emotion, but from an inability to contain and reflect over an excess of affective experience. [pp. 93–94]

Yet, even in the initial session with Mrs B, I had a sense that this was not quite the whole story. I felt I had caught a glimpse of something more tenacious in her, the part of her that the community worker had been in touch with, that which had held onto the idea of coming to the clinic, that had made very definite eye contact and had been able to know about and assert her need for continuity of contact. I wondered if this more hopeful part had been acknowledged, unconsciously, in her opening description of the pleasure she had felt, even if short lived, at moving into a place where family life could be re-established. Could this be a reference to her hopes for our work together, however split off they may have been; a hope that somehow contact with a maternal object could be re-established, a phantasy consonant with the African tradition of calling together the extended family at times of crisis? Nevertheless, I was in no doubt that what dominated her internal world was a terror and horror that provided no place for optimism or comfort. I understood that her wish for contact was being projected into the community worker and myself, possibly in the hope that there it would be understood, kept safe and nurtured.

MANAGING THE UNMANAGEABLE

At our first meeting I had felt troubled by her invitation to ask her questions and this had left me feeling uncomfortable. My experience was of being invited to participate in the cruel drama of her internal world, where I was being recruited to stand in line with the various intimidating officials and landlords whose questions she was obliged to answer, figures possibly linked in phantasy to her sado–masochistic husband. However, on further reflection, it now occurred to me that her invitation may have represented a wish that I would be interested in knowing more about her situation even if she could not bear to know about it herself (Steiner, 1993). Perhaps the discomfort I experienced related more to my wish to protect myself from exposure to my own sado–masochism which could be evoked by becoming more intimately acquainted with the violence and cruelty of her situation.

She continued to convey hopelessness, preoccupied by the pains in her body which seemed to take over her mind to the exclusion of all else. As I saw it, my task was to find a way through this pain that was rendering her mindless and make contact with her in a way that would allow some of my understanding about her difficulties to be of help to her. Cautiously, I suggested that, even though she, herself, did not feel able to think about her suffering, there was a part of her that wanted me to think about it. (The idea here is that she wants me to think about her situation even though she doesn't want to think about it herself.) To my surprise she readily agreed. Slowly, I began to share with her some of the thoughts I was having. I suggested that, perhaps, it had been difficult for the doctors to help her with her pain because it was a kind of mental pain, that belonged more to her mind, but that it had been too much for her mind to bear and so she had had to re-locate it into her body. Most often, these interpretations would be followed by long, agonizing, silences which left me feeling cruel and heartless, like the torturer of her internal world. Indeed, there were times when I felt considerably challenged by my countertransference, a feeling of being drawn into a sadistic enactment of cruelty which, at one level, she passively encouraged. Occasionally, the silence would be broken by a loud sob that conveyed an unbearable pain difficult for both of us to bear. During one session, when I suggested that my words were hurting her, she quietly insisted that this was not the case, willing me to continue in spite of her anguish. I became aware that her communications were taking on a different quality. Now, rather than belonging to the realm of masochistic acquiescence, they were beginning to convey an interest in finding out more about her pain. I wondered aloud if it was her wish that the doctors would find something physically wrong with her which she hoped they would treat medically and in this way take her suffering away. But, I continued, I thought that in part of her mind she recognized that her suffering lay in the terrible feelings of hurt and sadness she felt and she wanted me to know about them and how life threatening she felt them to be. She replied that she did not have a mind so could not think about these things, but her comment suggested that already these ideas were beginning to hold some meaning for her. A subtle change in atmosphere in the room supported my impression that she was reclaiming some space in her mind where her suffering could be held onto and encompassed rather than evacuated into her body, a space nurtured by meaning and understanding.

As fragments of her history gradually came to light she revealed an internal world dominated by an unforgiving, hostile mother threatening punishment and retribution for her transgressions. She, herself, closely identified with this figure who now held sway, a figure that had come to replace the supportive, life enhancing internal mother she believed she had destroyed by her anger and resentful attacks. It was her guilt at having been so defiant and rejecting in insisting upon her marriage and all its dire consequences, that now tormented and persecuted her and was making her ill. She insisted that she had brought this whole awful situation upon herself and her children and no amount of support from her external mother and family alleviated the intensity of her self-criticism.

Up until this time, around the sixth session, I had remained concerned about the children but it had not been possible to mention them; so great was her need for undivided attention. But now that she had brought them into the room, we were able to think about them together. With considerable emotion, she expressed her wish to become a better mother. I believe that her acknowledgement of this wish represented a change in our work. Internally, it symbolized a re-establishing of contact with a helpful object with a mind to look after herself and her children: a shift that was facilitated by her acceptance, in spite of her ambivalence, of my concern for her as someone who could tolerate her pain, bear to investigate its meaning and find a way of putting into words the intolerable feelings she was keeping at bay.

The crisis for Mrs B had come about by a tragic combination of circumstances. It was just as she was extricating herself from her marriage and feeling badly about the loss of her mother and her guilt towards her, for which she believed she should be roundly condemned, that she had been confronted by an external authority that confirmed her badness and sought to punish her through threatening the lives of her children. Both internal and external reality had come together to confirm her guilt which, in the absence of a forgiving inside voice which might otherwise have sustained her, had plunged her into hopelessness and despair. But a tiny part of her had remained alive and available and it was this that had made itself known to the community worker and myself. In a recent paper Rustin (2001) suggests that:

A traumatized patient ... needs to have a therapist survive what could be traumatic. The heart of the matter is that our moment of horror as therapists mirrors what the child could not cope with ... Bringing the trauma into the room, into the relationship with the therapist, is what may enable us to make a difference. To do the necessary work safely we have to ensure that we have time and adequate personal and professional support for ourselves. [pp. 283–284]

I believe that it was my knowing about and surviving her trauma in the room that had made the difference and enabled her to embark on the road to recovery, to reclaim her mind and become more concerned about her children. Engaging in this work is demanding and the pain being communicated can become almost unbearable, at times. The availability of supportive colleagues and access to a body of knowledge within which the process could be thought about and understood, became an integral part of the therapeutic framework. But it would have been difficult to sustain the work without the collaboration of the community worker who was available to offer practical support and to manage the external crisis.

I was in a position to provide the undivided attention that Mrs B required as I felt confident that the children's welfare and development were being firmly held in mind elsewhere. But without this conviction, my mind would have been, almost certainly, overwhelmed by their conflicting needs. It was the community worker who addressed the worries generated by the emergency hospital admissions, the threats of eviction and home-lessness and the impending dangers of relocation to yet another borough that would have jeopardized the family's fragile sense of security. Without her management of these anxieties my work would have been untenable as their urgency would have become the focus of treatment. But without the containment of her internally generated despair, I have a sense that the intensity of her projections would have challenged the resources of any community worker "however favourably brought up". The community worker and I needed each other, just as parents of a new baby each need the support of the other in providing for the child, and in this way we worked together as a couple, trusting and relying on each other's skill and competence as we fulfilled our respective tasks.

Facing reality

At a conference in London to investigate the educational attainments of Somali pupils (A report for Camden LEA, 2000), a university student reflected upon her childhood experience of becoming a refugee. What she recalled was having to flee "just as you are", without time to say goodbye, prepare for the journey or plan what luggage to take. It was during her stop over in Iceland that she realized she would not be going home again. For some young people, whose resources have been more keenly challenged, this painful realization can take much longer.

Case study: D

D was eleven years old when she left Eastern Europe with her parents and two little brothers to seek asylum in the UK. Her father had spent much time in hiding, a common occurrence within their community. As a small child she had experienced the early morning intrusions of police entering her home unannounced to conduct a search and enquire about father's whereabouts. On these occasions her mother would hide her upset and they never talked about it. After many upheavals, the family settled into permanent accommodation in London and were granted ELR (Exceptional Leave to Remain) status. At school, she picked up English quickly, was popular with her peers and demonstrated considerable ability, achieving well in class. However, as time went on, her teachers began to worry about her absent mindedness and the way she would drift off. They had an uneasy feeling that something was wrong but her smiling face and easy charm that sought to reassure all concerned that everything was fine, seemed to belie their anxiety. The first crack appeared when, aged fifteen, she failed to arrive for an exam, something quite out of character. She returned to school, some weeks later, offering no meaningful account of what had happened other than the fact that she had overslept. But something had changed. The concern of her teachers' grew and it was suggested that she might like to talk to someone. She was referred to the Refugee Counselling Service that had been established at the school. This in-school provision, which ran for a number of years, provided psychotherapy for refugee pupils and was resourced by staff from the Tavistock Clinic.

On first meeting, she presented as attractive and forthcoming and talked engagingly about friends and teachers with an idealized warmth and affection. From the beginning, I was aware that the ready contact between us had a strange quality. It gradually began to dawn on me that all the people she described belonged to the past yet she talked in a way that conveyed the immediacy of the present. This realization produced a disturbing effect as if something peculiar was happening inside my head. I did not know what to believe as her words and affect seemed to contradict each other. I had the feeling that my own experience was, simultaneously true and not true, a feeling of disavowal in which I was being drawn into a reservation that was free from the impingement of reality (Freud, 1924). On recovering my equilibrium, I was aware of a deep feeling of sadness. But I also felt under considerable pressure not to disclose my discovery as if to do so would be dangerous and disastrous. I suggested to D that it might be helpful for us to have more time together to explore what was happening and, somewhat reluctantly, she agreed.

During the sessions that followed, she complained bitterly about "all the fuss" that was being made about her failure to sit the exam. Then, one day she added that they did not really matter, anyway, as you never get the results. On exploring this apparently throw away remark, she explained that the morning she had fled to the UK with her family, she had been due to receive exam results, adding poignantly, that she still had not received them. With a little more encouragement she offered a fuller account of her departure. Her parents had kept their preparations secret until the evening before when they had informed her that they would be leaving early the next day. She felt shocked, angry and disbelieving and, initially, refused to accompany them. They put forward the explanation that secrecy had been essential on account of the volatility of the political situation and the dangers involved, for everyone, if their plans had been discovered. But she felt profoundly disturbed and betrayed and spent a sleepless night planning her escape. However, when morning came she felt coerced to join them. From the manner of her account it was evident that she had remained in a state of shock and I had a sense that, psychologically speaking, she had not yet arrived in the UK and was still in transit. But the recalling of these terrible events brought home their reality to her and she sobbed copiously.

The disavowal that she had employed to negate what had happened, and which had been so powerfully projected into me, began to break down.

She used our time together to express her hurt, pain, and rage towards me, the school, and her parents. The intensity of her distress was difficult to bear but less so than her utter denial of reality. Consciously, she tried hard to think of neither the past nor the future whilst, unconsciously, she inhabited a world in which past objects continued to be available to her as they had always done, as if nothing had changed (Britton, 1995). A belief that she had never left home, meant that only a superficial engagement with the world around her was required; I believe that it was this that accounted for the dreamy quality that had been noted by her perceptive teachers. I learned that, recently, her avoidance of reality had come under considerable strain following a letter from a friend back home that suggested she was living in the past. The letter described how as a group they had all moved on in their interests and friendships and this had shocked her deeply. The day of the exam at school in London followed shortly, triggering a flood of traumatic feelings and memories which she was ill-equipped to manage.

Her grief was profound but remained contained within our sessions as she struggled to protect her parents from its impact, feigning physical unwellness to account for her upset. According to her, her parents (like many refugee parents), sacrificed a great deal by going into exile and were consoling themselves with the idea that at least the children could put their losses behind them and get on with their lives, even if they, themselves, were unable to do so. In our work together I felt pained by the poignancy of her suffering and identified with the impotence and uselessness her parents must have felt in the face of her distress about leaving. But unlike her parents, I had available to me, through my learning and experience and the support of colleagues, the resources to continue to have a conversation with her about the reality of her pain and was able to introduce her to an idea of a world in which her pain could be tolerated and endured rather than damagingly avoided.

The next wave of understanding that impinged was a sudden, sharp realization that she had missed out on her life over these last four years, living neither here nor there. She mourned the fact that she would never get this time back and wondered if she would ever be able to catch up, wondering whether it was too late. Adolescent anxieties about relationships with girl friends and boy friends came to the fore. After some months, when she had found a boyfriend whom she felt she could talk to and who expressed a wish to help her, she told me that she did not need to see me any more. She expressed her appreciation for the help she had been given and explained that she now felt more ready to use the support of her peers.

It was with some concern on my part that our work together came to an end and I wondered if she was escaping, once again, this time into an adolescent world in which there was no need of parents, who, in any case, were experienced as depleted, inadequate, "has beens" with nothing to offer. I reflected upon her determination to keep her parents at arms' length and had no way of knowing the accuracy of her perceptions of them. I found myself wondering if her flight into the bosom of her friends was a flight away from a parental couple whose depression she found too difficult to bear. After all, they, like her, had fled under desperate circumstances and it was likely that their enforced secrecy had, additionally, served to avoid them facing the painfulness of their departure. Or was her flight in response to guilt about her passive hatred of them for taking her away or her triumphant educational success that left her despising their incompetence in her new world. Whilst there was much to remain concerned about, I believe a change had taken place. She had demonstrated a capacity to face reality and use support and I had the idea that she may seek out further professional help in the future, should the need arise, as proved to be the case.

Conclusion

The burden of the psychological pain suffered by refugees is enormous and its survival requires considerable resilience and a readiness to tap into whatever personal, social and agency support may be on offer. Whilst some refugees demonstrate an impressive ability to make use of this social capital, there are others for whom the availability of emotional, community and practical help may be limited or non-existent. But for another group, the problem is not so much the absence of support but their lack of capacity to use it.

In this chapter, I investigated the particular difficulties experienced in two such cases where a traumatic loss of contact with an internally supportive figure, in one case through excessive guilt and in the other through unresolved mourning and anger, resulted in a state of mindlessness that interfered with their contact with reality and their capacity to make use of the opportunities available to them. The psychoanalytically informed therapeutic work undertaken investigated their pain, bringing it into the room and their relationship with the therapist, where it could be thought about and survived. I believe that through re-establishing contact with a thinking object, Mrs B was supported in turning her attention away from the pain in her body to the toleration of the pain in her mind, a shift that enabled her to engage with life rather than remain overwhelmed by it. Similarly, through the work with D, she was helped to relinquish her disavowal in favour of bearing the painful reality of her departure from home and arrival in a new world.

I hope these case studies have demonstrated that where psychoanalytically informed psychotherapy is undertaken under the right conditions, a little can go a long way to make a significant difference to the quality of life of refugees.

CHAPTER SEVEN

Killing time: work with refugees

Valerie Sinason

"Oh earth, cover not thou my blood and let my cry have no
resting place"

The Bible, Job v. 16–18

"You tell me that if I leave this country
I can return
Again and again

The angry sea of customs and immigration
Will open up for me

And I will pass through
As effortlessly as a ghost through barbed wire"

"For the Stateless Person Getting a Passport". Sinason, 1987

General thoughts and introduction

I am writing this as the grandchild of refugees who came to the
East End of London from the pogroms of East Europe. I am
also writing this as a teacher, child psychotherapist and adult

psychoanalyst who has worked extensively with those living on the edge of mainstream recognition and services and who brings their experiences into public knowledge. That in itself is one of the reparative consequences of such generational transmission.

There were dynamics I most knew and noted from this history and recognized in people coming for help. Firstly, was the longing to be rooted in one place and one country and never to leave an assumed safe place. This would evoke fear of abandonment and catastrophe or rather re-facing in the present the past catastrophe. The fear of moving and letting go could also apply to belongings. Those who had experienced enormous poverty and hunger preferred to keep food, clothes, and other belongings long past their sell-by date for fear of there being nothing. Spending money could evoke a crisis of existential danger. All household items, such as string, bags, could be held onto as possible lifesavers in difficult times to come. Simplistic ideas of anal retentiveness or obsessional compulsive behaviour transposed to such behaviour, live in a different world to that of the reality of extreme starvation and other trauma. Secondly, was the opposite, the fear of staying when staying was equated with being annihilated. This led to a wandering life.

From personal experience, I can also corroborate the view "that far from having detrimental effects, the oppositional discourses [i.e. the opposition between loyalty to the country of origin and loyalty to the host country] may enrich and assist families to live more creatively" (Papadopoulos & Hildebrand, 1997, pp. 232–233). Additionally, it is important to note that an acknowledged political fact of attacks on any minority group does not necessarily traumatize all individuals. However, I am focusing here on some negative impacts of the refugee experience.

Fear of moving or letting go

ABDUL AGED TEN

> Abdul was diagnozed as having a severe attention deficit disorder and was sent to a school for emotionally disturbed children for his conduct disorder. Abdul clung onto every pencil and book he was given and would die rather than have it taken away. The end of any school lesson was "murder" to him. He fought any teacher or teachers who tried to remove these items.

It emerged in therapy that he had held onto his baby brother when his family had been massacred and, although he was only ten, he had never forgiven himself for his "weakness and cowardice" in eventually having his baby brother prised from his arms and killed. Additionally, he marched up and down classrooms at the beginning and end of lessons in a terrified state of hyper-vigilance. Once his courage and self-blame could be understood in therapy he was able to begin to mourn. A caring teacher also found ways of providing items he could keep and did not have to hand in.

VORJAT AGED TWELVE

Vorjat was not only a refugee who had witnessed terrible atrocities; he was also physically handicapped. At the end of his session his worker began to move his wheelchair out of the therapy room without preparing him. He looked terrified. He threw himself onto the floor out of his wheelchair and lay totally still. His carer apologized for not having warned him she was about to move his chair (something that regularly happens to physically disabled children and adults).

There was a powerful silence. He could not speak or move any part of himself. "Well done!" I said to him. "You are telling us you cannot be moved without proper warning. Good for you! You are lying down where there is nowhere lower you can fall to. You are already there".

He cried silently and I told him the poem of Janos Pilinszky. "Where you have fallen, you stay. In the whole universe, this is your place. Just this single spot. But you have made this yours absolutely" (1995). Then he was able to leave.

The nature of interpretations given is different in the light of the lived experience.

Fear of staying and identification with movement

The second dynamic was almost the flip-side of the first. This was the need to be identified with being a wanderer. American "road" songs can idealize the attachment to a lost and moving object who needs to be attached to the moving process itself because staying still can mean death. A rolling stone gathers no moss. Attachment to the world can make for fruitful internationalism at its best or for shallow roots.

STEFAN AGED THIRTY-SIX

Stefan saw himself as a loving womanizer. After a period of imprisonment and torture he had reached England and had a range of short-term relationships, which were all ended "because of my job". His job involved weekly travelling to Europe and long stays in the USA. "It is just not fair for a woman or future child to have to go through that". A little while later he could think how the moment he became attached he was terrified of loss of physical control (memories of torture flooding back) and invisible imprisonment—being forced to stay in one place. His mother and father and former fiancée had been killed and he saw their refusal to move as the key cause of their deaths. Moving on meant repairing and keeping alive all attachments at the same time, of course, as losing his new objects.

Stigma

The "adventurer" who seeks usually "his" luck in another country is admired in some periods of history. The Vikings who travelled to England for the sake of exploration are perceived differently from current "economic migrants" who desperately cling on to the bottom of channel tunnel lorries or trains in the hope of finding a better place for their families. However, schools are very aware of the language and cultural problems for "lucky" transplanted children. Army children, diplomatic children, boarding school children all face issues of cultural change and loss that need to be worked through. Adding on a different language, a different mother-tongue makes this process even more painful. However, moving without being a refugee does not inherently include the same level of trauma, where, that is, there is trauma.

A refugee has had to flee the place that was their home because it is no longer possible to be there—whether through natural causes (flood and volcano), man-made catastrophes of poverty and famine or man-made catastrophes of war and genocide. Just as the abuse victim is expected to feel gratitude at being "saved" from an abusive home (with no thought of the interwoven strands of love and corruption to mourn), the refugee is not allowed to be depressed, to pine for the beauty of their natural landscape, the different climate, views, language, sounds, assumptions.

Additionally, and particularly and again very like an abuse victim, a refugee is not expected to be hyper-vigilant, violent, traumatized, perverse, delinquent. Without any attachment and identification yet in place to the new country, the refugee is to be shamed at showing signs of their ordinary cultural behaviour. Countries that rank people according to their economic position create more shame and stigma for poor refugees.

ROSA AGED TWENTY-SIX

> A young Czech gypsy woman could not understand the hatred she received when begging with her baby on London underground trains. The baby was safe with her. Unlike the orphanage for gypsy children she was raised in, in the former Czechoslovakia, where there was a high death-rate of unloved abandoned babies, she was proud to keep the baby with her at all times. She could not believe money would come to her and not be taken away because her previous experience was to trust her own street-wise means of survival. Otherwise she and the baby would have been separated.

Nature of refugee experience

Refugees come in different ways from different cultures and events. Papadopoulos (2000b, 2001a,b) is concerned at the blanket way "refugee trauma" emphasizes one of the four phases of the refugee experience he has documented; these are: (a) "anticipation"; (b): "devastating events"; (c): "survival"; and (d): "adjustment". More specifically, he argues that the "refugee trauma" privileges the phase of "devastating events", without considering the other three phases. Moreover, as he points out, many refugees escape the actual period of "devastating events". This makes it all the more important to examine the meaning of trauma.

Trauma

My main concern here is those refugees who are bearers of trauma, wounds from external reality that we find very hard to bear. Part of our difficulty in bearing the pain of trauma means that we tend to punish the witness or message-bearer. Just as the abused child is hated for making us realize the meaning of abuse, the traumatized refugee can be pathologized by our definitions. This is something specialists in the field of refugee trauma (e.g. Papadopoulos, 1999a,b, 2000b, 2001a,b; Papadopoulos & Hildebrand, 1997; Summerfield, 2001) are particularly wary of; they examine the impact that the wider dynamics of families and socio–cultural discourses have on the ways that professionals tend to relate with their refugee clients. They show how the dominance of the refugee trauma discourse slants towards a pathologization of the refugee situation. Nevertheless, it cannot be denied that certain refugees are traumatized and this chapter focuses on my own experiences of this phenomenon.

Trauma comes from the Greek, meaning, "wound" from an earlier derivation meaning, "to pierce". It has long been used in medicine and surgery as meaning both an injury where the skin is broken as a result of external violence and as the consequences on the organism as a whole.

Regardless of the newer understanding of the meaning of the word (Papadopoulos, 2000b, 2001a), in using the term "trauma" psychoanalysis, followed by psychology, has utilized the three components involved.

(a) *An external stressor that comes suddenly and therefore cannot be prepared for.*
The human animal shares with others a life that involves many external stresses. Physical incapacity, mental incapacity, hunger, pain, separation, loss, death, and aggression are universal experiences. Where there is warning of impending catastrophe, preparations can be made and total helplessness is avoided. However, natural and man-made disasters that suddenly overtake the individual intrinsically cannot be prepared for. Suddenness breaks through even hyper-vigilant behaviour. Suddenness is therefore an intrinsic component of a traumatic incident.

On August 27th 1998 Hurricane Bonnie sweeping through North Carolina did not cause deaths as earlier awareness of hurricanes and how to deal with them had led to careful evacuation. The hurricane itself could not be as traumatic as those for whom there was no advance technological warning or human proactive planning. By contrast, a bombing of Planet Hollywood, an American-owned hamburger restaurant in a tourist area in Cape Town was traumatic (August 26th 1998). Whilst the South African population is psychically geared to the knowledge of an expectancy of violence the suddenness of an attack on an area used especially by children could not be prepared for. However, it is possible that the extreme visibility of this attack will lessen post-traumatic disturbance.

Significantly, there is some evidence that less visible man-made disasters are more likely to lead to post traumatic emotional disturbance (Scurfield, 1985). Natural disasters, when large in scale, are shared by others and can be seen in the environment. Floods and earthquakes, tornadoes and hurricanes, leave a public visible sign. The testimony of survivors is shared. Indirect man-made disasters, where human error has precipitated a shipwreck, fire or train crash are also more amenable to being processed. The experience of the "innocent" victims is shared in the same way as with natural disasters and the visible proof of the trauma is also shared. A personal man-made trauma is more personal, not always so visible and, especially when involving sexual abuse, shameful. Pynoos and his team (1995) have highlighted the significance of intentionality. Their research has revealed five basic parameters.

— Proximity to the violence
— Lethality of the instrument
— Intentionality
— Object of the violence, and
— Seriousness of the injury.

(b) *A stressor that is strong enough to break through the protective shield of skin and mind (Freud, 1920) which cannot be adequately mentally processed and affects the whole organism.*
Human beings from earliest infancy through to death have to face many painful experiences. Indeed, part of the ability to deal with difficulties and think comes from the experience of managing difficulties. However, a sudden overwhelming experience is not possible to process adequately mentally.

Indeed, it is important to note that some events can never be adequately mentally processed. For example a study of Vietnam veterans (Schlenger *et al.*, 1992) showed that twenty years afterwards, 500,000 individuals (15.2% of men and 8.5% of women) still suffered PTSD.

(c) *The interface with the individual's internal world including unconscious guilt and phantasy.*
Psychoanalytic theory adds extra complexity to this paradigm as it is possible for someone to experience intentionality that is not objectively present. In other words, unconscious and conscious anxieties and phantasies can transform concepts of intentionality.

Clinical examples

DONNA AGED SIX

Donna had Down's syndrome. Despite patient attempts by both her caring parents to explain the meaning of Down's syndrome, she stayed rooted in the idea "Donna is a bad girl and her face went bad". Donna took the blame herself in order to feel less helpless. There was also a gender bias in her taking such responsibility. She saw all stigmatization and trauma in her previous country as caused by her learning disability.

ADONIS AGED EIGHT

Adonis on the other hand, also with Down's syndrome, commented, "Daddy hates me. Gave me Down's syndrome. Greece hates me". Here, an additional cause for such a gender-biased view was that Adonis's father left the marital home, not bearing the personal pain of having a son with a disability and there were superstitious views about Adonis in the particular village he was born that led his enterprizing mother and aunts to get him to the UK.

However, it is important to emphasize in both examples, they did have an external reality impingement to deal with. The unconscious fantasy would never have had to be worked through without the intrusion.

Psychiatric definitions of trauma

It was in 1980 that the Diagnostic and Statistical Manual of Mental Disorders (DSM-III) first included a separate category for psychological trauma.

Criteria on trauma as defined by the DSM-IV
(American Psychiatric Association, 1994)

Trauma can be diagnozed when a person has experienced an event that is outside the range of usual human experience and that would be markedly distressing to almost anyone such as: a serious threat or harm to one's life or physical integrity; serious threat or harm to one's children, spouse or other close relatives and friends; sudden destruction of one's home or community; or seeing another person who has recently been or is being injured or killed as a result of an accident or physical violence.

Highly relevant to this thesis is the finding that life-threatening physical illness (Hartman & Burgess, 1985) and sexual abuse (Donaldson & Gardner, 1982; De Zulueta, 1993) have similar post-traumatic consequences.

The current criteria for a traumatic event add, "the person's response involves intense fear, helplessness, or horror. In children this may be expressed instead by disorganized or agitated behaviour" (DSM-IV 309, p. 81).

Multi-disciplinary shared views on trauma:
the breakdown of assumptions

Daily life depends on a series of theories about the world and ourselves. Of particular relevance to trauma are three assumptions. Regardless of knowledge of personal vulnerability and mortality we operate on an assumption of personal invulnerability. Indeed, illness and death are often called "life" events in the hope that by singling them out we will see them as a part of life. If they truly were experienced as part of life, we would not need to call them "life events".

Secondly, we operate on an assumption that the world and our experiences within it can be experienced as meaningful. Finally, regardless of unconscious doubts, we largely have a consciously benign view of our place in the world. Trauma calls into question all these ways of viewing the self and the world (Bard & Sangrey, 1970; Janoff-Bulman, 1985; Garland, 1998, pp. 9–31).

Lerner's (1980) "Just World" theory underlines the sense of a fair world in which people get what they deserve. A trauma causes a problem here. There are religious and social doubts activated after natural and man-made disasters. Disasters are not fair. They destroy the innocent as well as the guilty. Therefore, they disturb the assumption that there is a simple concept of justice at work. Indeed, Bloom (1997) emphasizes the need for justice and fairness in working with victims and perpetrators alike, in order to minimize post-traumatic stress disorders.

Finally, positive assumptions about the individual's place in the world are also eroded by trauma. Trauma reactivates negative self-esteem and stirs up unconscious fantasy (Garland, 1998).

Biological and neuro-biological aspects of trauma

In common with other animals, we share certain biological and neurobiological responses to danger. The fight–flight impulse, for example, is an instinctive biological response. This was the term coined (Cannon, 1914) to describe the appropriate bodily response to danger. Breathing is affected, the heart-rate increases as do alertness and vigilance. There is extra brain activity in the release of norephinephrine. Additionally, there are signals transmitted for the release of adrenaline. However, when the danger is inescapable, most animals respond with behavioural helplessness and the same bodily changes in later situations where escape was possible but a trigger existed or where aversive stimulus was mild (Van der Kolk, 1987). Hence, whilst an immediate response of a neurobiological kind to acute stress can be reversible where the trauma lasts or is of sufficient intensity or frequency (Perry, 1994) the changes are not reversible.

Regardless of the nature of the trauma, the human response is consistent. There is an intense response to any trigger reminiscent of the original trauma. In other words there is no ability to regulate a physiological response (Schore, 2001a,b). There is no function that enables regulatory modulation of affections so that anxiety and aggression are extreme, whether internally or externally directed. Life-threatening physical illness (Hartman & Burgess, 1985) and sexual abuse (Donaldson & Gardner, 1985; De Zulueta, 1993) have similar post-traumatic consequences.

The consequences in adolescent and adult life are profound. Perry (1994), in looking at changes in neurochemical regulation and physiological function in traumatized adolescents, hypothesized that prolonged alarm reactions in earlier childhood induced chronic abnormal patterns of catecholamine activity altering brainstem functioning, including cardiovascular dysregulation.

The amygdala can alter its danger-recognition set points and the hippocampus its memory-encoding properties. Additionally, the media prefrontal cortex can have its abilities to establish or reduce associational connections hampered (Horowitz, 1999).

Self-injurious behaviour in adults (Pynoos et al., 1995) together with suicidal behaviour might be a re-enactment in adult life of past trauma.

Attachment, trauma and child development

Childhood attachment is a pre-requisite to safety. Spitz (1945) showed how children in an orphanage, who were physically cared for but who had no attachment figures, were more vulnerable to dying. Attachment to an adult or adults protects children from danger whilst they develop the maturational skills to care for themselves. Where a parent is unable to screen a child from danger or is part of a dangerous experience for a child, these factors can alter or destroy a young child's perception of safety and of adult protectiveness (Pynoos et al., 1995).

Where the trauma is external but the parent is unable to mediate the experience because of her own traumatized experience or either minimizes or over-reacts (Bat-Zion & Levy Shiff, 1993; Pynoos & Nader, 1993), children experience more physiological and emotional anxiety whereas where a parent remains calm and appears in control, the child's anxiety before and after is lessened. It is the mother's response that is the most significant indicator in the development of symptoms in the child (McFarlane, 1987).

Hyper arousal (Van der Kolk, 1987; Field, 1985; Perry, 1994) in response to minor triggers also occurs after disruptions of attachment. There is a similar physiological disturbance and disorganization in infants separated from their care-givers. Spitz (1945) found that in an orphanage, despite impeccable hygiene, toddlers were more susceptible to illness and had higher mortality rates. Our understanding of the traumatic consequences of separation has been underlined by the pioneering research of Bowlby (1979).

Professor Allan N. Schore (2001a,b) brings together psycho-analytic research, attachment research, and brain research in showing how impairment of the right brain's stress coping systems due to relational trauma in infancy have damaging consequences for the future adult.

All of these issues need to be considered when dealing with traumatized refugees. Was the child's emotional experience filtered by the resilience of parents or family and friends? With secure attachment the impact on the young child's brain functioning is modified. What kind of attachment patterns did the adults have to their own internal parents or external ones if still alive? The most extreme level of dissociative disorder that I treat in my Clinic for Dissociative Studies is those without secure attachments who were so sadistically injured under the age of five that they fragmented into different states (Sinason, 2002), involving major neurological and brain re-circuiting.

A technical note

Those who have been chronically traumatized sometimes have internalized a painful dialogue that makes their emotional expression flat and lifeless. They have uttered a sound or communication of great human need and been met with blankness, retaliation or disconfirming. This two-person dialogue has then been internalized in a way that re-enacts the original trauma and tragically, all too often, brings in the therapist as the disconfirming object.

An assessment: cannibalism and killing time

A mother with her daughter from Rwanda newly arrived from an atrocity area somehow ended up in safety in the UK. They had been raped singly and together. Other siblings had been hacked to death in front of them. Before joining a convoy to safety, parts of the husband/father's body had been thrown at them. They had been forced to eat this.

Something of the unbearable nature of their experiences had meant there had been inordinate delays in housing them and providing them with adequate support. Distant relatives who were currently housing them in extremely cramped conditions were also overwhelmed by grief and secondary traumatization. Mealtimes were particularly traumatic with the daughter vomiting involuntarily. Blessings had been sought from religious figures over the taboo experience of cannibalism (just as the Andes survivors of an aircraft accident sought a blessing from the Pope after eating the flesh of a dead comrade in order to survive), but had made no difference.

It was my experience of working with abuse survivors who had been made to take part in cannibalistic acts that led to this referral. Local services were not willing to provide services until I had written a report, even though I made clear it would be damaging for the family to travel all the way to London to meet someone they would never see again. However, nobody wished to see these terrible witnesses without another professional having part-digested something of the inedible narrative.

A short note on cannibalism

> Fee fo fi fum
> I smell the blood of an Englishman
> Be he alive or be he dead
> I'll grind his bones to make my bread.

Whilst the oral stage was originally the oral cannibalistic stage, contemporary psychoanalysis appears to have removed that rather complex second adjective. McDougall (1995) speaks of Cannibal Love instead of "oral" love, reminding us implicitly of the censored missing word.

Cannibalism is a forbidden area evoked only by primitive jokes usually displaced onto a black other, or temporarily resurrected in looking at the behaviour of serial killers. Outside of head-hunting tribes, cannibalism has largely been seen in the forensic field at the most disturbed end and its tendrils in regard to babies—"so lovely I could eat her up" are more often tidied up in fairy tales where wolves who try to eat and incorporate mother's babies as one envious attack on her get their come-uppance by being filled with stones.

In the recent fighting in Borneo, the subject of cannibalism took on a painful contemporary note. When people offend against the "adat" they are not seen as humans but as animals, "Then we eat them as animals". Dayak warriors in Borneo could thus be seen casually eating the body parts of the Madurese they had just killed.

However, in the field of ritual abuse survivors, who I have called invisible refugees (Sinason, 1994) there is regularly talk of being made to eat human flesh—usually of a baby. It is this disclosure above all other that leads to enormous shame and guilt and precipitates self-injury.

This fear was actualized in the Goddess religions that Judaism and then Christianity tried to stop. The Goddess, as mother and creatress of the universe, demanded the sacrifice of babies. The Goddess, Innana/Ishtar is Goddess of heavens, fertility, judgement, war, sexual love, healing.

In mythology we have the primordial child who then incorporates the power of the God. Christianity, in struggling to reverse the Goddess religion, has the primordial child killed by the primordial father.

The Ogre in Jack and the Beanstalk is allowed to relish his cannibalistic impulses. "I'll grind his bones to make my bread". For him they are not symbolic, or even a symbolic equation. His larder is full of human meat. Like Cronus, he is the father who devours the young males who will eventually seek to destroy him.

How does this happen? Television commentators on the war in Kosovo have pointed out that without adequate food supplies the animals in Kosovo zoo had begun to eat their own babies. Cannibalism in China and Russia by humans and other species at times of starvation and terror is also well noted and is part of the background of a significant number of serial killers within the West. It, therefore, can literally be a survival mechanism even before we look at religious meanings concerning incorporating the goodness of the other. Spitz (1945) found that orphanage deprived babies without an internal constant object could not differentiate between a mother's body/bottle and themselves and would bite themselves. Indeed, biting, in child abuse, is a sign of a far more dangerous disturbance.

However, in order to avoid secondary traumatization, I am not going to provide a detailed case history here. Nevertheless, I consider it important that health service professionals intending to take on some of this trauma work can conceptually begin to consider the origins for such behaviour.

End of the assessment: mother thirty-eight and daughter thirteen from Rwanda

The mother and daughter had been told we would meet for one hour and thirty minutes and that I would then send a report to their local services. At the one-hour point I had also reminded them of the time constraints. I brought, I hoped, the meeting to a slow and gentle end and explained what would now happen with the local service and what I would put in my report. And now the time had gone and I had to admit I experienced relief. Their account was harrowing in the extreme.

"It is time", I said.

"No!" shouted the child. She looked at me with absolute horror and fury on her face. She remained seated, mute with despair.

"It is hard that now it is time to stop", I said softly.

There was an electric pause before she spoke in stiletto sharp words.

"You stopping. You. Not me. Not time".

There was a painful pause as I took in the correctness of her statement.

"You are right. I am saying we stop now. The time is not saying it and you are not saying it. I am sorry. It is hard for you that it is me who says we stop now even though you do not want to and you have so much to tell me".

The thirteen year old raised herself proudly to her impressive height and spoke words I will never forget.

"Easy say stop. Easy say dead. Easy say-now-kill. Say it is time. Orders. British fixed appointments. Refugee. Home office. Queue. Passport. Easy easy words. Goodbye killer".

With her pale-faced mother smiling nervously at me the thirteen year old left the room, leaving me humble and shocked.

The child was bringing Bosnia and Rwanda into the room and I was replying "English" without adequate attunement to her situation. Within therapy schools there is a shared culture that underpins meaning around time-frames. "We have to stop now". "It is time now". The fifty-minute hour was not invented by each practitioner anew, it was inherited, just as was ninety minutes for family interviews and groups. As inheritors, we have the luxury of only having to question when something does not work with the frame. Hale & Sinason (1994) found that ritually abused dissociative patients needed two hour sessions. As a result of that thirteen-year old, I have rethought my language in all kinds of settings. Winnicott's concept of punctuality being the way the analyst expresses hatred is worth exploring here.

Where bodies and minds have been chopped up, fragmented, what room can we make for attunement?

Conclusion

Working with the actual pain of external reality is not popular. Therapists used to the beauty of symbolic representation need to understand the achievement of even managing a symbolic equation. Lacanian concepts of "the real" come in here too. The person who has gone through systematic torture and loss knows only too well our fears and failings. Therapeutic language as a defence against pain (witness my inept "It's time") do not work. Also we have the pain of realising where our own actions are not symbolic. The East European woman being employed as a prostitute, the Middle Eastern boy being sexually abused by his mother and aunts with no social services action because such abuse was not recognizable, the severely learning disabled adult returning to a violent home, are not experiencing the end of the session as symbolic loss. It is a reality.

We have to acknowledge our own psychic limits at bearing indigestible narratives and be accountable for the pain our misattunements cause. However, if we do manage this, then we will have been enriched with the heart and soul of another and another culture and our defining of Statehood will have changed.

CHAPTER EIGHT

Transient familiar others. Uninvited persons in psychotherapy with refugees

Renos K. Papadopoulos and Violeta Hulme

T he aim of this chapter is to identify and explore a specific phenomenon in psychotherapy with refugees. This phenomenon refers to situations when refugees in psychotherapy bring to their session/s person/s who were not invited to come and without giving in advance any notification to the therapist. To our knowledge, this has not been examined before and it will be argued that it highlights important facets of working therapeutically with refugees. Although, admittedly, it may not be a very common phenomenon, nevertheless, it deserves attention not only because of the implications it has for the technical considerations of therapy when it occurs, but also because it can enrich our understanding of the nature, meaning and purpose of the psychotherapeutic work with this group of people.

The first author is a clinical psychologist at the Tavistock Clinic and (in addition to other duties) works therapeutically with refugees (individuals and families) and the second author is an interpreter who has completed the specialist course on "Working with Refugees" at the Tavistock Clinic, taught by the first author. We often work together with refugees from the former and present Yugoslavia who are referred to the Tavistock Clinic for psychotherapy. The first author is a Greek Cypriot who speaks Serbocroat and the second author was born in Yugoslavia of mixed nationality and speaks several languages including Albanian and Serbocroat.

In this chapter we present and discuss two case examples from our recent practice where the refugee patients brought unannounced persons to their sessions. The cases have certain similarities and many differences between them but both present interesting facets of the therapeutic approach with refugees.

First example

A is a Kosovan–Albanian young woman in her mid twenties who was brought to this country in 1999 after the refugee exodus from Kosovo. Her parents were arrested and subsequently murdered. She left home and joined the exodus of refugees, witnessing atrocities, on her way to Macedonia. In London, A was reunited and stayed with her older sister (in her late thirties) who was divorced and had been living here alone with her children for seven years. A had not seen her sister since she had left Kosovo for London six years earlier; her sister did not return home and A did not visit London prior to her arrival in the UK as a refugee.

Shortly after settling in London with her sister, A had a serious traffic accident and spent several weeks in intensive care. As a result, she now is afraid of doctors. She suffers from strong migraines, pain in one side of her body, in addition to having disturbed sleep, nightmares and flashbacks (of the accident as well as of the atrocities in Kosovo). Her general medical practitioner prescribed painkillers and antidepressants for her and she is still taking them. She has difficulties concentrating and learning, tends to be agitated and nervous, and gets easily frustrated.

Before her accident, A began attending school that teaches the English language to foreigners. She was quite disruptive in the classroom and demanded extra attention from her teacher. The teacher referred A to the school psychologist but they had difficulties communicating without an interpreter. Moreover, the psychologist soon realized that A's condition required specialist professional attention and she referred her to the Tavistock Clinic.

We were not very surprised to find her in the waiting room for her first session, with a female teacher from her school. It is not very unusual for refugees to arrive for their first session accompanied by friends or other workers who wish to assist them to find the Clinic, to ensure that they arrive on time, to wait in the correct waiting room and, in general, to oversee that everything goes smoothly. Occasionally, such persons also wish to have a word with the therapist in order to convey what they perceive is important information. However, we were a little surprised when the teacher said that it was A's wish that she joins the session. Even this is not very unusual. It is not infrequent that such accompanying persons request permission to join the first session in order to enable a smooth transition into psychotherapy. What surprised us most was that soon after the session began A said very clearly that she expected her teacher to accompany her to all her sessions with us. She said that in a very firm way as if she expected us to argue against it. We said that we did not object to her demand (because, in fact, it was a demand and not a request) and clarified that, for the time being, all four of us would continue to meet, and we would see how things develop and then decide accordingly.

A was extremely attached to her father. She had been the only child left at home and her father had a particularly close relationship with her. He was a professional man who was also politically involved in the nationalist movement of Kosovars and as a result he suffered discrimination and persecution from the Yugoslav authorities for many years. Her mother was a devoted wife and a well educated woman. During the chaotic upheavals in the period of the NATO bombing of Kosovo, her father was arrested by Serbian paramilitary forces. A remembers vividly the afternoon of his arrest. He was calm and assured her not to worry about him. He asked her to do her best to leave the country and join her sister in London, promising to unite with them, along with her mother, at a later stage. A keeps remembering the painful details of that parting, blaming herself for obeying her father and letting him be taken away. She knows, of course, that it is irrational to blame herself because she could not have done anything to prevent his arrest, but still she cannot forgive herself. Then, during the exodus from Kosovo, she lost her mother and later heard that she was murdered, as was her father. She has no other siblings apart from her sister in London. It was rather unusual for a Kosovar family to have only two daughters. Before the war, A was a student but, unlike her father, she was not involved in politics and was leading a rather quiet life, like her mother. Only her father was interested and involved in politics. He seemed to have been a charismatic and powerful man and both women must have been in awe of him. However, he appears also to have been a gentle and kind man, an intellectual and a devout Muslim. Neither A nor her mother had strong religious beliefs, although they clearly considered themselves as Muslims. They seemed to have been content to bask in the shadow of the powerful, assuring and protective presence of her father.

For the first few sessions A would come with her teacher and usually talk at us (rather than with us) mainly about two themes: complaints about almost everything in her current life, and information, in a rather detached way, about facets of her life and experiences back in Kosovo. Invariably, she would return to the theme of her parents and their premature death. This was the only subject that was accompanied by emotion; she would express strong anger in a contained way and she stubbornly would try, unsuccessfully, to hold back her tears. The teacher would then hold A's hand and give her tissues to wipe her tears, all in silence. The teacher would sit there awkwardly, as if eavesdropping on A's intimate accounts which now she could understand for the first time through the interpreter (the second author). A's spoken English is not very fluent and she prefers to speak in Albanian (and be interpreted into English) and also wants everything said in English to be interpreted into Albanian.

Although the therapeutic process was developing relatively well, we were aware that we felt rather paralysed by the multidimensional nature of the situation: the enormity of A's pain and the unusual setting with the teacher present. Gradually, we began to clarify, in our own discussions in-between sessions, the various constituent elements of the complex situation and the therapeutic dynamics, and started to feel freer and less paralysed. We reflected on our reactions to both A and her teacher and acknowledged our mixture of feelings: on the one hand, we were fond of A and felt extremely protective towards her, feeling deeply her pain and destitution and, on the other hand, we felt annoyed because we felt as if we were manipulated by a greedy child.

Although we were aware of the importance for A that her teacher was present, we felt uneasy and intruded upon, feeling that we were stuck with an arrangement we did not know how to alter. We also became aware of our impulse to become firmer and to demand to exclude the teacher from our sessions; but we realized that that would have been a counterproductive and indeed a symmetrical and impulsive response to A's original demand to include her teacher. Reflecting on the positive function of A's demand, we realized that it was a complex phenomenon of which we did not have a clear understanding; nevertheless, we sensed that it included at least three components:

(a) With reference to the actual teacher's presence—undoubtedly, the teacher created a sense of safety for A, although it was not an unambiguous situation. It was evident that A was, in fact, not very close to her teacher and yet she experienced her presence as containing.

(b) With reference to her relationship with us—we knew that she had a fear of doctors and her teacher's presence must have made A's contact with us more bearable.

(c) With reference to her decision—A, by making that demand, must have experienced her potency in shaping, at least, some conditions and in influencing some facets of her life; this sense of agency must have been considerably important for her, and it was in contrast to what had happened in Kosovo, when she was helpless to prevent the destruction of her family and the murder of her parents.

However, regardless of the original purpose of the initial arrangement, as the therapy was developing, both A and her teacher seemed to become increasingly uncomfortable about the arrangement but were unable to alter it. Accepting that we did not have, as yet, a clearer understanding of the complexities of this phenomenon, we continued working with the teacher present at our sessions, endeavouring to increase our insightfulness. Gradually, after several further discussions between us, we felt relatively clear to say in a session that we agreed that it was appropriate for A to keep bringing her teaching to the sessions "for the time being". In addition to having a familiar person in the room, we said that the teacher's presence seemed "helpful in making up for her parents' death" as well as for A "being away from home". We emphasized that although we did not "completely understand, why it made up for these losses, nevertheless, we felt that" her teacher's presence had that function. A covered her face up and cried unrestrainedly for a long time in silence.

> During the following session, the teacher spoke about her ambivalent feelings in sitting in A's sessions. On the one hand, she was willing to help A as much as she could but, on the other hand, she felt awkward being present in a space which was supposed to be for A in an exclusive and intimate way. Moreover, she admitted that she felt uncomfortable because she hardly knew A. They were unable to converse easily at school due to the language barrier between them and she explained that it was not painless for her to sit through the sessions and listen for the first time to the personal details about A's life and feelings in a setting where she did not have any role.

> A listened silently and thoughtfully and gradually the two women were able to speak to each other in front of us more openly about the arrangement. A expressed her need to be with her teacher but she also understood that it was not necessary to drag her to the sessions forever. Moreover, she was worried that her teacher may have felt blackmailed into joining A in her therapy.

> The whole climate of the therapy began to change and there was a genuinely open exchange between them about their respective positions. There was an obvious sense of relief in everybody that they were able to speak about this. Without rushing into altering the arrangement, we added our own viewpoint by identifying the various pressures that both women were under, and then focused in particular on A's needs, offering ways of dealing with them separately.

> More specifically, with reference to her physical symptoms, A always used to say that she did not know whether they were a result of her accident or of her traumatic experiences in Kosovo. Putting them in a new perspective, we said that we were not certain either of their exact causes but in addition to the two reasons she mentioned, we thought that there were further possible explanations for having these symptoms. We suggested that her pains were not unconnected

with the enormity of her losses (parents, home, country) and the realistic pressures on her now in this country in relation to her refugee status (she is still waiting for her application to remain in this country to be considered by the authorities), and the pain of having to begin a new life on her own here. Further, we emphasized that piecing all that together was not an easy task and it was not likely to be achieved very soon. Then, with her consent, we referred her for a specialist assessment to diagnoze the precise nature of the consequences of her accident, and we also wrote to her solicitor requesting information about the progress of her application.

A felt more held and understood and the quality of her contact with us began to change. The tone of her voice became more connected, she was able to talk more with us (rather than at us) and a smile began appearing on her face. It was an enigmatic smile of a little girl, partly helpless and partly mischievous. At about the same time, A and her teacher began expressing their uneasiness about continuing with the arrangement for the teacher to be present in her sessions with us. Once we saw that they were becoming clearer about terminating the arrangement, we assisted them by proposing an ending date within a couple of sessions and helped them to negotiate the kind of relationship they wanted to have after that end. Both seemed satisfied and felt safe enough to terminate the arrangement. It appeared that both had felt trapped in something that initially seemed good and appropriate but then gradually it had become a snare out of which they could not break free. Both women were able to express their relief as well as their sadness at the impending end.

We were most surprised when at the following session, A announced that she wanted another teacher to replace the first teacher joining her in her sessions. She had mentioned the other teacher previously as the only other person at her school that cared for her. We discussed her suggestion and proposed that this time the arrangement should be implemented in a more systematic and planned manner. Without questioning her reasons for wanting a replacement of the first teacher, we suggested that the second teacher should be contacted in advance and that all of us should negotiate an acceptable arrangement before her first session. In a telephone conversation with the second female teacher, she told us that she was in a dilemma because, one the one hand, she liked A and wanted to help her, but on the other hand, she was concerned about the boundaries of her relationship with her and did not wish to compromise her own privacy—she was newly married and pregnant.

Finally, we all agreed that the second teacher could come for only two sessions, which she did. During those sessions, A was able to express her awareness of the difficulties of the situation and accepted that it was not needed for her teacher to come again. Moreover, she was able to negotiate clear and boundaried limits to their relationship outside her therapy sessions.

When we began having sessions with A on her own, she started telling us more about her relationship with her sister in London. She felt disconnected from her and she did not relate well with her sister's children. Evidently, she found it difficult to share with her the pain of their loss; also, A did not wish to get close to her sister's difficulties with her own family and both seemed to live a painful existence next to each other without being able to share their anguish. It also emerged that their mother had a close woman friend in London with whom A developed a rather warm relationship but she was finding it awkward to talk about it in the sessions, as if she did not want to share her substitute mother with us.

It was then that A also began considering her relationship with her boyfriend. Before the war she had a boyfriend at home but this relationship did not appear to be particularly strong or deeply meaningful. After the war, he remained behind in Kosovo and at just about the time of her coming to the Tavistock Clinic they re-established contact. She was extremely distressed because, according to her, he rejected her and told her that he decided to terminate their relationship after only a couple of phone calls. The reason, she said, was that her boyfriend thought that she "could not lead a normal life after her accident". She was very upset and angry about his reaction, called him "big-headed" and blamed his rejection of her on his newly acquired "Muslim mentality". She was able to mourn the end of her relationship as well as to express her rage at his heartless treatment of her.

Slowly, A was becoming able to connect with the enormity of her pain. The obstacles that had prevented her from relating to her profound disconnection within herself seemed to be moving away.

Discussion

As the purpose of this chapter is to illustrate the phenomenon of uninvited persons in psychotherapy with refugees, the presentation and discussion of this example is, inevitably, limited to this purpose and it will not address many of the other important facets of our clinical work with A.

Although it would be imprudent to argue for a definitive and single explanation of this phenomenon, nevertheless it would be useful to venture into exploring some of its constituent dimensions.

There is no doubt that the two teachers A brought to her psychotherapy sessions served a useful function not only in stabilizing her in psychotherapy but also in assisting her to address some debilitating obstacles that prevented her from connecting with facets of her own inner and outer world. It could be said that both teachers, in their transient presence, served a transitional function in enabling her to feel safe enough to tackle the enormity of her pain and in ushering her into the next phase of her development. Both were familiar figures and actual people, they were not images of her fantasy or objects she carried around with her. It is important to note that both of them were not members of her family or of her ethnic group or of the staff from supporting services she was dependent on. This means that they combined a certain familiarity with a degree of otherness (Papadopoulos, 2002b). On the one hand they were close to her and she trusted them, but on the other hand they belonged to a different ethnic, language and cultural group. Therefore, it is proposed that such persons are considered as "transient familiar others". These two Transient Familiar Others seemed to have offered A an optimal distance, protecting her from the intensity of her own projections, thus preventing excessive identification and even fusion with them. Following this appreciation, it can be added that the teachers' age was equally suitable. Both were in their mid thirties which means that they were not close either to her own age or to that of her parents. Finally, it could be argued that A must have known, deep down, that these two teachers could not have been available to become her close companions; the first teacher had a stable partner and the second one was married and pregnant at the time. Both of them were leading their own independent and full social lives. The pregnancy, of course, must have evoked images of motherhood, home and parental, and more specifically, maternal intimacy. It could be hypothesized that the teacher's pregnancy activated strongly baby feelings in A who sought to reconnect with the sense of safety and protection.

Although our first interpretative intervention (about the importance of her teacher's presence and her function in "making up" for her lost parents and lost home) was a fairly simple statement of the obvious situation, it, nevertheless, seems to have brought home some basic awareness. A, overwhelmed and frozen by extreme emotional deprivation, frightfully alone and with an enormous amount of undigested experiences, developed a tyrannical greediness that was expressed in unboundaried ways. Our intervention must have created a combination of boundaried safety with accepting flexibility. Moreover, by admitting to our own limits in understanding (when we said that we do not fully understand the connections) we may have also brought some note of safe reality into the midst of highly charged projections.

Subsequent to our intervention, the first teacher was freed to voice her own limitations and boundaries in a way that also conveyed her genuine caring of A. That enabled A to express her own misgivings, and gradually, the oppressive fear of a destructive resolution of this arrangement began to ease and the whole situation felt for A safer and more manageable. When the central cluster of the arrangement was addressed, it then became possible for us to delineate A's specific needs and we were able to refer her to other appropriate sources of help.

The second "transient familiar other" was introduced in advance and, on the basis of the work done with the first teacher, we were able to anticipate some of the difficulties and create a boundaried framework within which it was still possible for A to derive the positive benefits of her second teacher's presence.

Evidently, A needed the experience of having two "transient familiar others" in order to become available to herself, to connect with her own inner world and to create a more fitting therapeutic frame for her and us. Then, she was able to address her current situation with her sister, her mother figure and her boyfriend. It must have been very difficult for A to have come to her sister's house and find not the home she had been yearning to re-establish but, instead, another source of pain and disconnection. However, even if she had found a warm and loving home in her sister's household in London, it is doubtful whether she would have been in a position to experience it as such and respond accordingly. Her own psychological "frozenness" would have prevented her from doing so.

Frozenness has been suggested as an apt term to refer to the refugees' psychological state of constriction, contraction and retrenchment when they concentrate only on the bare essential functions and processes for mere survival in order to minimize the damaging effect of multiple losses and disrupting experiences (Papadopoulos, 1997, 1998, 2002a). It has been argued that the overall impact of all the experiences throughout the phases of refugeedom (and not only during the phase of atrocities and devastating events) makes it impossible for refugees to digest them and, therefore, the only way to move forward with their lives is in a state of psychological "frozenness". Moreover, this state enables refugees to "conserve energy which helps them develop a reflective and meditative stance" (Papadopoulos, 2002a). Despite the similarities of this state to that of dissociation, essentially, it is of a different nature. Dissociation is a psychiatric term that implies pathology and, therefore, it is not applicable to this reactive and temporary state that can be overcome in due course.

Second example

Mr B is in his early-thirties and he comes from the former Yugoslavia. He was referred to the first author by a London mental health community team because they felt he required specialist attention. He had been diagnozed as borderline and was on antipsychotic medication.

He came to the first session with a younger woman, in her late twenties. Initially, we thought that she was a member of staff of the referring team. However, we were surprised when he calmly introduced her simply by her name, C, and as his "friend". She remained silent and when we asked tactfully who she was, he again replied "my friend".

B looked rough, unshaven and tired. His hands were shaky, he had a dry mouth and sipped frequently from a bottle of mineral water he had brought with him. He wore a rather heavy overcoat and rocked his body gently back and forth. The overall picture was that of a medicated person who was struggling to maintain a coherent conversation. Yet, he succeeded in conveying with considerable clarity his painful predicament.

B comes from an ethnically mixed family in Yugoslavia; his father is from X ethnic group and his mother from Y. He was brought up as a Yugoslav without a sense of ethnic identity or religious affiliation. Before the war he was a successful businessman, married (without children), respected in his community, and very politically active. He enjoyed reading and writing, and was leading the life of an intellectual. When the war broke out between X and Y ethnic groups, he tried in vain to remain neutral and not to get involved. However, the whirlpool of war could not leave him uninvolved and inevitably he suffered severely at the hands of both ethnic groups, escaping death miraculously. He was arrested and imprisoned by both sides, he witnessed close friends, men and women, from all Yugoslav nationalities being tortured, sexually assaulted, and murdered. Finally, he ended up in the safe haven of the territory of a third ethnic group, Z, because his grand father was of that nationality. However, he soon found himself in trouble again because he kept criticizing the activities of the Z police. He was imprisoned and witnessed many atrocities, including people being taken to their execution. In London, he is plagued by frequent flashbacks from all the atrocities he witnessed.

Since he arrived in the UK, he changed temporary accommodation many times, always remaining in London. His life is disturbed by insomnia, headaches, flashbacks, general symptoms of dysthymia, and an irritable mood. He is convinced that he is followed by people who could be connected with the secret police from the former Yugoslavia. In fact, he said that he brought his friend C to the sessions in order to confirm his stories. He emphasized that he was not crazy and that he had evidence that he was pursued by certain people. He mentioned examples, such as hearing his name being called out from the loudspeakers in a railway station. Whenever C was called to testify to the truth of his claims, she responded in a remarkable way that managed to achieve the almost impossible combination of validating his reality without, in fact, confirming his version of events. What was equally astonishing was his reaction to her responses: although he brought her to testify to the truthfulness of his narratives, he did not seem to mind that she did not corroborate his stories fully and unreservedly.

C sat in the sessions quietly without initiating any conversation and spoke only when spoken to. She had a calming and reassuring presence and her main concern was how to care for B. Gradually, we got to know more about her. She was an Australian postgraduate student who B first met in Yugoslavia just before the war. They became good friends, sharing similar political beliefs and cultural interests. They reconnected in London when B arrived here as a refugee and she came to continue her postgraduate work in a rather unsystematic fashion. B lives in sheltered accommodation and C spends a lot of time with him, looking after him, cooking for him and whenever she feels that his symptoms may be overwhelming for him she smuggles herself into his room and stays overnight. They had a special kind of intimacy which was difficult to fathom. They looked more like brother and sister rather than partners or lovers. In fact, as he told us subsequently, they were lovers for a brief time in the past but they were now bonded by a strong friendship.

Throughout the sessions we spoke in English. B's spoken English was very good. As the three of us (apart from C) also spoke Serbocroat, occasionally, he used expressions in his native language.

C's presence in the sessions became a regular event but we did not know how to find a suitable way to address it. She remained a silent observer for most of the time and whenever we tried to involve her in the conversation she first seemed to want to check with B that it was appropriate for her to speak. She did this in an unspoken way that underlined her loyalty to him. Throughout, her overall presence had the admirable effect of conveying both a validation of B as a person as well as a clear delineation between their different perceptions and realities. She was able to communicate this differentiation in a non-threatening and confirming manner.

We grew to like C and valued her presence in our sessions and despite our own discussions in-between sessions and our reflections on the dynamics of their relationship, we did not find a convenient way of addressing her attendance in B's psychotherapy. It seems that, somehow, we accepted her as his partner and almost conceptualized our work as therapy with a couple.

C did not attend one session with B because she went abroad. Her absence created an opportunity to address the issue of her presence. At an appropriate moment, we commented on how much he must be missing C not being in the session. After an initial hesitation, he gradually began to speak about C and their relationship. Although he tried to present it as if she did not mean much to him, his tone indicated that she was a most important person in his life; he seemed scared to acknowledge their intimacy and to make sense of the nature of their relationship. We interpreted to him his hesitations and fears and he remained thoughtful. We also added that her presence must have made him feel good for reasons that may not be entirely clear to him or us but somehow it made him feel safe. He agreed and went on to talk to us about his wife for the first time. He said how their relationship had deteriorated and finally broken down during the war; the strain was excessive for both of them. He felt that she was unable to understand and help him with the complexities of his confusion, feelings, loyalties and principles during the mad times of political upheaval and insane violent eruptions in his country. He spoke with sadness rather than bitterness and he realized that it was the first time he had ever thought of her in a serious way. During that and subsequent sessions, B was able to get in touch with his deep sorrow for the break-up of his marriage. She remained back in Yugoslavia and he hardly had any contact with her now. In contrast, C made him feel cared for and understood. Then, he spoke of other girlfriends who also had a protective role for him and he mused that he was perhaps looking for a mother substitute. He told us about his mother and father who never related to him in any close or warm way; throughout, they were busy building their illustrious careers paying little attention to him and his sister who were cared for by their grandparents. He had fond memories of his grandparents whom he considered good and warm people. His parents and sister (now with her husband and children) lived near each other outside London and he visited them very infrequently. Invariably during his visits he would get entangled in political arguments, his family pursuing nationalist ideologies and B reconciliatory pacifism.

C was going to be abroad for two more sessions, and in the third session that he was alone B said that he did not think it was a good idea for C to be present in our sessions any longer. He felt clearer that he wanted to pursue his psychotherapy alone with us. We suggested that her participation should not terminate immediately, but rather that she should be invited to come to at least one more session in order to have a proper ending. B agreed.

During her last session, we encouraged C to emerge as a person in her own right and not just as an appendix to B. She spoke about herself, her own studies and life in general and was able to speak candidly about her impressions of B. She said that she was aware of both his potential as well as his madness and criticized him for often slipping into the role of a "useless" person, unable to do anything for himself. B listened carefully and agreed with her. Then she said how much she gained from coming to the sessions; although she was silent and her main aim was to help B, she was appreciative of everything she gained for herself by attending our sessions.

In the ensuing sessions, B explored further his relationships with women especially discussing his difficulty in developing close and intimate relationships in the context of his problematic connection with his own family of origin. He seemed more reflective than ever before. At about the same time, he began identifying his paranoid thoughts as being paranoid thoughts and not as constituting his entire sense of reality. He was able to separate himself from these thoughts and even "laugh at them" when they emerged. Also, he began thinking of his life in a wider context and not in terms of "day by day survival", as he said. For the first time he began thinking of himself not only as a set of passive reactions to the distressing experiences he had had during the war but also in terms of his future and how to make the best use of his stay in this country.

Eventually, after several sessions with the three of us (i.e. the two authors and B) it became evident that there was no need for the second author to be present either, as our interactions were conducted in English and occasionally in Serbocroat. Therefore, therapy now continues only with the first author and B.

In one of our recent sessions, when asked for his permission to write about him in this chapter, he reflected on his own on C's function for him and said:

She has been helping me in many ways, but, one of the things she helped me with more than anything else was to offer me the possibility to care for someone; that has been most helpful to me, to know that despite everything that has happened to me and despite my own state now, I am still capable of caring for someone.

Discussion

There is no doubt that C is a very different person from the two teachers that A brought to her sessions. Nevertheless, they were similar in so far as C had a remarkable ability to be both distant and close to B and provided for him a useful source of support and containment. B felt safe to rely on her because, paradoxically, she maintained clear boundaries despite allowing herself to be used as an "intruder" in his therapy. Her ability to confirm and validate him as a person as well as her confidence in criticizing him and not sharing totally his reality, enabled him to have a reliable living presence in his life that offered a safe, containing and corrective counterbalancing function to his volatile borderline state. His constant struggle with his paranoid thoughts and ideas of reference were exhausting him and C's presence provided him with a much needed solidity. It is interesting that she remained a safe and stable presence in his life and at no time did she ever get entangled in his paranoid thoughts.

C's presence facilitated considerably our therapeutic endeavours. She was a most welcome ally to the therapeutic process. Without her coming along with him at the beginning of his therapy, most likely B would not have been able to come alone to therapy. It seems that she had an effective function as a catalyst in enabling B to settle in and reach a state when he could benefit from psychotherapy. Gradually, B was able to begin to write poetry again; occasionally he gave the first author some of his poems to read (always in Serbocroat and not in English), feeling good that he could access his "old self" (as he called it). Overall, his psychotic-like features were reduced although they did not disappear.

Ultimately, it may be impossible to state with any degree of certainty as to whether B's current state of mind was the result of a reaction to the multiplicity of psychological shocks he suffered during the war or whether he was already a person with a latent borderline condition. In a sense, this question is of academic interest because regardless of the original aetiology, B seemed to gain significantly from our psychotherapeutic work.

What is of interest in this example of a Transient Familiar Other is that B not only felt the holding support from C but also became aware of his own capacity to care for her. In other words, C managed to activate in B the function of mutuality, i.e. to reciprocate the caring he was receiving from her. To begin with, he first sensed the fact that he was also caring for her. That realization had a profound impact on B. Gradually, in subsequent sessions, he was able to describe situations where he was able to care for C in different ways, from protecting her in public places from potential danger by obnoxious men to being concerned about her accommodation. He also began to realize that, in effect, his concern for C often helped him come out of his paranoid system of thinking. He did not enumerate these examples in any systematic way but he began to warm up to the idea that, after all, he was not such a useless person and he was capable of caring for others.

Mutuality and reciprocity are important facets of the therapeutic work with refugees and requires further examination.

Transient Familiar Others

What is the essence of the phenomenon of Transient Familiar Others (TFOs), what are its functions and what are its characteristics? These examples illustrate two instances of TFOs with some similarities and some differences.

To begin with, it is important to emphasize that in psychotherapy with refugees one has to be extremely flexible in order to respond appropriately to the specificity and complexity of the situation. In short, simple logic suggests that if refugees are defined in terms of their loss of home, then what they require is not psychotherapy but the return to, or the restoration of their homes or something equivalent. Regardless of the simplistic nature of this logic, if we were to ignore it completely our therapeutic work with refugees would invariably suffer. The rationale, of course, is that in psychotherapy refugees would be offered the opportunity to address the complexity of their psychological reactions not only to their loss of home but also to a host of other unsettling factors. However, adding this rationale for psychotherapy to the equally sound simplistic logic outlined above could create a wider context within which we could obtain a more intricate composite understanding of the psychotherapeutic approach to refugees.

This means that we cannot afford always to be aware that the condition of being a refugee on its own is not a pathological condition. Consequently, their psychological response could be appreciated as "a normal reaction to abnormal circumstances" (Papadopoulos, 1998, 2001a; Papadopoulos & Hildebrand, 1997). This awareness could add a corrective element in the conceptualization of our therapeutic work with refugees. Therefore, the very technique and construction of our therapeutic frame should be shaped accordingly and become more flexible and open to creative constructions.

Referring to the psychological experience of displaced persons in the context of the wars in Yugoslavia, Vizek-Vidović writes that they:

> are pervaded with disbelief and incomprehension as to what has befallen them. They feel as if they were partially in close encounters with an imaginary future as presented in science fiction movies in which the inhabitants of a peaceful little town suddenly realize that among them, in the guise of their neighbors and acquaintances, live alien beings programmed to destroy them. [1992, p. 165]

This means that the experiences certainly of B (in territories of the former Yugoslavia), but also partly of A (in Kosovo), had a strong element of unreality in them that could easily have contributed to the creation of a psychotic-like sense of reality. Psychotherapists without field experience in working with people in war zones tend to overlook the fact that in the eyes of the refugees we work with, the very psychotherapy situation itself appears unreal. Therefore, under these conditions, the presence of a reliable person who represents a sense of continuity, stability and familiarity makes perfect sense. The onus is on therapists to find suitable ways of accommodating the presence of such persons rather than imposing blindly the usual conditions of the psychotherapeutic frame.

Moreover, as has been repeatedly emphasized (Papadopoulos, 1998, 2000b, 2001a,b):

supporting refugees is not simply a question of "treating their trauma". It requires an understanding of the complexity of their situation and of the adaptations they must make ... A conviction that mental illness, especially PTSD [Post Traumatic Stress Disorder], is usually present in refugees is unhelpful. [Richman, 1998, p. 179]

This means that there is a level of complexity that needs to be understood, and indeed properly addressed, in order to be effective in any form of therapeutic care with refugees. The overall refugee situation has been characterized as being "multifaceted and multidimensional", as it involves a mixture of dimensions and perspectives, ranging from the psychological and socio–political to financial, cultural and historical (Papadopoulos, 2001a), to name but a few.

One of the elements of this complexity is the appreciation that what is "traumatic" for refugees is not only the "devastating events" of the atrocities they experienced during the war but the totality of their situation, covering the entire span of time from the anticipation of the upheavals, the actual devastating events, the uncertainty of survival, to the confusing destabilization involved in adjusting to their new country (Papadopoulos, 2000b, 2001a,b). An exclusive focus on the devastating events tends to suppress the totality of their experience and creates a skewed perception of them, of their history and of their stories.

Refugees have a wide variety of painful, disrupting, and undigested experiences as well as a host of perceived and unperceived needs. Although it is impossible to address all of them in the therapeutic context, nevertheless, if at least therapists were able to hold them in mind, this would have a most holding and containing function for both refugees and their therapists. One of the main needs is connected with the loss of home along with everything that it implies. Home should be accepted, "as an important psychological and psychotherapeutic category (and not just as an epiphenomenon) in our therapeutic care for refugees" (Papadopoulos, 2002a). It has been suggested that home refers to a fundamental cluster of basic proto-processes, needs and abilities that form a "mosaic substratum" on top of which we build our sense of individual and collective identity (Papadopoulos, 1997, 2002a). Therefore, the loss of home creates for refugees a deep sense of lack, of disorientation and absence which is not easily identifiable either in terms of its nature or its effects.

It appears that the presence of the TFOs softens in some way the impact of this lack. However, it does not mean that TFOs necessarily restore the loss of home; this loss cannot be redressed easily. Their function seems to be far more complex than simply counteracting one deficit and, therefore, it will be useful to examine further some of their characteristics. TFOs tend to be persons who:

— Are familiar and close to the refugees but, at the same time, are different and distant in some important ways. It seems that refugees choose their TFOs in a way that they guard against too close an identification with them. The TFOs, in both examples in this chapter, illustrate clearly this combination of familiarity with strangeness, closeness with distance. A's teachers as well as C were of different nationality from the refugees they were accompanying and in a sense they guaranteed against the possibility of much closer contact.

— Although they offer seemingly unconditional support, nevertheless, they also provide a corrective function to the refugees' sense of reality. Their assistance to the refugees has clear boundaries, regardless of their ostensibly total and unboundaried devotion to them. This has been one of the remarkable features of all three TFOs discussed here. All three of them had the capacity to validate the reality of their accompanying refugees without sharing their illusory or delusory systems.

— Can enable a mutuality of care. Although TFOs appear to be the care-givers, they may also manage to activate in refugees an ability to care for them, as well. This reciprocity is a most important function. Refugees often try to find appropriate ways to reciprocate the care they receive from their therapists. Not familiar with the psychotherapy protocols and conventions, refugees usually carry with them the traditions of reciprocity from their countries of origin, according to which they feel the need to express their gratitude to people who assist them by offering them various gifts. This is a sensitive facet of psychotherapy with refugees that needs to be treated with delicate tact. However, it seems that at least with TFOs, refugees are able to exercise this reciprocity even if this is not always acknowledged consciously. This mutuality is more evident with C rather than with A's two teachers. However, with A there was a comparable mutuality which was of a more subtle form. Despite her overall attitude which resembled that of a greedy child, A was able to be sensitive to her teachers' needs and attempted to avoid imposing excessive demands on them. A, in connection with the second teacher, was most concerned not to tire her because of her pregnancy. The actualization of mutual care and reciprocity is most important for refugees to reconnect with their ordinariness and shed (at least partially and temporarily) the specialness connected with their refugee identity. The presence of TFOs is particularly apposite in facilitating the activation of this function because it is not easy to exercise this mutuality with one's therapist. Refugees, in a significant way much more than other patients, tend to offer gifts and other tokens of appreciation to therapists and this requires a most sensitive treatment which should not exclude the cultural considerations.

In terms of their function, it seems that TFOs:

— Are both transitory and transitional. This means that their own presence in therapy is not permanent; however, their temporary presence enables the transition of refugees into more advanced developmental stages. To begin with, refugees may not even come to psychotherapy if they were not accompanied by TFOs. Then, after the TFOs settle refugees in therapy, their presence helps the refugees address areas that were previously inaccessible to them.
— Play an important combination of contradictory roles sequentially and paradoxically. This is a function with a great deal of complexity. Initially, TFOs facilitate the stabilization of refugees in therapy by providing a reliable presence and continuity; this seems to have the effect of moderating the amount of pain refugees can afford to experience, but then, by continuing to perform the very same function, TFOs seem to retard the refugees' progress. This happens when TFOs carry on sheltering refugees from painful experiences that refugees are then in a position to process. As the refugees' capacity for processing

disrupting material increases, the importance of the presence of TFOs decreases until a point is reached that their presence becomes completely redundant; prolonging their presence at that time would, in effect, prevent refugees from progressing further. The characteristics of good therapy would be to provide the appropriate set of conditions so that refugees would be enabled to alter the initial arrangement and terminate the TFOs presence, thus remaining alone in therapy. Therefore, therapists will need to be vigilant in order to be sensitive to the signals for the timing of this transition and endeavour to enable it as smoothly as possible.

Needless to say, not all TFOs are the same and not all are like the ones discussed here. It cannot be denied that they may also have a negative effect, especially if they are unable to observe clear boundaries and if they over-identify with the refugees. Occasionally, TFOs' presence may even become tyrannical, abusing the privileges that refugees bestow on them. However, TFOs can be most helpful in enabling refugees to negotiate the transition into more advanced stages of psychological development and integration, as long as the therapists are able to sense correctly the situation, maximize the TFOs' benefits and minimize their damaging effects. Certainly, TFOs' overextended presence may work to the detriment of the refugees' development.

Overall, the TFOs' presence may inaugurate a preparatory phase that would assist refugees to enter into and benefit from more advanced forms of psychotherapy. This can be effected not only in terms of enabling refugees to attend therapy in the first place (which is the bare minimum, and yet most important benefit), but also in facilitating certain pivotal processes in the refugees' psychotherapy. These include the activation of the psychological components of the cluster of home and the thawing of the refugees' frozenness.

Since refugees are defined in terms of their loss of home, it is important to delineate the psychological processes connected with this specific loss and not to resort exclusively to theories of trauma in order to understand this phenomenon. Psychologically speaking, home can be appreciated as connected with a unique cluster of proto-processes that are fundamental to the development of our psychological mechanisms. To begin with, home as the proto-container, similar to the concept of "family envelope" (Houzel, 1996), can provide the possibility of coexistence of opposites through continuity and variability and thus prevent archaic forms of splitting (Papadopoulos, 2002a). Then, home represents the psychological structure and process that can "mediate between … the intrapsychic, the interpersonal and the socio–political [realms]"; this means that it can negotiate boundaries between inner and outer as well as personal and collective. In addition, home may also contain both "prospective and retrospective movements (towards the origins and the goals)" as well as facilitating the bridging between "tangible and intangible entities (physical and imaginary)", literal/material and symbolic/psychological dimensions, and promoting not only an external settledness but also an internal one by "reconnecting with one's sense of self and accessing the dis-membered parts of one's personality". All these processes can be enabled by the provision of a reliable, stable, and safe presence which provides continuity (Papadopoulos, 2002a).

As has been shown in these examples, TFOs can contribute substantially to the development of these potentialities. If the therapeutic process makes appropriate use of their presence, it is possible that they can promote most of the positive functions that the psychological cluster of home can enable. In these examples, the catalytic effect of the presence of TFOs facilitated refugees to re-member and reconnect the various dis-membered parts of their history and sense of self. Moreover, the TFOs' accepting capacity of refugees' realities enabled them to experience a solid and corrective presence that facilitated their transition into more advanced developmental stages.

The presence of TFOs challenges the traditional understanding of the therapeutic frame and boundaries. If therapists insist on adhering to the usual format of the therapeutic frame, then the very phenomenon of TFOs would not exist at all. Purist therapists would not allow uninvited persons, who are not part of a planned intervention, to contaminate the therapeutic process. However, working with refugees exposes us to a host of unexpected situations which challenge us to address them in impromptu and creative ways. The phenomenon of TFOs is just one of these unpredict-abilities. Appreciating the complexities of the multifaceted and multidimensional nature of the refugee situation, therapists should abandon purist external forms and concentrate on translating the complexities into the fundamental elements of the therapeutic processes (Papadopoulos, 1999a). In this spirit, therapists may allow the inclusion of TFOs in therapy and then monitor carefully the quality and meaning of therapeutic interactions, ensuring that the TFOs' presence does have any anti-therapeutic effect but, on the contrary, maximize their benefit.

One specific benefit from the TFOs' presence is their contribution to the "thawing" of the "frozenness" of refugees. In so far as frozenness constricts refugees and limits their repertoire of functions, their interaction with TFOs, especially in the context of psychotherapy, may be facilitative in expanding that repertoire. The blend of psychological distance and proximity that TFOs combine, can contribute to the gentle thawing of this frozenness. Moreover, TFOs can provide refugees with an important connection to a wider spectrum of activities and connections in life whilst maintaining the sense of safety and containment; this combination can speed up the thawing considerably.

Finally, TFOs assist with the identification of other, non-therapeutic needs of refugees. Within the confused state of frozenness, refugees tend to merge and muddle up their various needs. Obvious needs such as housing, medical, legal, financial needs etc. tend to be clearly identifiable from the beginning of the therapeutic work. Then, usually, therapists delineate the therapeutic realm by addressing these needs separately (cf. Fox, 2002; Garland et al., 2002). However, in difficult cases, refugees may be unable to identify such needs at the beginning and the presence of TFOs enables this differentiation during the course of therapy. This was the case with the two examples mentioned here.

The phenomenon of TFOs appears in psychotherapy with refugees whenever therapists appreciate the complexities of the totality of the situation and do not insist on adhering strictly to traditional forms of the therapeutic frame. Then, this seemingly untidy phenomenon may not only not interfere with the work but it can positively enhance it, if therapists endeavour to follow vigilantly the deeper and finer nuances of the therapeutic process, rather than adhere rigidly to external forms of the therapeutic frame. Clinical experience suggests that the therapeutic process with refugees will need to be conceptualized in its uniqueness and it should not be approached routinely as any other form of psychotherapy. The specific features of this process are related to the psychological meaning of home and the impact of psychological frozenness which are highlighted by the presence of the TFOs. By privileging these distinctive features, over an indiscriminate application of the theory of trauma, it is possible to approach the psychotherapy process with refugees as a unique endeavour.

RESEARCH

CHAPTER NINE

"We have to blame ourselves"— refugees and the politics of systemic practice

Chris Glenn

A long hot summer

June 2001: The Labour Party, in Britain, is re-elected with a second massive majority. A feature of the campaign was of the two main parties vying with each other to be tough on refugees and asylum seekers, but the shock of the 2001 General Election was the electoral breakthrough made by the British National Party in Oldham where in one constituency they gained 11% of the vote and in another 16%. Much of their campaigning was based around the assertion that poor white people were being denied resources which were given instead to refugees and local Muslims.

July 2001: In Genoa in Italy, hundreds of thousands demonstrate against the leaders of the eight most powerful nations on earth. A central demand is for them to drop the debt repayments imposed upon poor nations. On one of the days of the Genoa protests 70,000 people demonstrate in support of refugees and asylum seekers. Riots hit Bradford (a town in England) as Muslim youth clash with racists, many from outside the area.

August 2001: A Kurdish refugee is stabbed to death on a deprived Glasgow council estate. In Afghanistan an estimated five million people face starvation in the coming winter.

September 2001: On the front page of the *"Guardian"* newspaper of September 4th, it is announced that the Labour Party, elected and re-elected on a pledge to improve educational standards, has cut spending on schools and colleges "to the lowest share of national income since the early 1960s" (Stewart *et al.*, 2001). A work colleague tells me that he has stopped his direct debit payment to the Labour Party and has written to them outlining his reasons. He comments that the government must be pleased that the papers and the TV news are so full of articles about asylum seekers as it deflects attention away from the performance of the government.

September 11th 2001: In the USA, the World Trade Centre and the Pentagon are attacked leading to a horrific loss of over 2780 lives (CNN news update 28.01.2002), including many of New York's fire-fighters as well as catering and cleaning staff.

In Britain, in the days that follow, an Afghani cab driver is attacked and is paralysed from the neck down; mosques around the country are attacked; and many female Muslims, including school-girls, are afraid to wear traditional clothing in the streets for fear of being assaulted. Meanwhile, Aid agencies estimate that worldwide 24,000 people a day continue to die of hunger and that 6000 children die daily from diarrhoea and measles, both preventable diseases.

The subsequent bombing of Afghanistan creates new waves of refugees fleeing to Iran and Pakistan to join the estimated two million Afghanis already in these countries.

How many Britons faced with a seemingly unending prospect of poverty and a future with no hope would seek to make their way to other lands?

Ethics and values

What has all this to do with those such as myself trained in family therapy and with other practitioners in the caring professions?

It is my contention that certain important issues need to be considered when working with refugees and by implication other groups in society.

The first important issue concerns the relationship between practitioners and how they view the world we live in. I consider the implications of this for the field of family therapy—although professionals from other traditions and backgrounds may *also* wish to reflect upon the relevance of the issues raised.

Within this chapter, it is argued that a consistent focus upon the wider social and political context may paradoxically lead to a deeper appreciation of the lived experience of individuals and families. This should also lead to the continuing development of an anti-discriminatory practice based upon the recognition that inequality and oppression are features of British society. The second, related but more specific, issue concerns where practitioners position themselves in relation to refugees and the asylum question.

As part of my family therapy training, I interviewed a number of women, refugees from Somalia, about how they and their children experienced the British education system. The interviews took place in a Saturday school which they ran in an inner London borough.

An immediate issue for me was the importance of recognizing the inequalities inherent in the research process, amplified by the disadvantaged position of groups of refugees.

I am a white English male who, on the level of appearance, represents the majority culture in this country. The women were Muslims from Somalia fleeing a country devastated by civil war, seeking refuge in a country in which significant forces within politics and the media have sought to develop a view of Little England being taken advantage of by scheming asylum seekers.

Such are the myths attributed to the motives of refugees arriving in this country that it seemed an ethical issue to me that from the outset of the research I stated my position that "Refugees are welcome here".

Failure to do this would have left the Somali women uncertain of my motives and beliefs. Just as clients are uncertain where practitioners position themselves in relation to issues of inequality and oppression until they declare themselves, so this may be mirrored within research.

As well as recognizing an ethical dimension, it is also likely that this position would aid my access to the experiences of the women and children than a stance that was distant and unstated or perceived as unsympathetic.

In attempting to contextualize the testimonies of the Somali women, I will try to show how behind the words lay a wealth of political arguments and debates.

Education and language

The issue of language was viewed by the Somali women as being of crucial importance. Unsurprisingly, the extent to which they and their children were able to communicate with education professionals was seen as central to their ability to negotiate the education system.

One mother spoke of the dilemmas of both children and teachers in communicating with each other:

> "The teacher, she's English and she doesn't speak Somali and he [the child] doesn't speak English."

Another woman explained:

> "My brother he didn't understand the French lesson because the language of French they explain in English—he don't know French and he don't know English. How can he understand?"

The women shared stories of what the children had told them about the experience of trying to learn in school in the face of the language barrier. One mother gave her daughter's description of what it is like to sit in class and not understand:

> "My daughter she said 'I'm deaf'. She was thinking she was deaf, she said 'Mum, the people is talking and I don't know what they say', and after a few months she say 'I maybe feeling my ears are opening up a little bit'."

This experience was echoed by another mother who described how:

> "The children tell me that some people who is just talking to them they can see their mouth and whenever the teacher is writing they can understand nothing."

Other mothers described their children's experience of secondary school in particular as "awful" and "very very painful".

The lack of a common language was also felt by the Somali women themselves:

> "There is no connection between the teachers and the parents at all ... the teachers they don't speak Somali and the parents they don't speak English."

The efforts that schools made to communicate with Somali families were recognized but examples were given of how these attempts to bridge the gap between home and school could in themselves lead to humiliating experiences if professionals do not take care to check out the level of language acquisition.

A point that was raised by all the women I spoke to was that it may also be the case that, as well as not understanding English, the children and their families may also not have the skills of reading and writing in Somali. One of the women who had a good grasp of English and supports other mothers in their contact with schools described what happened when the daughter of a Somali woman was being permanently excluded from secondary school:

"I was at the school last week and there was a woman, her child is being permanently excluded, the woman she doesn't know what is going on. They brought up a lot of things. The mother she doesn't know if she's seen the psychiatrist in education, psychologist in education, if she's getting assessment from local government. And when the teachers or governors ask 'Do you have any questions to ask us?', she doesn't know what's going on ... They phoned me because I was an interpreter for her a while ago. The school has arranged for me to go with her and I went with her many times, the first time she received a big pile [of papers] in Somali language, she never read or write Somali language and they thought because she has received this in written Somali language she must know what's going on, but she doesn't know what's going on."

The issues of the exclusion of Somali pupils from school and the way in which some schools refuse to admit "difficult" children was highlighted. The same woman recounted how she tried to find a new school place for two excluded boys. When she contacted schools, she truthfully explained that they had been excluded from another school. Each school replied that they did not have any spare places. She then decided not to tell the schools that the boys had been excluded and was now told that places were available. But then the boys' previous school was contacted, the truth of the exclusions was discovered and the woman was then told by the school that they had made a mistake and that places were not available.

A further incident shows how it is not only the lack of a common language that hinders effective home–school communication. It may also be the assumptions of school staff that they know the parents' relationship to the English language. Following an incident involving her son, a mother describes a meeting that took place in school with the deputy headteacher:

> "She was talking to him ... and then she left the meeting. She never talking to me because she thought I can't speak English."

The importance of learning the English language was emphasized by all the women, "because if you don't know the language you can't understand anything about school", and led to calls for extra classes in English for the children.

The women had another very practical suggestion to resolve the communication difficulties occurring between members of the Somali community and the schools—employ Somali teachers or home–school liaison workers to work in schools or to make the link between families and schools, "because if someone represents us ... our children's problems will be less", and they were also aware that some other neighbouring boroughs were already providing these services.

Discussion (1)

Communication between the Somali community and education professionals occurs through language. The less the access to a common language the more painful and humiliating the experience of refugees' contact with schools is likely to be.

Therefore, it would seem straightforward to suggest that strengthening acquisition of and literacy in the language of the host country is of over-riding importance. However, there are political implications within this position.

Some argue, for instance, that this should be done at the expense of a commitment to multiculturalism. Ray Honeyford, a former Bradford headteacher who refused to implement the council's multicultural policies, attempted to explain the clashes that occurred in that city in the Summer of 2001 between white racists and Asian youths in terms of the council's language policies:

> We must stop believing that Asian and other ethnic minority children must be accorded special treatment. We must see them for

what they are: British children, whose future lies in adapting to British culture and society. The necessary first step is kicking out multicultural nonsense from schools. English needs to be established as the basic language of education and instruction, and the efforts to translate everything into Asian dialects need to be ended. [Honeyford, 2001]

This echoes arguments, summarized by Davis (2000), that have been put forward, for example, in California where a referendum proposing that English be the only language used in classrooms became law in June 1998, despite the opposition of 63% of Spanish-speaking Latino voters, the largest group in the state for whom English was not the first language.

In fact, there is an increasing body of evidence that suggests that whilst immersion in English from an early age is beneficial, for older children bilingual education is more helpful. Cummins (1984) points to "strong evidence that promotion of L1 (first language) literacy skills can facilitate the overall academic achievement of minority students" (p. 265) and that there is an interdependent, recursive relationship between the level of skills acquired in one language which will help in the acquisition of the other. Similarly, Thomas & Collier (1999) claim that "the growing research base on long term outcomes clearly demonstrates" (p. 46) that developmental bilingual education, which uses the resources of family and cultural community to develop true bilingualism, is most effective in raising attainment levels.

This suggests that practitioners, when working with those for whom English is not the first language, should take a keen interest in the extent to which they are able to read and write in their first language as well as that of the host community. It also suggests that, if the government and educationalists are truly interested in raising attainment levels, resources should be put in place for both the speedy acquisition of English *and* the development of skills in the first language. Finally, it seems eminently sensible that whilst communication difficulties occur between two communities, those who are bilingual should be mobilized to bridge the gap. As the Somali women suggest: Why not employ a taskforce of bilingual workers from their community?

Again, however, one enters the arena of political debate—this time over the funding of public services. How is it possible to fund such posts if, as has been claimed, the proportion of the country's wealth being spent on education is actually falling rather than rising?

This is not simply an abstract question for practitioners, including teachers as well as others who work with refugee children. The current teacher shortage is mirrored in other areas such as the child and adolescent mental health services where waiting lists for appointments are often notoriously long due to understaffing. In this sense practitioners and refugee families are both victims of an under-resourced system. The professionals are unable to provide an appropriate and adequate service, resulting in the painful and humiliating experiences of the refugee children and families—and, of course, many black and white British children and families suffer too from the lack of resources.

Further political issues arise such as the use of league tables to measure "success" and indeed the structure of the school system itself. It is inherent in a system of competition that the strong triumph over the weak. In Britain the school system is highly stratified. At the top of the pyramid are the private schools where parents pay to avoid their children being prey to the perceived problems and difficulties of state-funded schools. Below this are a layer of selective, religious and popular schools that are able in one way or another to decide who is allowed a place. At the bottom are the schools that have to educate the rest of the school population including the excluded children, the "low achievers", a disproportionate number of children with special educational needs, those children who have moved into the area because they have moved to a new foster family or with their mothers are fleeing domestic violence—and the refugee children.

The more "successful" schools undermine the efforts of the less "successful". In turn, the efforts of these schools to compete regularly results in those who cannot contribute to raising the levels of exam success being humiliated, belittled, and excluded. Just as with teacher shortages, long waiting lists, inadequate housing, poverty, and so on it is not only refugee families that suffer but many black and white British children and families.

However, the hysteria whipped up by the political parties and the media encourages the view that refugee families are taking resources away from poor British citizens. The attacks and murders

continue as the deprived fight each other for scarce resources whilst
the rich and privileged look after themselves and their children.
We may now turn to yet wider themes.

Culture and identity

In my research, the women talked about religion, language,
clothing, food, and the contrast of being Somalis in Britain with
memories of Somalia as aspects of their cultural identity.

One of the women talked of the attempts to get a school to
recognize the dietary needs of the Somali Muslim children whilst
she and others spoke of the dilemmas of their Muslim children
attending Christian assemblies:

"They go but really I don't like it because it's not my religion and
we do not believe what they believe—it's wrong because their mind
is a magnet when they are a child, maybe they'll believe this is
true."

This mother knew that she had a right to withdraw her children
from the assembly but decided not to do so:

"But when they come home ... I tell them 'Don't believe this'. I
think leave it ... it's not good all the time to be complaining
continually in my opinion, so I tell them what's the truth, what's
wrong, after school."

The complexities of the interactions between mother, children,
and school in the context of their relationship to two distinct
religious beliefs becomes apparent:

"They look at the Christmas party as fun, so I say 'Go, but listen to
me, that's not your religion' ... because the children they hate me if
I say 'Don't go this, don't go that' they hate me for it."

Another mother described pressure from a teacher to persuade
her to allow her daughter to attend a Christian service:

"One of my children, I told her not to go to church and one of the
teachers said 'Why are you stopping her from going to church?' I
said 'I have got rights' and she said 'I know you've got rights but it

would be such a shame if she doesn't go to church'. What about the women that doesn't know?"

Another reason for providing Somali workers was because:

"I want them to know about our culture, our own way of doing things, our own sets of ways of living our lives as Muslims. We have rights to be respected for what our beliefs are. I want them to know where we're coming from, let them be aware of who we are, then they can help."

The Saturday school has become an important place for members of the Somali community to hold on to and develop aspects of their cultural identities:

"They learn the Koran because Saturday is the only time that they have, they miss the language because all of the time they speak in the school English they lose their Somali language."

For this mother maintaining a distinct Somali identity was not a matter of symbolic significance but of practical importance with significant implications for the future:

"It's important because we are temporary here, this is not our country, when we come to our country how can we speak to our parents or our family?"

When asked if parents or family will already see her and other Somalians in Britain as different, the mother replied: "Really different".

The international context

The reason for the influx of Somalis into Britain is the intensification of the Civil War in Somalia in the years following 1989 and the ensuing famine conditions. Whilst the children and their families have escaped the physical dangers of the war, images of the war have accompanied them to Britain.

"When the other children are watching television they getting teased from the other children 'Did you watch the TV, all the Somalians starving'."

When I first made contact with the Refugee Network, I was told the tale of a primary school girl who was shoved in the side by another pupil and then fainted. The explanation given for the fainting was that in a camp in Somalia she had been shoved in the side by a soldier with his rifle butt. As one mother told me:

> "These children they're not like English children, they've had and they've seen many problems and they've had many bad experiences, but they're not getting any help or any concern for their physical and mental health, they're just put in a class of thirty children."

As well as being clear about the terrible experiences that the children had endured, the women stressed the importance of maintaining an alternative narrative to that of violence and famine:

> "I know that not all Somalis are starving or killing each other."

> "We have a nice country, long beach, we hope our country will come back with freedom and government."

One mother had this to say about where responsibility lay for their situation:

> "I have to blame ourselves first, we have to blame ourselves, we caused this problem for ourselves."

A narrative of Somalia

One response to the statement that "we have to blame ourselves" might be to explore the roots of the crisis that has led to thousands of Somalis seeking refuge in Britain.

Possibly the best starting point for practitioners who wish to begin to understand the social and political context of the different refugee groups in Britain is Jill Rutter's book *Refugee Children in the Classroom* (1994). In a succinct guide to each group, Rutter provides information on each country of origin covering ethnic groups, languages, names, religion, education system, economy, a chronology of events, and details of refugees in Britain. Much of the information below is taken from this source.

Somalia is placed at the mouth of the Red Sea and in the nineteenth century began to attract the attention of colonial powers because of its strategic importance. At the Berlin Conference of 1884 the African continent was divided up between various European imperial powers. The northern part of Somalia became a British colony whilst the Italians took control of the south.

Much of the cause of present-day catastrophes in Africa may be traced back to the arbitrary carve-up—note the number of borders of African countries that are straight lines, drawn with a measuring ruler on a map—by imperialist powers which disrupted the more-or-less peaceful co-existence of Somali and other nomadic clans. Western governments, however, have an interest in explaining the plight of refugees as being the result of: (a) natural disasters, such as drought, which cannot be controlled; (b) a barely understandable aggression that leads to mass torture and killing which occurs amongst backward and primitive peoples but not in civilized countries (Alexander, 1987). This may then mean that refugees are encouraged to blame themselves—and their irrational compatriots —for their fate rather than the impact of wider systems upon them.

During the Second World War, British Somaliland was used as a base to fight the Italians in Eritrea, Abyssinia and Italian Somaliland—many Somalis joined the British armed forces at this time and helped to capture Italian Somaliland. In 1950 with UN backing, the Italians returned to the south whilst Britain continued to administer the north.

Following growth of a Somali nationalist movement in the 1950s, Somalia gained independence in 1960 and united to form one country. Despite great poverty, the different colonial and administrative systems of the north and south, and deep clan and political divisions, the Somali Republic was a democracy and human rights were respected.

In 1969 a military coup took place and shortly afterwards the Somali Democratic Republic allied with the Soviet Union which as well as providing financial aid turned the army into one of the largest in Africa. In 1977 the Soviet–Somali alliance ended and the USA stepped in to continue to provide arms to the government.

Having pumped massive numbers of arms into the country, the superpowers laid the basis for the killings that were to follow. There are eerie parallels with the situation in Afghanistan during the 1980s when the Russians backed one faction, the Americans another (in which Osama Bin Laden was a prominent figure) and during the ensuing years the country descended into civil war and famine.

In 1978, as oil price rises hit Somalia very badly and the country fell deeply into debt, the leader of the coup, President Barre, began to experience the first opposition to his rule. By the 1980s Civil War had begun and Somali refugees began to seek asylum in Britain in increasing numbers.

Somalia has a population of some seven million. The effects of the chaos and bloodshed of civil war have been enormous. In 1988 72,000 people were killed in the town of Hargeisa with 400,000 fleeing as refugees. In 1992 the International Committee of the Red Cross warned that four million Somalis were at risk of starvation. Half a million, including half of all children under five, died of starvation. By the end of that year one million Somalis were internally displaced (cf. Vernez, 1991) and a further one million were refugees in Ethiopia, Kenya, Yemen and European countries.

Since the mid-1980s more than 20,000 Somali refugees have arrived in Britain to join small Somali communities which were established in the early twentieth century when sailors from British Somaliland settled in London, Cardiff and Liverpool. The vast majority are Muslims and may well come across prejudice against Islam.

Somalian is the mother-tongue. Many rural Somalis are not able to read and write and many children who would normally have learnt to read and write in Somali schools have not attended for many years, if ever, as due to the Civil War many schools have been closed.

The largest Somali community is in Greater London and almost every London secondary school and many primary schools now contain Somali refugee children.

Discussion (2)

If one only considers the interactions between those directly involved in a relationship, the context of the relationship is not clear. Within systemic thinking, a tension exists between two positions: the first regards a focus upon the immediate family relationships and interactions as being sufficient to gain a view of the nature of the problem; and the second stresses the importance of exploring the social and material context of people's lives in order to gain an understanding of particular situations.

Many systemic practitioners would regard these two positions as being interconnected rather than mutually exclusive and may rather stress one position at one particular time whilst bearing the other in mind. Nevertheless, the tension exists in a way which is not only creative but also may lead to the exclusion of, in particular, the part of systemic thinking that stresses the wider social and political context. The danger is that it is relatively easy to concentrate upon those relationships that are within view, whereas widening enquiries to include social and political considerations often requires a conscious shift in thinking that may be extremely difficult to achieve—especially if practitioners believe that the world we live in is basically a fair and equitable place.

In the development of family therapy and systemic practice, for instance, a clear strand exists from Minuchin's (1974) stress upon placing the father at the head of the family and the Milan Associates' focus upon the strategic battles taking place within families and between families and practitioners; to Cecchin's assertion that "therapy is not the place for politics" (Mackinnon & Miller, 1987, p. 143) and the idealist position that "there are no "real" external realities" rather that "problems are in the inter-subjective minds of all who are in the active communication exchange" (Anderson & Goolishian, 1988, p. 374).

What links all these positions, despite their often competing theoretical underpinnings, is their lack of recognition of the social and material context of interpersonal relationships.

In recent years, social constructionism has had a significant influence upon systemic theory and practice in Britain. From a social constructionist perspective "because there can be no truth, all perspectives must be equally valid" (Burr, 1995, p. 81) and therefore to seek to privilege one explanation over another would be viewed as antithetical to working co-constructively with families. Practitioners adopt a "not-knowing approach" (Anderson & Goolishian, 1988) that is curious about the meanings that inform family members' beliefs about particular behaviours.

Whilst one very positive effect of this position is to check the tendency of professionals to impose their views upon those they work with, another may be to become becalmed in an "endless sea of tolerance", as advocated by Gergen (1992, p. 163), a leading theoretician of social constructionism, that adapts to a given set of circumstances and pays little if any attention to the real world in which people live—celebrating difference may become a means to ignore inherent inequalities.

An example of the logic of this approach within systemic practice has been the attempt to theorize the struggle between Palestinians and right wing Israelis as being one between two more or less equally balanced protagonists (Shamai, 1999). When such thinking goes unchallenged, the danger is that practitioners, witnessing only the immediate pain and suffering of both sides, will uncritically support the maintenance of an unequal relationship (Glenn, 1999a).

Nevertheless at the same time as increasing attention is being given in systemic thinking to the detail of personal interactions, for instance, between clients and practitioners (e.g. *Journal of Family Therapy*, 1997) the pole of systemic thinking that gives due weight to the social and material context continues to develop.

Dowling & Osborne (1995) place the joint systems approach to education problems within the context of wider changes in the education system, such as the National Curriculum and the introduction of league tables for schools based upon examination results. They note also that the application of systems theory to the contexts of family and of school has developed separately and assert that "there is still a considerable need for this linking work to be done" (p. xv).

In an example particularly relevant to the attempts of schools to cater for a pupil population whose characteristics are continually changing and developing they show how a school that has success in integrating, for instance, pupils with particular educational needs may lose popularity with parents of "high achieving" pupils. This may then lead to a lower position in examination league tables and pressure being brought to bear not to offer places to "difficult" children. Such is the logic of competition within education.

Feminist practitioners have encouraged the use of the lens of gender to consider the unequal relationship between men and women in society where previously this had been ignored (e.g. Goldner, 1985; Burck & Daniel, 1995) and have critiqued the ideas of

Minuchin and the Milan Associates mentioned above (Leupnitz, 1988).

Black therapists have argued that race and culture are crucial factors that have previously not been given due prominence (Hardy, 1990). Boyd-Franklin (1989) has developed a multi-systems approach to consider the impact of external forces upon black families which I would argue is also applicable to other groups.

Family therapists are also coming to recognize how issues of social class intertwine with other forms of oppression. McGoldrick (1994) asserts that:

> family therapy ... has been structured in ways to support the dominant value system and keep invisible certain hidden organizing principles of our lives, including culture, class, race and gender. [p. 131]

The "Just Therapy" group write eloquently of the dangers that practitioners face in colluding with an unequal society:

> So people came to us depressed in bad housing and were sent away undepressed to the same conditions. After all we were only therapists! We sent them away to be happy in poverty! As we reflected upon this we realized that we were unintentionally but nevertheless very effectively, adjusting people to poverty ... by not relating the therapeutic work directly to the political, economic, gender, social and cultural structures, we were colluding with those systems in society that oppress, deprive and de-humanise families. Furthermore we were encouraging in the families the belief that they, rather than the unjust structures, are the authors of their problems and failures. [Waldegrave & Tamasese, 1994, pp. 194–195]

Within a British setting, a special issue of the family therapy publication *Context* entitled "The political and social context of systemic practice" (Glenn, 1999b) attempted to draw together the strands of social class, gender, race and sexual orientation. Burck & Daniels (1994), whilst focusing upon issues of gender within family therapy, take particular care to acknowledge issues of race, culture and class. An integrated approach to issues of oppression and inequality is essential if, for instance, one as a Westerner is to avoid the trap of assuming that Muslim women feel oppressed by Islam and that they need to be saved by those from more "civilised" cultures.

Papadopoulos & Hildebrand (1997) have applied systemic thinking to their work with refugees and considered the dilemmas at the heart of this process. They observed that it is thought that within refugee families some family members may hold on to a yearning for a return to the homeland whilst others are relieved to have found a place of safety. However, they argued, "these divisions in reality are much more complicated and less clear-cut than it first appears" (p. 227) In families they interviewed they found that different members of the family "took it in turns to represent each one of the two oppositional directions, without being aware of it" (p. 230). This shows that unless therapists examine more closely the families themselves as well as the wider contexts that impinge on the families, they are likely to adopt, mostly unwittingly, the various stereotyped versions that exist in our societal discourses about refugees.

A dilemma for practitioners is "how to establish and maintain a sensitive balance between clinical and political dimensions in this work" (Papadopoulos, 1995) and the losses and gains of maintaining neutrality when working with refugees. Moreover, "unless therapists appreciate the importance of their own systemic connection with the wider political issues, they are likely to slip into unexpected blind alleys" (Papadopoulos, 1999a, p. 118). On the one hand, practitioners may wish to contribute to redressing the injustices done to refugees, on the other, they may become drawn into political complexities of which they have little knowledge. An example relevant to casework is the use of interpreters. Families may be reluctant to be seen with an interpreter from their own community because of a concern that information about their circumstances may then become known. Additionally, they may be very worried that the interpreter belongs to a particular political faction within the community that could lead to them being placed in danger.

Woodcock (2001) has integrated political analysis with systemic and psychoanalytic ideas and concludes that the complex interactions with families:

> can place the therapist in conflict with the aims of government policy. In Britain, the government's harsh asylum legislation or its policy on refugee children who are excluded from the benefits of the *United Nations Convention on the Rights of the Child*. [pp. 147–148]

From pathology to resilience

It is a paradox that much writing on refugees' mental health is based upon those who present for treatment whilst the vast majority of refugees are not in this category.

Muecke (1992) states that the data and conclusions about refugee health in the literature are exclusively negative. "Absent is the study of refugee health or of healthy refugees" (p. 520). What is needed, she argues, is attention to refugees' capacity to change and to the meanings that change has for them. Refugees may then be seen not as passive acted-upon victims but as "extraordinarily resilient human beings" (p. 521) who are participants in clarifying the processes and meanings of human change. Further, the importance of participatory research between researchers and refugees to highlight the authentic voices of refugees is stressed.

Beiser *et al.* (1995) in their research on immigrant and refugee children in Canada comment that, "the mental health literature implies that the absence of disorder is the most important index of successful adaptation" (p. 70), but that these children's parents are as concerned about evidence of positive adjustment, such as self-esteem and school achievement. Rutter (1987) and Gilligan (2000) also emphasize the importance of positive school experiences for the development of resilience.

In a fascinating article outlining the setting up of a school-based mental health service for refugee children, O'Shea *et al.* (2000) describe how in an inner London primary school with ninety refugee children amongst the pupil population, fourteen refugee children were identified as having a severe psychological problem or special educational needs. This is quite remarkable as it implies that the large majority of primary school-aged refugee children have developed sufficient resilience to adapt to a new cultural setting and have levels of disturbance little different from typical inner London school populations.

A number of researchers (e.g. Rutter, 1987; Eisenbruch, 1990; Muecke, 1992; Keane, 1996) have been led to search for protective factors and to oversee a shift in focus from "vulnerability to resilience" (Rutter, 1987, p. 316). Rutter places the concept of *resilience* within an interactive frame which allows for a good fit with systemic thinking about how problems and solutions may occur. He asserts that resilience cannot be seen as a fixed attribute of the individual. Rather it is the case that "if circumstances change, resilience alters" (p. 317) and he urges a focus upon the processes that occur rather than a search for a list of positive or negative variables that may lead to greater or lesser vulnerability. Thus, "resilience is now understood in its wider context, as a product of a close collaboration and mutual co-construction between the individual and the collective" (Papadopoulos, 1999b, p. 327) and not an attribute of a tough individual.

Connecting theory and practice

Thompson (1998, 2001), a leading authority on anti-discriminatory practice for social workers and others in the caring professions asserts that "contemporary Western societies are characterized by inequality ... the worker can play a pivotal role with regard to the service user's experience of the discrimination and oppression arising from inequality" (1998, p. 1). He further asserts that practice which does not take account of this "cannot be seen as good practice, no matter how high its standards may be in other respects" (2001, p. 11) and that therefore good practice must be anti-discriminatory practice.

There are many practitioners who recognize the inequalities of the world we live in but find it difficult to find a way to bring this into the therapeutic relationship. Below are a number of questions and statements that may be adapted to differing contexts and provide a message to individuals and families about the practitioner's relationship to oppression and inequality in society:

- What was it like coming along today? For some families it can be very worrying coming along to an appointment especially if they are used to being treated badly/not listened to.
- How have you managed to cope for so long in the face of such adversity/unfair treatment?
- When faced with so much prejudice it is easy for family members to become depressed or start to argue more with each other—how does it affect you and your family?
- We know that the situation for Islamic families may be very

frightening when some people in this country show anti-Muslim feelings—has anyone been frightened in this family?

● It can be tough for members of refugee families when other people have little idea what they have been through—how do you manage to deal with that?

● If you were able to choose, what are the things you would like more of? (Better housing; more money for shoes for the children; more money for shopping and toys.) This is very interesting because it shows that if families could be given better housing/more money there might well be less problems.

● We know that there are concerns that black men are more likely to get heavier sentences in the courts—do you think that's what might have happened to your son?

● Sometimes when family members have felt humiliated by the system they can turn on other family members. They can't influence those more powerful than themselves so they might try to influence those near to them.

● Sometimes families that have been torn apart by events outside of their control can start to tear each other apart.

These questions and statements attempt to combine a general statement of the practitioner's relationship to issues of oppression and inequality through the use of the third person whilst allowing individuals and families the freedom to express their own unique experiences.

The dialectical unity of "not knowing" and "knowing"

It may be argued that only a systemic approach that places itself firmly within a tradition that considers social and political context as central and recognizes discrimination and oppression as reality is likely to be relevant when working with refugees. And if this is the case with refugees it is also true for all other groups.

I cannot "know" what the individual experience of anyone else is. In this sense, I agree that it is of enormous value in all interactions to adopt a "not-knowing" position (even if at times some of us find this difficult!) and to be curious about the narratives of others. However, simultaneously I hold beliefs and values that inform what I say and how I say it. I know, or think I know, about certain aspects of the world I live in. Along with everyone else, I have a view of the world I live in, the nature of society, its fairness or otherwise and so on.

Dialectical thinking is based upon the unity, or interpenetration, of opposites (Rees, 1994) and as such is able to acknowledge that both "knowing" and "not knowing" approaches may co-exist at one and the same time.

The dialectical approach that is at the heart of classical Marxism—the idea that all institutions and ideologies are in a process of constant change; that all aspects of society and nature are interconnected; and that it is the contradictions between the different parts of this totality that give rise to change—has also been theorized by systemic thinkers (see e.g. Boscolo & Bertrando, 1992; Cronen *et al.*, 1985; Keeney, 1983) and many systemic practitioners will recognize it as particularly relevant to their own thinking. It is expressed within the concept of "both/and" thinking—an idea incidentally not invented by family therapists and utilized, for instance, in the nineteenth century by Marx's co-thinker Friedrich Engels in *The Dialectics of Nature* (1934).

Bateson (1979) and Glenn (1995) have highlighted the similarities in epistemology between classical Marxism and the systemic approach. Relevant to this is Marx's dictum that people "make their own history, but they do not make it just as they please; they do not make it under circumstances chosen by themselves, but under circumstances directly given and transmitted from the past" (Marx & Engels, 1976, p. 103). This is an excellent example of externalizing the problem which has not been improved upon as a contextual marker by systemic practitioners. Interestingly, in a collection of essays commemorating Bateson, Rieber (1989) reflects upon Bateson's intellectual activity and involvement in human affairs and concludes that: "We should have to pin Bateson closer to Marx than to the run of social science academics" (p. 45).

What differentiates the Marxist dialectic from the systemic approach of family therapy's first theoretician is its clarity that, in the last resort, social context influences personal interactions more than the other way round, that collective rather than individual responses are more likely to have a greater influence in changing individuals' relationships with their social context, and the assertion that efforts to consciously change society for the benefit of the weak and poor are to be actively welcomed. This contrasts with the view of Bateson and many of his followers (cf. Carr, 2000, for an excellent and much-needed clear explanation of Bateson's ideas) that concerted, collective efforts to achieve change should be distrusted because of the unforeseen outcomes that will occur as a result of this process.

Conclusion

The dialectical relationship between past, present and future—and between underprivileged and overprivileged, weaker and stronger and so on—is a feature in all our lives, even if most of the time we may not think of it as such. For refugees, as they compare where they have come from with where they are now and where they are going to, this connection is likely to be much more explicit.

Kunz (1981) provides a succinct description of these connections and the influence that those in the host country may have upon their well-being:

> However much the newly arrived refugees are under the influence of memories of home and transit, they rarely remain fully captives of the past. Unless they are irrevocably broken by trials, they will soon begin to explore the surroundings, assess the attitudes of the hosts, and endeavour to find a niche for themselves in which they can feel consistent both with their background and with their gradually changing expectations. *In doing so the nature of the country of resettlement and its population will be of vital importance.* [p. 46—my emphasis]

Acknowledgements

My thanks to Clotilda Gundonia, who at the time of my research was coordinator of the Lewisham Refugee Network and arranged my contact with members of the Somali Women's Action Group; and to Dick Blackwell of the Medical Foundation for the Care of Victims of Torture who provided comments on a draft of this chapter.

CHAPTER TEN

Two phases of the refugee experience: interviews with refugees and support organizations[1]

Pamela Griffiths

Introduction

For the last six years I have spent several weeks each year on a Greek island off the coast of Turkey. The area has seen many waves of population movements, both voluntary and involuntary, as well as changes of sovereignty: prior to 1912 the island was Turkish. It remains border territory, emphasized by the presence of army conscripts guarding remote beaches. During this time, when shopping at the local market I have often noticed a busy gathering in the adjacent walled compound. Through gaps in the metal fencing I have seen dark-haired men, women and children seated at trestle tables or waiting in line. They were not Greek.

Soon I understood that what I was observing was part of a chain of movement of Kurdish refugees from Turkey, Iraq and Iran to Greece, and often onward to Western Europe. After paying large sums to be brought to one of several Greek islands, these asylum seekers are interned by police and later transported to a refugee camp near Athens. I have often counselled refugees in London, including a few Kurds, and realized how little I knew of their

189

journey into exile. I resolved to explore the process in order to understand more of their experience.

My cultural background is British and I have lived for several years in South Africa and America. In these countries I have worked with refugees, and had refugees amongst friends and colleagues. Usually they were in later phases of exile, but my knowledge of early phases was more limited—except in retrospective accounts. I recognized that people may be less inclined to speak in early phases due to fears of harassment or rejection and a consequent desire to remain invisible. However, in subsequent accounts (in therapy) the narrative of the journey into exile, following an often violent and abrupt change, is often highly charged, revealing extremes of emotion and the beginnings of a new identity. I felt that it was important to hear the refugees' voice at this time, as well as in later phases when they were becoming established in a host country, in order to illuminate this "transitional space" (Grinberg & Grinberg, 1989) that a refugee may go through. The considerable external changes—loss of country, social networks, language, family institutions and basic shelter—are more familiar from media reports. I wanted to gain some insight into the less documented internal changes experienced by the asylum seekers and refugees. Also, such an undertaking was very relevant to my studies as I was registered for a PhD degree at the Tavistock Clinic and Birkbeck College (of the University of London) doing research on the wider issues of the refugee experience. This paper presents the findings of the study carried out during the summers of 1996–1998 in Greece and the UK.

Background to the study

In 1996, at the inception of this study, there was a substantial increase in Kurdish refugees entering Europe. This was primarily due to economic and political instability in Iraq, and Turkey's violent campaign against the Kurds in Turkey. The Kurdish homeland is split over five countries and since the aftermath of World War I they have suffered considerable human-rights abuses, with many forced into exile (McDowall, 1992; Bulloch & Morris, 1993).

Many Kurdish refugees make their way to Greece initially, via sea and land, and most plan to move on to Germany, UK, Scandinavia and the Netherlands. In the summer of 1996, increasing numbers of Iraqi Kurds were sleeping rough in one of the main squares in Athens. Numbers eventually reached about 700 people. In October they were transferred to an unused children's summer camp for the winter, about thirty kilometres from Athens, and during this time an estimated 1300 men, seventy women and eighty children were in residence. By June 1997 the Red Cross could no longer continue their support and the refugees were moved to Mount Pendeli north of Athens and provided with army tents. Two adjacent camps were created: one run by the Médecins du Monde, the other self-administered by the refugees. At the time of the interviews in these camps, in late 1997, the number of people in the first camp was estimated to be 115–180, and in the second camp around 520 people. In the summer of 1998, the second camp was closed and refugees again began to sleep rough in an Athens square. The only official refugee camp (and the only refugee reception centre in Greece) at Lavrio, south of Athens, already sheltered a population of approximately 350 refugees and asylum seekers: 250 Turks, and 100 Kurds from Iran and Iraq, as well as some people from other countries.

The context of the Kurdish refugee experience

According to the UNHCR, as of early 1998 there were 22,376,300 refugees, asylum seekers, returnees and persons displaced within their own countries. This figure represents one out of every 264 people on earth. For Europe alone the figure for 1997 was 6,056,500 (UNHCR, 1998).

In 1998 this total had risen to 6,212,620 partly due to the massive exodus from Bosnia and Herzegovina. The largest exodus during the late nineties had been from Iraq (UNHCR, 1999): mostly Kurds and from the Arab Christian minority. Several European countries received substantial numbers of asylum seekers and refugees from these areas. Other smaller groups seeking refuge in Europe in recent years include peoples from Vietnam, Somalia, Sudan and Afghanistan. Kibreab (1999) argues that the evidence of societies excluding people they consider as "other" has never been greater, reminding us that refugees are essentially created by political factors.

The refugee experience, particularly in the early stages, can be characterized by extreme loss and pain. Papadopoulos & Hildebrand (1997) argue that we have not yet developed a model to normalize the suffering due to war and, inevitably, this leads us to formulate the refugee experience within the context of a pathology and a deficit paradigm. Their analysis shows how: "when war breaks out ... mental health professionals [tend to] ... find themselves trapped in a disabling syndrome. This consists of a powerful and yet fuzzy mixture of political and moral considerations" with "attempts at psychological theorising, disbelief, numbness, relief, ... shame and guilt, impractical idealism, omnipotent fantasies, etc" (Papadopoulos & Hildebrand, 1997, p. 209).

Muecke identified two dominant approaches to refugee health: "the objectification of refugees as a political class of excess people, and the reduction of refugee health to disease or pathology" (1992, p. 515). She argues for the inclusion of a new paradigm based on the resilience and fortitude of refugees. In this respect, affirmation of the resources and traditional coping skills of the refugee population is advocated by the UNHCR (1994).

Western attempts to understand the refugees' transition tend to focus on trauma. The most commonly used category to address mental health issues of refugees is Post-traumatic Stress Disorder (PTSD) (Van der Veer, 1998). Its emphasis on disorder and questionable applicability to other cultures has been a subject of concern (e.g. Marsella *et al.*, 1994, and Manson, 1997). Amongst alternative models of constructing the refugees' experience "cultural bereavement" (Eisenbruch, 1990) and "nostalgic disorientation" (Papadopoulos, 1997) have been proposed. Although both proposals attempt to normalize the refugees' suffering, neither addresses the re-construction of identity that may be experienced by the refugee.

In order to gain insight into the experience of the asylum seekers and refugees the following research question was proposed: How do asylum seekers and refugees experience their journey from their country of origin to their adopted country? The key areas to be explored by the research participants comprised: the main difficulties they face, differences in experience between genders, sources of sustenance and support, emotional responses, and opportunities to maintain their cultural life. These areas were also addressed with the support organizations, as well as looking at how staff coped and the main challenges and rewards within this work.

Method and rationale

Two fieldwork locations were used in Greece (Athens and environs) and one in the UK (London). Greece represented the experience of early exile (mainly asylum seekers): days or weeks after arrival. UK represented later phases of exile (usually refugees): often several years since leaving the country of origin. Persons persecuted for political reasons have the right to claim asylum. They are usually not permitted to work or to benefit from educational programmes. Refugees have been granted full citizenship rights within the country. Most refugees begin their journey into exile as asylum seekers.

Papadopoulos (2000b, 2001a,b) developed a classification of five main phases of the refugee experience which is relevant to this study. His point of departure was his argument that the "refugee trauma" discourse is so dominant in our society today that it tends to colour not only the way the mental health professionals' work with refugees, but also the very way refugees perceive their own situation. In other words, it is easier for everybody to focus on the terrible events that forced those people to become refugees in the first place. Papadopoulos called that phase the phase of "Devastating Events". Further, he argued that by privileging of the "Devastating Events", professionals and refugees themselves tend to underestimate or even ignore the impact that other phases of the refugee experience have on the refugees' overall psychological state. He then proposed the following three additional phases:

> "Anticipation"—when people sense the impending danger and try to decide how best to avoid it; ... "Survival"—when refugees are safe from danger but live in temporary accommodation and uncertainty; and "Adjustment"—when refugees try to adjust to new life in the receiving country. [Papadopoulos, 2001a, p. 5]

Following this classification, it was important for this study to identify and compare the experiences refugees had in these two distinct phases of their overall ordeal. The refugees' stay in Greece corresponds with Papadopoulos' phase of "Survival" whereas their stay in the UK with the phase of "Adjustment".

A qualitative study was designed where semi-structured interviews, intended to stimulate a broad discussion, were carried out with three groups of respondents: a sample group of Kurds (mainly asylum seekers) in Greece in early phases of exile, a sample group of Kurds (mainly refugees) in the UK in later phases of exile and a sample group of support organizations in each of the two fieldwork sites.

Face-to-face interviews were essential where refugees had no address. This method also elicited a high response rate from overstretched support organizations. Media views and discussions with friends and colleagues in Greece and the UK helped sensitize the researcher to the dominant discourse at the time. A journal was kept to note observations at the refugee camps and community centres.

Collecting data from Kurds in early and later phases of exile, as well as the support organizations, made it possible to access different perspectives of a complex experience and to enhance the validity of the findings. Data was analysed by means of content analysis to identify common themes.

Locating the sample

Network or snowball sampling, often chosen in sensitive research where the target population is hidden (Biernacki & Waldorf, 1981), was used to locate the refugees and some of the support organizations. Participants were found through referrals amongst people who shared similar experiences, i.e. refugees or support organizations.

Gatekeepers (Bloch, 1999) were used to make contact with possible respondents. Gatekeepers were people who worked for and with support organizations, refugee camps in Greece and refugee community centres in London. They were often able to facilitate the research by encouraging the participation of people in their organization or work sphere. A drawback of snowball sampling is that only persons within one friendship network of the population may be interviewed (Welch, 1975). To reduce this possibility varied starting points were found with different Kurdish groups and different support organizations. Starting points for support organizations were also found in newspapers and phone directories.

The interviews

All the interviews were carried out by the researcher in order to enhance validity and reliability. An interpreter translated the responses from the participants, where necessary. The interpreters were briefed as to the purpose of the research and were asked for some detail about their background, e.g. were they Kurdish, how long had they been in the current country and where had they travelled from.

These details were necessary in order to provide an awareness of the context of their translations. All the interpreters were Kurdish refugees except for one interpreter who was a Greek national.

The questions for the asylum seekers and refugee groups were:

— What are the main difficulties or problems facing you as a refugee?
— Are these difficulties different for men and women?
— What sustains or supports you?
— What are the main emotions that are present for you?
— Are there opportunities to maintain your customs?

The questions for the support organization group were:

— What is the role of your organization in supporting refugees?
— Are the issues for men and women refugees different?
— What are the main mental and/or physical difficulties of the refugees?
— How do your staff cope with the effects of working in this area?
— What are the main challenges or rewards of working in this area?

The questions were used to stimulate a broader discussion. Initially, plans were made to tape the interviews; however it became clear from the first interviews that this approach was inhibiting the respondents and raised suspicions as to the real purpose of the research. It was therefore decided to write down the responses. This process was facilitated by the extra time provided while the responses were translated. Responses were regularly clarified or repeated back verbatim to the respondents for confirmation. This process enhanced the validity of the data.

The main location for the refugee respondents in Greece was the refugee camps, and in the UK the main locations were community centres. Data was collected in Greece during June and September 1996 and September 1997, and in the UK in May and September 1996, October 1997, and September 1998. Completion of analyses, including triangulation, and writing up took place in 1999 and 2000.

Research participants

A total of twenty-five Kurds (mainly asylum seekers) in the early phases of exile were interviewed in Greece and twenty Kurds (mainly refugees) in later phases of exile in the UK. Respondents from eight support organizations were interviewed in Greece and the same number in the UK. The sample of Kurds in Greece comprised sixteen men (64%) and nine women (36%) and their average time spent in Greece since arrival was seven months. In the UK the group comprised thirteen men (65%) and seven women (35%) and their average time in the UK since arrival was six years. Respondents in both countries included Kurds from Iraq, Iran and Turkey.

Respondents from a range of support organizations were interviewed, comprising (in Greece): the UNHCR (United Nations High Commissioner for Refugees), the Red Cross, the Red Crescent, the Greek Council for Refugees, Médecins du Monde, the Medical Rehabilitation Centre for Torture Victims, the Social Work Foundation, and the Counselling Service for the Centre for Mental Health. In the UK respondents from the following organizations were interviewed: the Refugee Council, the Medical Foundation for the Care of Victims of Torture, three Kurdish Community Groups, an Immigration Law Firm, Nafsiyat (a counselling organization for ethnic minorities) and a refugee hostel manager.

Results: I—The asylum seekers' and refugees' responses

The most frequently cited items are given for each question. The number in brackets indicates how many people expressed the same theme.

G = Greece: Respondents in early phases of exile (mainly asylum seekers) ($n = 25$); (20% did not require an interpreter).

UK = UK: Respondents in later phases of exile (mainly refugees) ($n = 20$); (40% did not require an interpreter).

a) What are the main difficulties or problems facing you as a refugee?

G—All respondents cited the traumas of the journey to the camps and described it in detail. Examples include: "We were eight or nine hours in a boat. The whole thing was very dangerous". "You flee— it's the only way to save your life". "We were kept for twelve days at the border without food or money—twenty people in one small room". "We walked for three weeks—our child died on the way".

In the camps the deficiency of food (in Mount Pendeli one loaf of bread per person each day being the allowance), lack of adequate sanitation and no work were the main themes (25). In Lavrio occasionally refugees earned some money helping local tradesmen but at Mount Pendeli they had no currency at all.

UK—Most respondents (12) felt the main difficulty they faced was being able to express themselves and be accepted: "We want to feel accepted". "We want to know our rights as well as our duties". For some of the respondents it lay in building a new identity (9); many reflected with insight on their transformation: "I felt naked, stripped of my identity", "my ego felt so small", and "my old identity had fallen away, then I felt a bit desperate".

Later, on learning a new language, "slowly the construction of my new identity began".

b) Are these difficulties different for men and women?

G—The majority thought that "women have a more difficult time" because they have more responsibility, e.g. child minding (17).

UK—There was agreement that it was more difficult for women (18), a common reason being that "they feel imprisoned at home".

c) What sustains or supports you?

G—Most responded that it was "the struggle" and the hope to return to the homeland (19). "We feel so sad that we can't go and fight" was a common refrain.

UK—Talking together at community centres was the main support (20). "We need a place to feel safe and not threatened" was a key reason why the centres were such an important factor in their lives.

d) What are the main emotions that are present for you?

G—Fear was the dominant emotion expressed (25)—of the police and of the military. Some had been chased by dogs at the border. In Mount Pendeli in particular fear of the cold in winter was a concern (9). Parents (8) said that children were afraid of the dark and thought that there was a monster on the mountain.

UK—Fear of those in authority was cited (16). Examples included policemen: "when I see a policeman I hide—though I've no reason to" and "even a clerk in an office". Fear could occasionally turn to anger such as towards a "rude bus driver" but was more usually directed towards politicians. Flashbacks could occur e.g. on hearing a helicopter "I was transported—I wanted to shoot it down" or on seeing a policeman "I feel they're going to come for me" (2). Parents (7) said that children were afraid of being bullied.

e) Are there opportunities to maintain your customs?

G—After some thought many referred to music being organized occasionally in the camps by the asylum seekers and refugees (15). A few referred to the difficulties of arranging a traditional burial in Greece (5). It appeared that in some cases arrangements for the body to be returned to Kurdistan had to be made.

UK—There was general consensus that sometimes music and Kurdish food was organized, and classes for language and dance were held in some Centres (20). A frequent comment was: "We talk about the news broadcast on Kurdish TV". (MTV, a satellite channel based in Belgium, which was taken off the air during the time of the research.)

Result II—The support organizations' responses

G—Support Organizations in Greece ($n = 8$)
UK—Support Organizations in the UK ($n = 8$)

a) What is the role of your organization in supporting refugees?

G—All the organizations were involved in negotiating shelter and/ or basic health care for the refugees (8). A few offered psychological help or counselling (3).

UK—All the organizations offered some guidance regarding legal support, benefits and/or housing and skills training (8). All the respondents spoke of the development of long term projects within their organization (8). Most of the organizations offered counselling (6).

b) Are the issues for men and women refugees different?

G—Many of the organizations commented that women were more able to trust and "open up" and begin to "flourish", "they learn new skills and wear ear-rings". They found that men appeared to have lost more in terms of status e.g. "men are degraded—they were the glory of the world" (6).

UK—There was consensus that women (particularly single women who "have less to lose") were able to adjust more easily to the new country. Women were seen as being more able to support each other. Men, particularly those with higher education, were seen as having "more to lose" in terms of power and authority, and may often have to accept a lower-status job (8). A few organizations (3) noted that more women than men come forward to take up counselling.

c) What are the main mental/physical difficulties of the refugees?

G—All the organizations agreed that the main difficulties were related to shelter/food and financial assistance (8). Several organizations felt that the central difficulty was that many of the refugees were in shock and were unable to talk about their feelings, preferring to talk about what they cannot do e.g. "I cannot work" (due to a lack of official papers) (5). A few noted the frequent somatization of feeling: "mental health comes out as a somatic problem like fatigue or pain" and "they try to extinguish their feelings to survive—they can't afford to be depressed" (3). One organization noted that the refugees experienced some relief in talking about their journey and having some affirmation "at least of what has happened" (1).

UK—There was agreement amongst all the organizations that housing was the prime difficulty. Bedsits (i.e. one room apartments) were often sources of disillusionment e.g. "This room reminds me of my prison cell" (8). Many noted difficulties in couples' relationships as a frequent issue described variously as "painful" or "like emotional torture" (7). Hyper-alertness with a lack of trust was noted. This was particularly evident with authority figures e.g. "If they see a policeman they try to be very polite or hide because they are always scared of authority figures" (6); other difficulties comprised anger and "obsession" with past memories (5), men with professional skills often having to accept low-skilled work (5) and bereavement issues (5).

d) How do your staff cope with any effects of working in this area?

G—All the respondents recognized a need for staff support (8). However only a few of the organizations held a regular support group to talk about the effects of their work and "express anger" (2). One of the organizations had a system of supervision in place (1).

UK—All the organizations offering counselling had staff supervision (6), in addition a few organizations also ran support groups for staff (3). A couple of the organizations had no formalized system of support in place (2). Each group also cited "colleagues" as part of "our support system" (8).

e) What are the main challenges or rewards of working in this area?

G—All the respondents cited disappointment and burnout as the main challenge. Several also added "language barriers" as a challenge (5). The main reward was agreed to be fulfilling a desire to do something to help the situation (8).

UK—There was consensus that the main challenge was frustration at bureaucracy and politics (8). The main reward was doing something to help the situation (8).

Field notes

These were kept during the interviewing process to provide contextual data. Asylum seekers and refugees in the early phases in Greece were more desperate to tell their stories than those in the UK. The narration of the journey to Greece was often accompanied with much emotion, fast speech and hand gestures used to emphasize the words. By contrast their current difficulties—a deficiency of food, a lack of sanitation and no paid work—were described in a resigned, quiet manner. This manner also communicated their sense of not belonging as in "When you don't have a homeland, you have no place in the world, no homeland, so no identity, no passport".

Many men were sleeping when I visited the camps in the daytime, conveying an impression of mild depression and enforced helplessness. However, in the UK one refugee remembered his early experience as: "I slept and slept—it was such a relief", sleep was the culmination of physical and mental exhaustion. Interviews with the refugees in the UK often evoked lengthier responses and were sometimes cathartic. I also met refugees who had no voice—for example, one woman in Greece was in deep shock and unable to speak. She had been on a refugee ship abandoned by the captain in Italian waters in 1996.

Sometimes the lack of "voice" may have reflected disappointed expectations in the new culture. One refugee despaired "my wife hasn't spoken since we arrived", another exclaimed, in tears, "they should help us—we don't deserve this". Most people in the camps in Greece appeared to be in a state of limbo where general activity, and communication channels with a wider world, were greatly reduced.

A lack of contact between asylum seekers/refugees and support organizations was apparent in both Greece and the UK—but particularly in Greece. Technically, as in most cases of people fleeing persecution or disasters, most of them had no official papers and were therefore illegal immigrants. I was frequently asked in Greece "How can we get help?"

Efforts to connect with local populations were being made by the refugees in both countries. In Greece one camp put on an exhibition of their art work, often poignantly describing their journey e.g. "This is the time the group left me and I am only myself". Demonstrations were staged in a city square and some refugees went on hunger strike. In the UK a play was performed at a community centre and a demonstration took place in a city square.

Both demonstrations were to inform public opinion and were peaceful.

Ambivalence about revealing a "true" identity was evident particularly in the early phases. Consent for me to take photos in one refugee camp was subsequently revoked. Sometimes names were given, sometimes not. When contacting a few of the refugees in the UK to arrange appointments for the interview I found that I was given frequently changing contact numbers—it seemed that a pattern of moving on to safe houses was perhaps continuing.

Those support organizations with supervision and/or support groups in place demonstrated more insight into their interactions with the asylum seekers and refugees.

All the support organizations expressed considerable frustration but responded to it in contrasting ways. In Greece the frustration appeared to remain more within the individual organization. In the UK organizations were more active in political lobbying and representation.

There were times when I felt angry at the complacency of some support organizations and politicians. At other times I felt despair when asked by asylum seekers and refugees how they could get help and realized how difficult it was to reach supportive organizations with no money, little knowledge of the language, no phone or understanding of the host culture. I participated in a short-term support group for those working with refugees, an experience which I found valuable in helping me to identify my emotional responses, and motivation for working in this area.

Discussion

The key findings of the study include—amongst the asylum seekers and refugees—the desperate need, in the early phases, to have the story of their traumatic journey to Greece witnessed and validated by an outsider; the differing experiences of men and women; a change in identity over time; and considerable fear which was evident in early and later phases. Moreover all the support organizations expressed pronounced frustration but responded to it in different ways. Those organizations with supervision and support groups in place demonstrated more insight into their interactions with asylum seekers and refugees. Each of these findings will now be discussed and the counselling implications drawn out.

The need for validation of the traumatic journey

In the early phases the need for the asylum seekers and refugees to recount their journey, even though I had not specifically asked them to do so, suggested an urgency to have their position validated by an outsider. I was a stranger to them, apart from indicating my intention of communicating their needs to a wider audience. If I had taken the approach of asking them to recount the details of their journey I would have been following the model of psychological debriefing. This is an approach widely used following major traumatic events in an attempt to reduce psychological sequelae. However, the timing and rationale for this intervention needs careful consideration as recent research has indicated that it could traumatize the individual further (Bisson *et al.*, 1997; Mayou *et al.*, 2000). Being guided by the refugee allows him/her to regulate the degree of exposure to traumatic memories.

Following this approach, Papadopoulos describes how he made himself available to talk with Bosnian medical evacuees in a UK hospital: "I did not expect them to speak to me about their experiences or see me at set times ... I left them entirely free to interact with me in any way they wished" (1999a, p. 112). Papadopoulos saw his role as providing "therapeutic witnessing". This was also a term suggested by two of the support organizations who provided counselling: "They need you to be a witness: what's most important is to believe them". The nature of this approach is not to question, but to listen as a witness to their experience. Within the unconditional witnessing, refugees can begin to reconnect with the disparate parts of the traumatic experience creating a narrative where they can begin to position themselves in a context. White & Epston (1990) have shown the potential of the narrative to be used therapeutically to explore the dominant story. They point out that this approach is different to pathologizing the client and can lead to empowerment and the co-evolution of new or alternative stories.

A further dimension of the need for witnessing was introduced by a support organization: "Perpetrators have put them into a victim position—they're not believed. They've either had to hide the truth from their torturers or what they know, e.g. to save a brother. Now they want to tell the truth". This perspective highlights the need for a sensitivity to power issues in the therapeutic relationship on the part of the counsellor, as refugees may be hyperalert to prevent further abuses of power. A client-centred approach witnessing the meaning for the refugee is indicated. The counsellor needs to be aware of the values, attitudes and beliefs they hold and refrain from any assumptions which may over-pathologize the rehabilitative process. Refugees may not wish to provide full names due to fears of safety or security, and counsellors may need to work within this constraint. For those who want to talk, safety may be enhanced for some refugees by working in a group context. A long-time representative of a support organization in the UK noted that many refugees "don't like to be seen as individuals" in earlier phases of exile indicating a need for the provision of group models of therapeutic work.

Gender

The asylum seekers and refugees' view that women have the more difficult time seemed to be based on the continuation of their roles (e.g. childcare, cooking) whereas the men had lost roles they held in their country of origin. The support organizations, in both countries, recognized this loss of status in the men as well as their more restricted emotional expression and thus saw the men as having the more difficult experience. A recent study of displaced people in western Georgia found a similar imbalance in gender roles where the displaced men had "a reduced role and an apathetic response to the situation" (Vivero Pol, 1999, p. 349).

Although non-working refugee women may become isolated and depressed due to having less opportunity to learn the new language (Ekblad et al., 1986), many support organizations felt that in general women were more able to support each other. They suggested that this factor enabled them to cope more effectively in the new culture. A 1997 study of young, white men in America (Fischer & Good, 1997) found that they had difficulty recognizing and processing their emotions, which was strongly linked to traditional masculine gender roles. Similarly, male refugees may be bound by socialized gender roles which restrict their emotionality and ability to self-disclose.

Counsellors may need to consider approaches to working with male refugees in ways which enable them to experience themselves as emotional beings. For example, cognitive approaches could reinforce traditional masculine socialization. Consideration of the gender of the counsellor may be an important factor in this process, e.g. a male counsellor who can model emotional expression may be indicated. Conversely, revealing emotions to a female counsellor may be less acceptable within cultural models.

The implications of different experiences for male and female refugees in transition may contribute to the evident strains on couple relationships, noted by support organizations in the later phases. A few respondents linked the "emotional torture" observed in some relationships to earlier atrocities in one of the couples' experience. Clearly this behaviour could lead to the break-up of the relationship, which has implications for dependent children. Different standards between home and host culture were also cited as a source of conflict between parents and adolescents. These findings suggest a particular need for the availability of couples counselling, and possibly family therapy, for refugees.

Identity

In the early phases, sustaining influences were unanimously identified as "the struggle" and the "hope to return to the homeland". The homeland was often described in an idealized manner e.g. "the unity of the people". Similarly constructions of Western Europe could be idealized: "I was fascinated by Europe and what they've achieved". In later phases there was evidence of disillusionment both regarding views of the homeland and Western Europe: "I felt disillusioned about what I'd been fighting for" and "the working classes are still suffering here". This view was reinforced by some responses from the support organizations in the UK and may reflect some of the harsh experiences of life as a refugee as well as a different life-stage. Certainly the age, educational level and length of time since leaving the homeland are key factors to consider in understanding the perspective of a refugee in the counselling context.

There was evidence that some refugees, particularly in the later-phase group, moved between the perspectives of disillusionment and idealization regarding views of the homeland and the host country. For example, the homeland could be "a virgin and beautiful land" as well as eliciting comments of "I feel sorry for the people there".

Europe could be a "utopia" as well as the opposite; references being made to "Europe's shame". Movement between these positions conveyed an uneasy restlessness, demonstrating their attachment to their homeland and their identity forged there, as well as acknowledging increasing integration in the host country. A need to re-unite with those they knew at times of great trauma, e.g. when hiding in the mountains, was expressed in plans of annual reunions where a common bond elicited much emotion in "singing, talking and eating".

Although the notion of territorially based identity is disputed, Kibreab demonstrates that it is "critical to human well being" (1999, p. 407). He also points out that how people feel about their place of residence is "inextricably linked with the cause of displacement" (p. 404). Most of the refugees in this study left in great haste, without farewells, which compounded their loss and grieving. Some recognized that they can never return to the homeland they remember: "Many of the kids who grew up together perished".

Papadopoulos & Hildebrand (1997) identified a similar dilemma in Bosnian refugee families. Part of the challenge for the counsellor is to recognize these positions and facilitate integration. The use of narrative to build bridges between old and new identities, which Bruner (1990) refers to as forging links "between the exceptional and the ordinary", can enable ongoing psychological movement. Horticultural projects recognizing the universality of land and the cycles of growth are also being used as a means to connect disparate experiences and identify commonalities in an alien culture (Webb-Johnson, 2000).

Refugees in later phases in the UK, who had experienced counselling, reflected with insight on their transformation. Amongst a few who had become more settled in local communities, a new theme emerged of wanting to help those left behind in the homeland, sometimes accompanied by survivor guilt. The need for safety during such a sensitive process is paramount. The counsellor needs to create the necessary psychological space where the client can experience a continuity of what one refugee called "my sensual self", and an assimilation and accommodation of past and current experiences can become possible.

For many refugees in exile "juggling identities" can be a feature of their urban life. This is often in response to harassment, or the threat of harassment (e.g. Malkki, 1995). Thus the response of the local community is a key aspect in enabling confidence and self-esteem to build.

The conflicting approaches of the host community, who were seen to be operating with different agendas in this study (e.g. immigration officers, army personnel, social workers and counsellors) can only exacerbate the asylum seekers and refugees' trauma. In the context of their political struggle their trauma had meaning, and was perhaps more manageable. However, disappointed expectations in the new cultures could be experienced as deeply traumatic.

Fear

The asylum seekers and refugees in Greece initially answered the question concerning feelings in concrete terms e.g. "I cannot work". After further discussion it was evident that a fear of authority figures, or people abusing their power, clearly lasted into later phases in the UK. Support organizations, which had a medical background, were more likely to recognize the somatization of feelings in asylum seekers and refugees in the early phases. When fear is expressed, one organization emphasized the need for normalization, as in "of course you feel like this". This approach suggested a way to de-medicalize PTSD and apply the model to the refugees' experience of trauma. Understanding the nature and meaning of the trauma for different cultures, as well as recognizing its manifestation, is essential for any counselling intervention.

The refugees in the later phases in the UK were more articulate about their feelings and vividly described their fears, including a "fear of death" during their earlier experiences which had been "unacknowledged". My non-refugee status was highlighted in: "We are haunted by our experiences. You as a European are accustomed to the simple fact that you can walk on the street without being bothered by anyone—but it is very dear to us". This comment emphasized that I, as a European, would not be seen as someone who could understand their experience.

This perception could affect the counselling relationship, and counsellors would need to ensure that they could comprehend the refugees' experience and convey this understanding effectively.

The ethnic background of the counsellor may be significant in terms of the counsellor's awareness of the refugee's culture, and regarding the political stance of the culture the counsellor is seen to represent. A counsellor who is a refugee, and particularly a refugee from the same culture, may be seen as being more able to understand the extreme and alienating experience of the client thus quickly engendering trust. However a counsellor from an ethnic background allied to, or of, the oppressors would be unacceptable. The position of the counsellor as an authority figure representing the host country needs to be carefully considered in the context of the counselling relationship. Regular supervision is an important resource for this discussion.

These principles could also apply to interpreters who may be required in sessions. The choice of interpreter needs to involve the client's consent. It should not be the client's children, although this is sometimes the easiest option as children may develop their language skills in the school system faster than adults. This was an option some support organizations in this study had used.

Counsellor training could include guidelines for working with interpreters as well as a sensitization to the issues of refugees through role plays, presentations from refugees and exploration of transcultural models.

The support organizations

Most support organizations in Greece cited "disappointment" and "burnout" as the main difficulties of their work. Organizations offering counselling reported that so far there was a limited understanding of this area in Greece with "no training here in counselling skills and supervision". The few organizations offering counselling had difficulty finding a resource for supervision in Athens, although one had a weekly support group. There appeared to be less experience of working with refugees in Greece than in the

UK, and the marked increase of asylum seekers and refugees entering Greece in recent years has been a phenomenon that the Greeks were unprepared for. Greece is a less multicultural country than the UK and its refugee protection framework remains underdeveloped (Sitaropoulos, 2000).

In one over-stretched organization I was aware of staff becoming angry with the refugees as the latter battled to explain their predicament. Support organizations could misunderstand the despairing anger covering fear and grief. This particular organization had no system of support or supervision in place. Burnout could be accompanied by feelings of being de-skilled. The despair, and rage conveyed by some staff in these organizations could be seen as "vicarious traumatization" or "traumatic countertransference" (McCann & Pearlman, 1990). Sleep disturbance, somatic complaints and inner conflicts are also possible (Benedek, 1984; Van der Veer, 1998).

Those organizations with support groups and/or supervision in place cited their value in helping staff to recognize these feelings and understand them. A review, or updating, of approaches to counselling and therapy with refugees could re-establish a sense of valued contribution.

Ensuring that their case-load is not exclusively asylum seekers and refugees may allow counsellors to strengthen and re-evaluate their resources, enabling their work to become more effective.

Limitations to the study

There are several limitations of the study to be noted. The sample focused on young and middle-aged adults only. No young children were interviewed although they were seen in a makeshift classroom and playing in the camps and centres. A few participants were probably in their late teens. No elderly were present in the camps or at the community centres and therefore their views are not represented in this study. Concern about elderly family relatives in Kurdistan was expressed by some refugees in the UK. Welch's concern (1975) regarding the limitation of the snowball or network method was counterbalanced in the study by locating networks at different locations. However, very isolated refugees were probably missed.

In all cases but one, the interpreters were Kurds. One was a Greek national. Interpreter bias may have occurred in a few instances. This was minimized by briefing the interpreters as to the purpose of the study and interviewing them first regarding their views.

Inconsistencies, e.g. between the respondents' body language and the translated response, were challenged and checked out at the time.

Conclusions

Counselling asylum seekers and refugees is an issue which is central to European life at the beginning of the twenty-first century. All counselling training needs to include preparation for working with asylum seekers and refugees. Counsellors are also well placed to help effect more humanitarian approaches to refugee movements. The extent of distress in this group of people can be easier to ignore, or hide. In reviewing and updating policy and practice regarding refugee counselling, discussions may be initiated in organizations which can engage inter-professional teams in many countries. Dialogue amongst organizations within, and between, countries can enable learning, support and a greater coherence of policy. The facilities of the internet, video-conferencing and a willingness to network, even where policy agendas differ, could reduce the potential ongoing trauma of the "Adjustment" phase.

The key findings of this study have important counselling implications. The desperate need of asylum seekers and refugees in the early phases to tell the story of their traumatic journey helps them to begin to connect to the host community and to re-establish a sense of self. Guided by the asylum seeker or refugee, the counsellor can witness the narrative, being open to the meaning for the client, within the context of the client's culture. Thus, the findings of this study support Papadopoulos' observations and views that it is imperative to enable refugees to acknowledge the wide spectrum of their experiences during the different phases of their ordeal, rather than focusing only on one phase:

Distinguishing these four phases shows that the idea implied by a single traumatic event is erroneous. Counselors should not attempt to track down the single event which "caused" all the "trauma". The whole of this sequence of phases can be most traumatic. Thus, the work of the counselor becomes more complex and attempts to elicit the meaning of suffering people give to their experiences of all these phases. In this way, it could be said that one of the main objectives of the counselor would be to provide the appropriate therapeutic space within which the suffering person could explore the variety of feelings from all phases and not to impose (unwittingly) an expectation to hunt down "*the*" cause of trauma. [Papadopoulos, 2000b, pp. 97–98]

Understanding the difference in experience for men and women asylum seekers and refugees, can enable more appropriate counselling provision to be put in place. For example, approaches to familiarize men with the support offered in counselling, setting up a mens' support group or providing a couples' counselling facility could be considered.

The asylum seekers' and refugees' changing identity over time, and oscillation between positions, is fundamental to a counsellor's understanding of therapeutic movement over time. Counselling approaches need to address ways of working which are compatible with the client's culture in this respect. Non-verbal approaches may be indicated for early phases when the client may have no "voice". The fear of authority figures experienced by asylum-seekers and refugees, in early and later phases, requires the counsellor to be particularly sensitive to the client's perception of power in the counselling relationship.

The support organizations raised concerns regarding their frustrations, disappointments and possible burn-out. The study indicated that those organizations with support groups and/or supervision in place demonstrated more insight into their interactions with asylum seekers and refugees. Counsellors could be proactive in helping support organizations to set up support groups and/or supervision. International resources can be drawn upon to offer training programmes for countries with less experience in this area. As suggested earlier internet facilities and video conferencing can be one aspect of such co-operation.

Areas for further research include exploring the experience and needs of child asylum seekers and refugees and investigating ways to work effectively when counselling with an interpreter (leading perhaps to training programmes for counselling interpreters). Finally more attention must be given to developing models of counselling which are less tied to Eurocentric historical traditions and belief systems, particularly involving non-verbal approaches, in order to enable a greater understanding of cross-cultural counselling practice.

Acknowledgement

I am grateful to Brunel University for a grant towards the cost of this research and to all the participants who contributed to the study.

Note

1. This chapter is a slightly modified version of a paper entitled "Counselling asylum seekers and refugees: a study of Kurds in early and later stages of exile" which appeared in the *European Journal of Psychotherapy, Counselling and Health*, Volume 4, Number 2/August, 2001, pp. 293–313.

FIELD PROJECTS

Some assumptions on psychological trauma interventions in post-conflict communities

Natale Losi

General background

This chapter attempts to develop some reflections on the intense experiences in working in Kosovo between the summer of 1999 to date. More specifically, this work consisted in the setting up and implementation of a project by the International Organization for Migration to assist the region in the period immediately after the cessation of hostilities; the project was called Psychosocial and Trauma Response (PTR) and it represented a first concrete application of my ideas on post conflict interventions in the field of mental health and psychosocial issues. During this project, of course, the initial ideas were enriched and modified first by the experiences themselves as well as by the encounters and exchanges with other colleagues working in this field; these colleagues included also non-psychological professionals as well as lay people sharing with us in our endeavours to assist with the suffering of an entire population. Fundamental to this project has been the contribution of the Tavistock Clinic both as an institution as well as through some members of its staff who are duly acknowledged below.

Through the experience of PTR, we tried to develop an interdisciplinary approach with the aim of revisiting the sterile debate between professionals who advocate the mechanistic application of pre-packaged tools (e.g. programmes combating PTSD) and their radical critics, who reject the idea of trauma altogether.

It will become clear, when reading this essay, that I disagree with the tendency to use indiscriminately PTSD as a culturally-independent diagnostic category (cf. Chauvenet *et al.*, 1996; Crossley, 2000), but at the same time I have been concerned by the lack of positive answers, by those who deconstruct this category, to the real problems of collective psycho-traumatic suffering. Thus, another aim of this chapter is the revisiting of this debate from a different and positive perspective and on the basis of our experiences from an actual large project.

To begin with, it would be useful to offer a brief description of the activities included in the PTR project, in order to give to readers a general context of reference.

As soon as the war ended, in my capacity as head of the psychosocial unit of the International Organization for Migration, I contacted a selected group of international experts in the field and organized a Conference in Geneva at the Headquarters of the IOM in order to plan an appropriate response to the plight of people in Kosovo. From the outset, the plan had been to develop a meaningful partnership with our Kosovar colleagues in order to avoid the usual pitfalls engendered in the implementation of such programmes by outside experts. It was important to work in genuine partnership with the beneficiaries and, therefore, a group of Kosovar mental health professionals participated actively in this Conference. Subsequent to this meeting, a smaller working group was formed which developed to varying and deferring degrees the plan of the project. The essence of the project was to develop a training programme, as multidimensional and comprehensive as possible, for a group of Kosovar Albanians in order to equip them with the appropriate tools to address the plight of their people and to contribute to the reconstruction of their country.

The actual training programme was offered jointly by the IOM and the University of Pristina, in collaboration with several universities and centres of excellence from around the world. The Tavistock Clinic played a key role in many facets of the project, including offering accreditation of the training. This means that the graduates received certificates which included signatures from the Tavistock Clinic. The training itself consisted of multiple modules of theoretical courses, experiential workshops and practical fieldwork. These included the participation of communities and individuals in need of support. The training course was repeated, with some modifications, for a second year to another group of trainees and both courses qualified a total of seventy-five psychosocial counsellors. The basic format of the training consisted of the following five modules:

1. *Archives of memory: from an individual to a collective experience.*
   This began with a workshop which consisted of an open discussion on the memory of war; the participant trainees were helped to enrich their individual experiences and perceptions of the war by the experience of a collective sharing. Gradually, more collective forms of memories were developed. This work formed part of a long term research, the results of which have been recently published (Losi *et al.*, 2001).
2. *Theatrical workshop: the exiled body.*
   This module was implemented in order to use the theatre as a communication tool and to help individuals' self-knowledge of their own bodies. In addition, this module assisted trainees to symbolically reunite what had been torn—their inner world, their families, their country—as well as to mend the fracture between reality and imaginary. This module addressed several levels. Beside the clinical value for individual experiences, the connection between personal and collective narratives, this module also resulted in an actual theatrical performance at the National Theatre in Pristina, which was one of its first post-war performances.
3. *Psychiatry and family psychotherapy: a community based approach.*
   This included a range of family therapy approaches and it used different clinical situations ranging from direct consultations with families in the community or in our Pristina training venues to networking with relevant services and agencies.
4. *Ethnopsychiatric approach to large traumatized populations in post-conflict countries.*
   This module consisted of a presentation and the application of the ethnopsychiatric approach (Losi, 2000a; Nathan, 1986, 1994;

Pandolfi, 1994; Sironi, 1999). This included the principles of cultural mediation and the clinical role and functions of clinical mediators. Central to this approach is the understanding of cultural differences and healing practices of local populations and the exploration of the development of possible collaboration with actual local traditional healers.

5. *Training in the professional duties of the psychosocial counsellors. Assessment of psychosocial needs and the role of the counsellors in the community and mental health services.*

This module focused on equipping our trainees to assume the role of professionals in the newly developed mental health services in Kosovo. This included not only the teaching of assessment and therapeutic approaches but also the familiarization with the various related services, agencies, and bodies and ways to collaborate in connection with referrals and preventative programmes. Finally, issues of populations surveys and programme development and service monitoring and evaluation were also included.

Starting from the summer of 2001, the PTR project added two important components:

I. *The establishment of seven psychosocial mobile teams.* These cover the entire territory of Kosovo and are part of the local mental health system. The IOM continues to provide a specialist in-service training and supervision of these graduates, who are now employed by these mobile teams.

II. *The development of a psychosocial support programme of activities for ethnic minorities.* Following the war, there have been serious violations of the human rights of the ethnic minorities in Kosovo and the IOM wanted to redress the balance and offer specific programmes to assist the besieged ethnic minorities, mainly, the Serbs, thus actively paving the way for eventual reconciliation.

Introduction

In my experience, both in Albania and in Kosovo, I was astonished by the general context of the environment. I was struck by the difficult life conditions, the tension and instability, the suffering and anguish which was so evident in all aspects of the people's everyday lives. Most striking, however, was the arrogance and thoughtlessness of most of the international experts, who swarmed the entire territory. Pandolfi (2000), referring to Appadurai's (1996) notion of *mobile sovereignty*, defines these transnational formations as *migrant sovereignties*, which serve to link transnational forms of domination to local political practices (cf. Cuisenier, 1991; Ranzato, 1994). With reference to this issue, she states:

> This new dimension, ... has been so thoroughly mediatized that it has become difficult to select a field of research ..., and we are then faced with a double problem. On one hand, the anthropologist runs the risk of sinking into the interpretative logic of the media, which emphasizes violence, chaos, war, and hopelessness, i.e. "balkaniza-tion". On the other hand, (especially in Albania and Kosovo), we are confronted with other presence, like the International workers, NGO's, the Council of Europe, NATO militias, etc. All of these occupy the territories, usually after forgetting that they are intervening in a country at a vulnerable point. [Pandolfi, 2000, p. 32]

Most of these new sovereigns (I especially refer to those in the fields of the psychological interventions) had arrived with toolboxes of pre-packaged instruments, of which PTSD (Post Traumatic Stress Disorder) was the most popular. The acronym alone felt perturbing and invasive to me and seemed to cause conflict. Therefore, after much discussion, we decided to adopt the word "trauma" alone to refer to the suffering of the persons.

This was probably one of the strongest forces behind my attempt to design a project in Kosovo, aiming to overcome the limitations of the usual Western intervention programmes. This required moving on grounds, which were, literally, tumultuous and mined. The project was and still is a great challenge, intensified by the fact that, despite the rich range of critical literature available on humanitarian interventions in the field of psychic trauma, texts have mostly limited themselves to criticism, falling short of proposing alter-native intervention constructions.

Through our work in Kosovo, we have attempted to move towards the creation of different projects more respectful of the context and better adapted to local culture. We have considered the objectivization and the de-contextualization of symptoms as obstacles to progress, and have therefore rejected both. The elimination of these methods has compelled us all to join into this venture, prepared to be attentive, to observe, and to forgo the easy defence available to us in the form of ready-made answers and solutions.

Our approach, as well as our awareness that we did not bring pre-packaged "scientific" tools to be used as comfortable defences, exposed us fully to the powerful emotions and suffering of our students and of our colleagues at the University of Pristina as well as, of course, of the families and communities we went to visit with them. Their emotions were accepted as legitimate, their feelings were recognized, and their own interpretations of events, heard. We learned to value their common and unexplored resources, interpreting them as alternative means of understanding the suffering linked to their experience.

To put into practice this alternative approach, the methodological frame of the project started with the following logical and operational structure:

Entering the field

At the inception of humanitarian intervention programmes lie some basic common assumptions. These, which ordinarily tend to be accepted as foregone conclusions, find their way into the formulation of the methods used, and in certain cases they can have destructive consequences:

1. A reductive assessment of the refugees' plight,[1] limiting their needs to primary necessities, such as food, clean water, basic health care, and restricted reparations. Any responses to more complex and layered needs, tend to be delayed and are dealt with only in the form of "plans for the future".
2. The victimization of refugees. This begins with the conviction that the local population is not capable of surviving without our help, and then only to the degree that they adapt passively to receive our assistance as homogenous "victims", leaving behind their culture and their personal and emotional histories, their family dynamics, their individual professional backgrounds, etc.

3. A shift in the interpretation (and understanding) of the refugees' experiences, where the reasons for their exile are no longer socio–political, but belong to a more neutral, "technical" dimension. This often occurred after a de-contextualization of the refugees' experience, when these lost languages and concepts are replaced by medical jargon and obscure terms. In other words, the refugees' experience tends to be transferred from their "lay narrative" to a dialect of narrow clinical psychiatric definitions.

One particular case of this tendency might be found in the so-called diagnostic category PTSD (Post-traumatic stress disorder), which has become acceptable only because it is so widespread. In the last few years, particularly consequent to the wars in ex-Yugoslavia, the genocide in Rwanda and the war in Kosovo, the phrase has been widely used, often inaccurately and without judgement, upon a multitude of cases.

In the last fifty years, concepts like "stress" and "trauma" have become part of a discourse that is used commonly, in the media's coverage of war, conflicts or natural disasters. On the one hand, this has brought many to a fuller realization of the plight of the displaced or immigrants and of the psychological dimensions of their suffering. On the other hand, this dialect has also transferred the responsibility of the suffering and their care entirely to physical or mental healthcare professionals, thus reducing social problems to individual psychological process (cf. Papadopoulos, 1999a,b, 2000b,c, 2001a,b,c).

There is no doubt that psychologically, traumatized people all over the world require help. They need help in order to define and understand their trauma and to develop social and cultural-specific strategies for dealing with it. Imposing pre-packed "universal" interpretations, definitions, tools and approaches to human psychological suffering does not bring them the help they need. Moreover, by doing so, international aid workers run the involuntary risk of converting themselves into traumatizing agents, while they label some individuals as "psychologically impaired" and tear others away from the potential protection of their own resilience as well as from their community's traditional means of coping with trauma.

Currently, people find it difficult to discuss their difficulties in their own terms, and therefore fall into using an alienated language. This eliminates the particular, individual, social, cultural and historic characteristics of their suffering. Paradoxically then, the magical belief in "science" and in the power of the international scientific community is so strong that it tends to marginalize local knowledge.

A community based–cultural sensitive approach

From the western perspective, trauma is viewed as highly relevant. In the context of war and persecution, however, it becomes necessary to overcome individualistic approaches to trauma and attempt to bring the problem back to where it belongs, within its own social and cultural context. In order to illustrate the importance of this context, students in our first training programme were asked to define trauma, according to their different culture, background and knowledge. These descriptions, ranged from "a deeply spiritual disorder" to "a painful reminiscence", and touched upon many different ideas in between.

The definitions proposed by the students, indicate the wide range of meanings attributed to trauma, according to the complex cultural and individual perceptions. Behind each interpretation of "trauma" lies shared experiences and different traditions of real women and men, who finding common ground in this terminology. In opposition to this, and in an extremely near-sighted manner, a diagnosis of PTSD suggests a set of clearly identifiable symptoms, a clear way in which the illness develops and, therefore, implies clear circumstances under which it can disappear. However, in reality, none of this can be applied to the survivors of war and persecution.

Although many people present with symptomatology that can fit the PTSD category, many others are afflicted with different kinds of problems. Various kinds of somatic and psychosomatic illnesses, for instance, have been known to appear alongside psychological symptoms. The occurrence of these symptoms varies in timing; they might appear a few days after the traumatic experience or surface many years later.

This "classic" symptomatology is often hidden in young people who, instead, tend to reveal their affliction through anomalies in their social behaviour. They might have conflicts at work, drop out of school, use and abuse mind altering substances, or put themselves in situations of unnecessary risk.

In survivor families, a set of typical problems can usually be identified. These do not, however, fit the criterion for a diagnosis of PTSD. Indeed, family problems *a priori* are not even included in the notion of PTSD. To further complicate the definition, problems on a family level tend to appear and disappear, often following patterns which are not recognizable at the individual level but which seem to relate much more with wider social processes.

In other experiences,[2] the use of alternative concepts has proven more accurate. Among these are Bettelheim's "extreme situation", Khan's "cumulative trauma" and Keilson's "sequential trauma". Another interesting term is "extreme trauma", which is defined by Becker as:

An individual and collective process that occurs in reference with and in dependency of a given social context: it is a process marked by its intensity, of extremely long duration in time, and the interdependency between the social and the psychological dimensions. It exceeds the capacity of the individual and social structures to address adequately this process. Its aim is the destruction of the individual, his sense of belonging to the society, and of his social activities. Extreme trauma is characterized by a structure of power within the society that is based on the elimination of some members of this society by others of the same society. The process of extreme trauma is not limited in time and develops sequentially.[3]

Using this concept of "extreme trauma", implies a shift in our focus from the symptoms to the traumatic situation itself.

At the level of treatment, the conceptual change also requires a shift, away from individualistic approaches and towards working with the wider community. This does not mean that we should forget the individual; such a stance would only cause a repetition of the trauma. Each of us, within each community, should constantly rediscover what constitutes trauma for the specific group at hand, and create a strategy for addressing it, accordingly.

Constructing institutions where multitudes of professionals attempt to treat wide scale suffering is full of pitfalls. We can learn only in the communities themselves how to help its members, how each individual, within a group, can be a "trauma specialist". It is restrictive to plan "treatment" which is exclusively limited to closed consulting rooms; instead, our approach should take place in schools, in families, in community meetings, with employment, and through functions of the community. The basic task of professionals will then be to facilitate collective recognition of the psychosocial dimensions of their problems, to help overcome fragmentation, and to favour communicative processes, identifying key situations. Without forgetting their specific knowledge, psychotherapists might thus add to their therapy room the community and work with promoting processes of empowerment, rather than, unwittingly, encouraging victimization.

The psychosocial concept proposed here is an attempt to overcome the traditional (individualistic, psychological and PTSD-oriented) means of assessing and dealing with the problem of trauma, and to reconsider it within its socio–political context. From observation and experience on the field, we believe it necessary to work within the communities, viewing them as the base and unit model of the field. On the other hand, this cannot be done if we deny the complicated inter-psychic processes at work in the event of traumatic breakdown. These forces must be acknowledged, and even integrated within our approach.

The focus point of the programmes should, therefore, stem from a discussion on how these diagnostic categories might be used, not from their outright denial. Each of us, as we face the task of offering intervention programmes and we attempt to help, must consider these categories of diagnosis, the strictness or flexibility of their application, the process of identification and diagnosis itself, and the importance given to culture, as well as the suffering persons' ability to explain their problems in their own words.

Three axes of intervention

The project in Kosovo has been built from a methodology based on the above views which have their origin in the "learning through practice" approach inspired by Freire's pedagogical ideas (e.g. Freire, 1996, 1998). Within this framework, are three principal axes of intervention, each structured to hold a number of activities:

- Pycho-sociocultural;
- Historical-anthropological; and
- Clinical.

This division is not intended to be rigid. The different dimensions: psycho–socio–cultural–historical–anthropological–clinical, are not separated nor do they have a strict and temporal sequence. Moreover, partial elements of each of these dimensions mingle with each different training activity. At the same time, the training activities already have some operational value: during the different periods of the fieldwork, for instance, students in each axis undertake closely supervised support activities for those in need.

The psycho–socio–cultural axis

The activities that make up the psycho–socio–cultural axis of the programme were undertaken at two different times, both within the context of the module which we called "The Archives of the Memory: From an Individual to a Collective Experience". The first series of activities began with a period of introduction to the Archives of Memory. The second set of activities was run parallel to the theatre project, also within the programme. These two training sessions were carried out between December 6th and 17th 1999, and from February 7th to 25th 2000, respectively. In addition to this, in January 2000, the students began a four-week, supervised fieldwork.

The first training period of December 1999 was especially effective, in that it allowed us to establish a relationship of trust with students, but it was also fundamental to the programme, as through this trust, a community emerged and a group was formed between students and trainers.

In this first intervention, our primary objective was to show our students that the memory and the sharing of painful, even traumatic experiences had value. The shifting of this recollection from the past of the individual to the experience and memory of the collective, allowed for a certain "de-psychiatrization". Through these shared experiences, the students were allowed to express feelings linked to possibly traumatic events of their own past, within a contained, protected situation accompanied, led, and supported by the group and its facilitators. This experience, activated by role-playing, discussion of cases and fieldwork, allowed us to verify that this exchange of intense feelings was legitimate and therapeutic. Also, each of the students and trainers had been given the chance to experiment with psychosocial working tools like group discussion, which are held in a "conversational" setting.

In the next section of the training programme, the first part of the theatre project—known as the "exiled body" was attempted, and shown to be especially valuable. Besides giving the students another tool in the use of theatre and *mise en scene*, the project strengthened the solidarity of the group and their conviction they were doing something they believed in, something to which they were strongly committed.[4]

The historical–anthropological axis

Another axis of the programme, which was dealing with historical anthropological methods, was created mostly from the Archives of Memory module. This was the anthropological perspective as it relates to memory and its contexts.

The clinical axis

The shift in attention from the individual to the community in this programme has allowed us a similar shift in the clinical axis, from the symptoms of the patient to their context. For this reason, our training intervention has been geared to provide clinical activities and to use therapeutic techniques which would favour this movement. Given this chosen approach, the roles of suffering person and therapist must find new interpretations, new schemes of interaction.

More specifically, taking into consideration my previous clinical experiences, I endeavoured to promote an approach within which the suffering persons would feel encouraged to refer (consciously or otherwise) to any form of traditional, original, and familiar thought and understanding of the world that includes theories of illness and cure. Accordingly, the suffering person's disturbance is then identified as the rupture in his bond to family and community.

In this type of interaction, neither the healer nor the therapist act directly on the suffering person; they play the role of mediators between the persons and their social and cultural group. The objectives of the care lie in the search for deep-rooted belief systems, shared within local cultures and traditional means of curing the person's upheaval. This kind of intervention allows the suffering persons to represent their "illness" to themselves, perceiving the illness within their own ideas, according to their culture (allowing for re-affiliation and a sense of belonging) and to re-insert themselves in their original families and social network, thus renewing family bonds.

Further considerations on post-conflict constellations of violence and the role of rescuers

The conversations, the stories that people exchange and construct in situations of conflict, are clearly important, whether they influence the conflict's resolution or, on the contrary, contribute to its perpetuation. When these stories are woven into the context of an international conflict situation, such as that which overcame Kosovo, even international personnel, often unwittingly, get involved actively in their construction and furthering. This is especially the case for those sent to work "on the ground". Aside from these co-producers and co-narrators of conflict situation stories, the constellation, the set, the essential typology available and necessary to actually give meaning to the conflict, is made up of three principal players: the aggressors, the victims and the authorities. In the particular case of Kosovo, the international personnel saw themselves as placed in this last role, whereas, in fact, they were perceived, according to the different points of view and independently from their own intentions, as either saviours or as aggressors. Many of the international personnel indeed con-tributed to the domination of a constellation, which was advan-tageous to the perpetration of the *premise* for conflict. In other words, by their very intervention, the international actors risked perpetuating the narrative scheme aggressor/victim/rescuer (cf. Papadopoulos, 2000b, 2001a) which, itself, is an integral part of the conflict, and it perpetuates the very conflict they attempt to resolve with their intervention.

The pervasive nature of this triangle in conflict situations has become an object of observation in many different disciplines. Anthropologist R. Thornton suggests that:

> Narratives of violence have a specific social and cultural function. By narrating events, we link a series of actions—whether by chronology, conspiracy or psychological predisposition—into a comprehensible framework. In this way the violent event that has radically disrupted the flow of normality appears to have been predictable, and the moment of chaos that has challenged order is tamed. [Thornton, 1999, p. 3]

In other words, when we "clothe" an experience or a situation of chaos with a story or narrative, we transform it, give it sense. We tame chaos. This does not happen alone however, as Feldman notes, "Narratives not only explain events; they are integral to how we decide what is an event and what is not" (Feldman, 1991, p. 27). More specifically, with reference to destructiveness, Papadopoulos observed disturbingly that:

> Within the cloud of the inherent epistemological confusion and the anguish emanating from the unintelligibility of ... [these complex phenomena], the theories mental health experts advance in attempting to understand destructiveness may ultimately amount to being not much more than ornate psychologisations and pathologisations which are intended to ease the resulting distress. Thus, unwittingly, I would argue that we are used by society, as experts, to explain away the disturbing complexity of destructiveness and replace it with sanitised theories. [Papadopoulos, 1998, p. 459]

Similar concerns are expressed by Sironi (1999) and Viñar (1989).

In the case of Kosovo, the recurrent pattern that Bruck so well described, writing that "The human community needs to be split into perpetrators or transgressors, objects or victims, and authorities and responsible" (Bruck, 1992, p. 72), was endemic, present within almost every type of organized intervention, with the "humanitarian" aim intrinsic to the different agencies and NGOs.

The media exposure/transformation of wartime events that was so particular to the Kosovo crisis also allowed the journalists to meddle with the diverse versions of this basic conflict plot. The media's tendency to break up the facts and then put them back together to produce a telling story, found its best description in the term "mythinformation",[5] a word which evokes the means by which stories can be tied to objects, intentions, and events in a strong blend that appears true and credible because it is familiar; and it is familiar because it includes the fundamental triangle: aggressor/victim/rescuer. Our intervention did not arrive within a neutral situation, but rather in one where "mythinformation" had effectively fossilized the environment, interpreting it through the plot: aggressor/victim/rescuer, as mentioned above.

The Psychosocial and Trauma Response project, through the Archives of Memory and the other interdisciplinary modules as part of the three axes outlined above, tried to offer the different players involved in the Kosovo intervention a series of possible stimuli to help them break away from this rigid and limiting constellation.

Rescuing the rescuer

One of the main tasks of our intervention in Kosovo was, indeed, the attempt to alter the disabling effects of this limiting constellation. As Papadopoulos noted, in working with traumatized individuals in these settings, "the ... triangle of victim–saviour–violator tends to keep perpetuating itself creating endless variations with different people in the same roles" (2001, p. 8). As international mental health professionals, our only chance to modify this triangle was the possibility to dislodge from its rigid role only one of the constellation's components, i.e. "Rescuer". To be able to break away from this set function, he or she who plays this part first must be aware that the "Rescuer" model can be hidden or masked under a multitude of figures and scenaria. Below, I will attempt to describe briefly these possibilities, beginning with the guise pointed out by Enriquez, the figure of the "Trainer". Only if the humanitarian workers are able to have an awareness of their pre-selected role in this triangle (i.e. as rescuers), can they offer other members of the constellation (such as the "Victim") solutions that are not repetitive and fatal; otherwise, the "solutions" they will offer will inevitably reproduce the same dynamics of violence that created the initial conflict.

In other words, it is by breaking away from the set figures that the rescuer/trainer might help construct a future less exposed to the systematic repetition of violence.

Every act of international co-operation, especially if it occurs in the context of humanitarian intervention in a transition situation immediately following a conflict, and even more so in the field of psychosocial support, implies both a series of explicit models, and "ghosts";[6] these models and ghosts confer upon those who carry out this work its simultaneously passionate, worrisome, and frustrating aspects. The work's attraction probably resides in contemplating and sharing the desire of omnipotence with the fear of impotence, in being (at least in intention) a bearer of life, but also a bearer (usually unwittingly) of repetition and death. The models and ghosts interacting in psychosocial humanitarian interventions therefore may be coupled with those described by Enriquez (1980), when the humanitarian worker/trainer can be seen as a figure who:

1. Offers a good model/form (trainer);
2. Heals and restores (therapist);
3. Gives light to, helps emerge (midwife);
4. Interprets, makes aware (interpreter);
5. Helps act, change, move (militant);
6. Is dedicated to something, takes on problems (repairer);
7. Is free of taboos, prohibitions (transgressor);
8. Acts so as to render the other mad (destroyer).

I would like to briefly discuss these images, with two aims in mind. The first is to show that if the humanitarian worker chooses to adhere completely to one or a few of these models/ghosts, he or she (though in our case we could call this person a psycho–sociologist) contributes to the creation of a world of doubles, in which violence inevitably rages, through the repetition/re-imposition of this constellation. This will occur, even if the person's selfless intention was to contribute to the creation of a better humanity. The second reason to discuss this list is to show how, through the use or interaction with the Archives of Memory, it is possible to offer humanitarian workers a series of possible settings that reduce the risk of perpetuating the rigid role of rescuer, therefore releasing the other implicated players (aggressors and victims) from the bond of their reciprocal role as generators of violence. Let us look briefly at what could be a series of variations in the role of rescuer in humanitarian situations:

1. The trainer

The trainer is interested in "forms" and intervenes to re-form, trans-form, de-form, etc. If the humanitarian workers' representations of themselves fit within the common category according to which they view themselves as "model figures", they propose *de facto* to deprive their interlocutors of their own experiences, their difficul-ties, their anguish and their trial-and-error progress, to substitute these for a "good form" that is fixed, repetitive, deadly. Enriquez notes that this temptation is alive and well, above all among psycho–sociologists, "in that they believe to have realized, in the balance reached, a particular ideal that they wish to transmit, as is the case with educators, who desire to reform those who were ill-formed ..." (Enriquez, 1980, p. 116).

2. The therapist

In cases of humanitarian intervention after a conflict, it is easy to feel immersed in a universe that is considered "abnormal", and to therefore assume an attitude which attempts to readapt the individuals affected by or involved in the conflict. It is easy to feel a duty to restore them, to heal them of their "behavioural insufficiencies", and to help them lead a "normal" life. This is the case for most organizations that have worked with trauma. Implicit in their idea of this affliction and healing, is a model that:

— Assumes the person to have been in a stable state (health status) which was then upset by external agents (in this case the violence and aggression of war), and that by applying the appropriate therapy to such persons, they will be restored;
— Therefore presupposes a perfect reversibility of the organism: that once healed, it will not feel the consequences of the "illness" (aggression).

It is important to reflect upon the roots of this model, this ghost. In fact, at the basis of this *restitutio ad integrum* obsession, we find a very real tendency in our society to form a dichotomy with the "sick" on one hand, and the "care-givers" on the other. This model tends to be exported into international actions, when international actors medicalize the social with each glance they cast at it.

Papadopoulos expressed this dynamic as follows:

> ... inevitably our identity as mental health professionals imposes on our observations the ... constraints [of] ... the pathology-health polarity; this results in us combining the causal-reductive approach within the oppositional narrative of pathology and destructiveness which then together produce an inevitable psychologization and pathologization of destructiveness. By no means do I wish to suggest or imply in any way that destructiveness is "normal" or acceptable. But is placing it on the "normal"—"abnormal" polarity the only way out? ... Perhaps the first step towards such a deeper understanding would be for us to appreciate the fact that we are indeed trapped and imprisoned by and within these constraints where the pathology narrative occupies a key position. [Papadopoulos, 1997, p. 460]

3. The midwife

The objective of those who adhere to the maieutic model is not to restore or heal but rather to give birth to or favour development and maturity, and to permit the realization of prohibited or repressed potentials. Implicit in this approach is an idea of man as essentially good. In this context, the humanitarian will not try to impose form, but rather share a bond of trust with the interlocutors, who can let their (true essence flow), liberating themselves from the elements that oppressed them.

The maieutic model, which idealizes human nature, has an important corollary in that it also idealizes the humanitarian worker, thought to be the incarnation of goodness. The understanding (maieutic) attitude that they adopt and propose implies an enhanced image of themselves and others, diverting their gaze from the catastrophic situations in which they work.

4. The interpreter

Briefly, the vocation of an interpreter is to (interpret everything), sometimes changing (everything) due to the pervasiveness and popularization of psychoanalysis. The corollary is that the interpreter will find a cause and reason/justification for every behaviour.

5. The militant

This is the ghost that believes it possible to intervene everywhere in order to bring about social transformations. In this role, humanitarian workers proceed by somehow comparing themselves to a kind of prophet, confirming the participants' idea that evil comes from outside, that everything is due to society, or to the part of society which plays the role of aggressor, and casting aside the fundamental problem of possible connivance between dominator and dominated, persecutor and victim of persecution.

At the time of our very first training session for the psychosocial counsellors participating in our course, I vividly remember a conversation with a young interpreter who already, at that time, (in December 1999), clearly pointed out the mutual support between victim and persecutor. In her opinion, she said, this would shortly become evident. She said:

> "While the Serbs were still here everything could be blamed on them. Now that young women are disappearing from the streets, we need to accept the idea that there is evil also among us."

6. The repairer

Their objective is to promote activities by which the community can be reborn, through the reparation of damages suffered. They will sacrifice themselves for others, will not waste time and energy, and will lose themselves in their work, which they see as a true mission. The question I ask myself about these workers is, first, who invested them with this mission? Further, will the act of restoring, helping, saving, and dealing with the "victims", not help to perpetuate structures of exclusion? What secondary benefits do those who thus sacrifice themselves receive? It might be suspected that the repairer, through sacrifice, also sacrifices the others, by dealing with their problems, and "devouring them" with affection. In this privileged relationship, the repairers end up alienating the very people they were trying to help. They somehow live through the death of others.

7. The transgressor

Although this figure is part of the typology proposed by Enriquez and which was then "adapted" to situations of humanitarian intervention, it doesn't seem to me that this model, at least in the case of Kosovo, was present in a significant manner. I will, however, describe it briefly so as to offer a comparison to the reader. The fundamental calling of this model is to favour the emergence of spontaneity, festiveness and protest of institutions. In a humanitarian context, this model "expresses a sort of megalomania of being the father, the parent that generates the unknown and promulgates transgression and generalized instability" (Enriquez, 1980, pp. 126–127).

8. The destroyer

The destroyer model functions, essentially, at an unconscious level, in a kind of interpersonal interaction that tends to encourage or favour a conflict of affections in the other. According to Enriquez, who refers to Searles (1978), "This kind of desire is present in every affectionately healthy individual", and therefore comes into play in every therapeutic or training relationship. I will add that in a therapeutic relationship, as is often imagined by humanitarian workers, their perceived function as "helper of "unfortunate peoples'" and their desire to heal the other, might be reactive training: a defence mechanism responding to the desire to make the other mad. The desire to form can be affected or induced by the opposite desire to de-form, break, and shatter the other.

After all, how could humanitarian workers avoid the risk of this contradiction? Their position is such that they could, on one hand, give their group of "assisted people" an incentive for autonomy and encouragement to search for their own resources, but the workers could also refer back to their own closed interpretative system, leaving them with a situation of interpretative regression and dependency.

With this brief review, I intended to indicate that every trainer (and the humanitarian worker often refers to this figure for guidance) is very likely to be possessed by one or more of these ghosts. It is therefore imperative that trainers recognize these ghosts and question themselves about their impact on themselves and on others. Otherwise, by offering their services as "rescuers", unwitting trainers are likely to transform their interventions into dangerous situations that perpetuate violence.

The specificity of the Psychosocial and Trauma Response project

The specificity of the Psychosocial and Trauma Response project has been characterized by the acute awareness that we have on the issues discussed above, from the very conception of the project, back in its initial, planning phase. We knew by then that we had to actively address the likely formation of these ghosts and that we should have no pre-fabricated instruments to reach the main objective which we had established: the psychosocial support to a population traumatized by war and its horrors, through the training of psychosocial counsellors. It followed that the same training course could not be pre-coded. To apply any kind of training curriculum, even for psychosocial counsellors coming from the best Western universities, would have meant once again falling into the contradiction that I have repeatedly attempted to express here.[7] From this awareness, we have therefore tried to create innovative paths, starting with the essential observation/conviction from which, later, the idea for the Archives of Memory was born: the notion that traumata, though experienced individually, cannot find a positive response if their significance is forcibly reduced to an individual dimension. The Archives of Memory has proven to be one of the means of implementing this basic idea. Other means included the social or community theatre and the community transcultural clinical approach, respectively.[8]

From individual to collective experience

As discussed above, the Aggressor/Victim/Rescuer constellation occupied the dominant story in Kosovo, and its pervasiveness did not leave room for other narratives about either individuals or communities affected by war. As Papadopoulos (2000b) clearly describes, after a traumatic event, the people and the community tend to block and fix their understanding and interpretations of the event, the meaning of their lives, to the precise moment of the traumatic episode. The periods that preceded and indeed anticipated the event as such, tend to be cancelled, just as are all the other phases that follow the phase of the devastating events. What remains fossilized is the phase of the devastating events which then is used to fix meaning to everything. To be able to help people and communities that have endured these shattering experiences, it is necessary to offer suggestions so that they might offer possibilities to reconsider their histories and therefore the potential for their future, beyond the reduction of all of their resources to the ashes left by the devastating events. It is also necessary to help them consider "something different" that they might look to, once these hardships have passed.

The Archives of Memory, as well as the theatre, have been a precious source of this "something different". The Archives, and the other tools/actions taken during our experience in Kosovo, orient us towards a reconstruction of the complexity of the experience in Kosovo and of the Kosovars,[9] which it is not possible to reduce to a dominant constellation. They offer starting points, even in clinical work, to begin re-narrativizing, and re-story-ing (cf. Papadopoulos, 1999b) in the communities and families damaged by unhealed wounds and deaths. They offer less restrictive and more vital alternatives to the fossilized story, frozen around the dominant constellation which is maintained by the tyranny of the phase of the devastating events.

Conclusion

We know that among the members of the professional community to which we belong exist different positions, some critical of an approach like ours, which emphasizes the collective dimensions of the traumata suffered. Yet, our emphasis on the collective dimensions of the problem does not mean that we have excluded the individual experience. Instead, we have endeavoured to locate these in a context from which it is possible for them to take on culturally shared and appropriate meaning. Individuals are created by stories as well as creating stories (Papadopoulos, 1999b). We not only give sense to our lives through stories, we not only tell the stories of our lives, but our actual lives are the makings of stories—stories that often no one has asked us to tell, stories in the making, stories that are part of other stories, repressed stories, stories untold; stories that can make us mad and stories that can profoundly heal the wounds of the spirit. It is within this perspective and in this spirit that the Psychosocial and Trauma Response project and the Archives of Memory need to be placed.

Acknowledgements

I wish to express my gratitude to Professor Renos Papadopoulos for his generous intellectual and human participation in this project. Through his efforts, we were able to connect with the Tavistock Clinic and the project has benefited enormously by this collaboration. More specifically, I wish to thank Professor Andrew Cooper, Jenny Altschuler and Sue Rendall for their helpful input to the project, on behalf of the Tavistock Clinic and Dr Anton Obholzer, the Chief Executive of the Clinic, who supported this collaboration, throughout.

Notes

1. In the case of Kosovo, from a theoretical point of view, we assimilated local population's needs as constituting the needs of refugees. In effect, at least at that time, people were living as refugees in their own country.
2. I mainly refer to experiences quoted in a unpublished document developed by the Istituto Latino Americano de Salud Mental (ILAS) in Chile.
3. Again in the document developed by ILAS.
4. The theatrical group has produced videos and other didactic materials related to their specific intervention. In particular the third Psychosocial Notebook (in preparation) will be covering the wider experience of the use of arts and theatre in post-conflict situations.
5. This word was coined by television producer Danny Schelchter (Fordred, 1999, p. 12).
6. This term is used by Eugène Enriquez (Enriquez, 1980). I use his word and notion of "ghost" to refer to the trainer figure, in order to offer an alternative to the rigid constellation in which the "rescuer" can find him/herself as a part of.
7. For a more exhaustive description of the PTR approach, see Losi, 2000b.
8. Apart from the volume mentioned in the preceding note, two further volumes of the Psychosocial Notebooks, are in preparation. The first

will be dedicated to theatre (a sample video tape will be included) and the second, to clinical work.

9. All of the materials collected for the Archives of Memory (interviews, diaries, letters, drawings and pictures) will be soon available on a special website http://www.kosovomemory.iom.int . The research for the Archives of Memory was also extended outside Kosovo: in Italy and in Serbia (two of the regions most concerned by the migratory flow that occurred during and in the aftermath of the war) interviews were collected among the communities of Kosovar refugees. Research was conducted in Serbia by the Italian NGO Arcs—Arci Cultura e Sviluppo (under the direction of Nicola Mai) and in Italy by the European University Institute (under the direction of Luisa Passerini).

CHAPTER TWELVE

Strangers to ourselves

Andrew Cooper and Sue Rendall

T his chapter reflects upon two visits to Kosovo by two members of the Tavistock Clinic staff, for the purpose of chairing the final assessment presentations of students on a programme of Psycho–Social Trauma Counselling and offering some teaching on the programme. The visits took place separately, in January 2000 and the second in November 2001. The authors work from different discipline bases and from different theoretical frameworks in their own clinical practice (social work and adult psychoanalytic psychotherapy, and educational psychology and family systems therapy). The reflections presented in this chapter describe the shared and different experiences of the authors, and consider in particular the position of the visiting "expert" working with an indigenous student population from a country itself recently traumatized by war. Many of these students had themselves been refugees during the war, and were now training in order to provide a basic capacity to respond to the trauma of both "returnees" and those who had stayed behind. We take the view that the visiting "experts" in such a situation must be themselves capable of tolerating their position as the "stranger" if their expertise is to be rendered meaningful and helpful to the trainees, and not be experienced as intrusive or imposing and thus be rejected" as refugees themselves often feel they are.

The background to the purpose of the visits is grounded in a relationship between the Tavistock & Portman NHS Trust, and the International Organization for Migration (IOM). The latter negotiated with the University of Pristina the setting up of two one-year training programmes in Psycho–Social Counselling for Albanian Kosovar graduates of the University. The Tavistock was approached to contribute to the teaching programme and to provide joint recognition with IOM and the University of Pristina. The Tavistock was asked to provide the Chair for the Assessment Commission at the end of each of the two cohorts. Apart from contributing to the teaching programme, it was in this role that the two visits, which are the subject of this chapter, took place. Each Assessment Commission panel comprised local university tutors, representatives from IOM and the Chair. Each Assessment Commission included three and a half days of individual student presentations (forty in cohort one, and thirty-nine in cohort two). Each presentation was followed by questions to the student from the staff present. On the evening of the fourth day there was a presentation ceremony, with invited guests and students' relatives and friends. Successful students were awarded a Certificate of Psycho–Social Counselling.

Beneath the skin

These are the reflections of the first author, who visited in January 2000, a year or so after the end of the NATO campaign.

It is 7 o'clock on a cold, wet evening in Pristina. A small electric fire provides the only source of warmth in the large university lecture room where we are gathered. Everyone present is wrapped up against the cold. The students have worked in groups under the leadership of a local tutor for the practice component of their training, and each student makes a half hour presentation of his or her work, supported by the presence of the rest of the group who sit at some distance from the table around which the assessment panel are gathered. When they present, the students summarize the written case study they have prepared and show a short video extract of their work with a family or client, before answering questions from panel members. A pair of interpreters work tirelessly to communicate between the Albanian speakers, myself and my Italian colleague. Each presentation tells the story of some terrible traumatic loss, or escape from death, at the hands of the Serbian police. All the accounts of the worst atrocities reported in the Western media are brought vividly alive. Most of the Kosovar students and teachers in the room have themselves lost family, friends or neighbours in this way. Yet each student presents their work with professionalism, dignity and coherence. I detect no trace of obvious bitterness, desire for revenge, or sentimentality. The atmosphere of proceedings is sober, thoughtful and businesslike. Suddenly, becoming aware of this atmosphere, of my part in the process of judging or assessing the students' work, and of my accumulating mental pain as the impact of each new story is piled upon the last, I am overtaken by a powerful sense that what I am really participating in is a war crimes tribunal.

The impact of this thought concentrates my growing awareness that what I am involved in is taking me to the very limits of my experience. As a member of the international team of teachers and assessors for this training programme, I am an important part of the structure which has organized, resourced and conferred credibility on its life. I have come here bringing "specialist" understanding and experience, the status conferred by my home institution to evaluate and assess the work of these students, but the truth of my experience is that I feel myself to be a stranger in a strange land whose inhabitants have individually and collectively undergone almost unthinkable trauma. And when I leave, I find that this is what I take away, because for the next two weeks whenever I think about these experiences and in particular when I speak about them to others, I find I cannot prevent myself crying.

I have often thought that an essential but usually unrecognized function of the formality of court room proceedings is that they serve as an institutional defence to cope with the extremely primitive, powerful and sometimes perverse states of mind associated with grief, injury, loss, murderousness, and revenge which dominate the minds of victims and perpetrators, and which will inevitably be communicated to those responsible for justice. What most impressed me about the work of the newly trained counsellors in Kosovo was their seemingly straightforward ability to concentrate on the task of simply bearing the emotional pain of their compatriot clients, in the service of mobilizing the emotional resources of bereaved and traumatized people so that they could once again feel and think in areas of themselves which had become frozen and inaccessible. Perhaps, when a whole country is devastated by the impact of war, invasion, massacre, and bombing, the "dispassionate" presence of the stranger is positively helpful in organizing the resources of the relatively less afflicted to be capable of offering something genuinely emotionally restorative to those whose suffering has proved unbearable.

Because of the extreme emotional violence experienced by both clients and trainees, I am proposing that the structures—which is really to say the system of relationships—organizing the experience of trainees is required to be particularly resilient, but also flexible and permeable to emotional experience. In psychoanalytic terms, following Freud, it is usual to think of trauma as an experience which has "punctured" the psychological skin of the victim (Freud & Breuer, 1955). A process of violent projection and intrusion has occurred; the likelihood is that correspondingly powerful processes of projection will flow in the other direction, into trainees and from them into staff and trainers. The psycho–social function of the system of relationships which constitutes the training structure is to act as a well bounded "ego" capable of accepting, processing and making at least some sense of these primitive emotional processes. However, much the educational or training process is organized around the "transmission" of theories, skills or methodologies, these emotional processes will inescapably embed themselves within the training process. If trainers and tutors do not or cannot recognize and understand these processes, then they are likely to seriously disrupt the capacity of trainees to learn and make use of more cognitive aspects of the programme. But more importantly, the trainees' own capacity to receive and tolerate primitive emotional communications from their clients will be impeded. And if the development of these capacities is impeded, then the central task of working with traumatized people—of enabling unthinkable experiences to become thinkable once more—would have been undermined. Training counsellors to do this kind of work is not in itself a therapeutic activity. But attention to the same principles and processes which makes for good therapeutic work is vital to the design and delivery of the training process itself, precisely because powerful projective and introjective processes, like traumatic intrusion itself, have no respect for the ordinary boundaries of role, task and authority.

In his paper, "Holding, containing and bearing witness: the problem of helpfulness in encounters with torture survivors", Dick Blackwell (1997) says:

> I do not believe we are here, or that we should be here to "help" our clients. I believe we are here to bear witness ... It is much harder to bear witness than it is to be helpful. Good intentions are not hard to come by; so trying to be helpful is easy. Nor is it difficult to convey a helpful attitude nor to find something one can do that a client might experience, in the first instance at least, as helpful. It makes them feel better and it makes us feel better. Bearing witness, on the other hand, may well make both ourselves and the client feel worse, at least in the short term.

This idea of "bearing witness" seems to make sense of the core of my own brief but intense exposure to events in Kosovo. Trainees themselves often appeared to have done little else than seek out potential clients, and then engage with them through sustained attention to hearing their stories in both narrative and emotional terms. This simple but extremely demanding form of engagement often appeared to have allowed seriously traumatized people to recover some degree of emotional autonomy. Bearing witness in this context seems to mean several things at once: the capacity to be able to bear to listen, to tolerate the grief, rage, helplessness and so on which the clients' communication of their experiences evokes in oneself; but also to bear, in the sense of carry away, and be a bearer of some portion of this feeling; and finally, be capable of managing this pain rather than passing it on yet again for someone else to bear. Thought about in this way, it seems to me that this was the process into which I was drawn as I sat through, and at times endured, the seemingly endless series of horror stories told by the trainees in the course of presenting their work for assessment. On reflection, I too was called upon to bear witness, and perhaps this is why the image of the courtroom and the war crimes tribunal imposed itself upon me with such force.

When we work therapeutically with people whose damaging experiences lie beyond the limits of our own experience, or with people whose cultural origins are very different from our own, or whose language we do not share, we are faced with questions of how we understand and how do we know that we understand? Much emphasis tends to be laid upon the idea of "culture" and the necessity of attaining cultural "competence" in order to reliably bridge the potential gap in understanding. This seems to me to be a mistake, because the problem of achieving therapeutic understanding under any circumstances might be framed as one of bridging the gap between ourselves and the different, apparently opaque world of the "other". Cultural sameness is no guarantee of a capacity to achieve understanding, and cultural difference is an added dimension to the difficulty of the task rather than a qualitatively different kind of obstacle. Faced with the task of understanding someone from a different culture, I believe the question is whether we want to recognize and know about this particular dimension of "difference" or whether we remain blind to this. And this is likely to be about the presence or absence of racism in ourselves.

When we work therapeutically with people in severe mental pain, our aim must be to get beneath the surface of its manifestations, in effect beneath the skin of the person who is suffering. If the nature and origins of emotional pain and damage were understandable and treatable through attending only to its surface manifestation or presentation, then people would be better able than they are to treat their own distress, and cognitive and behavioural therapies would work better than they do. Traumatic experience disturbs and disrupts mental functioning precisely because it has punctured the skin or protective surface of the mind and exposed the individual to deeper levels of experience in themselves which often take a non-verbal or pre-symbolic form. People afflicted in this way will communicate their suffering to those around them, including therapists, in corresponding non-verbal and poorly symbolized ways. These are the levels at which we must listen and understand, and paradoxically it may be that the language of such processes is more universal or at least more invariant than is spoken language or the other symbolic systems which constitute "culture". When we work "beneath the surface" in this way, we respect those areas of human experience and connectedness which are woven through our differences and join us rather than divide us. When we allow our responses to be organized by surface manifestations of difference such as skin colour, language or seemingly incomprehensible patterns of thinking, then we fail to do this. Skin colour is one, but only one of the visible forms of "difference" into which we may project our hatred of difference (Davids, 1996).

How do we teach therapeutic theory and practice in contexts where its principles and assumptions are not well established? Psychoanalysis as a theory and practice is often accused of deploying "eurocentric" concepts and assumptions. But again, the danger is that if we treat this allegation too concretely, we may simply replace one allegedly "essentialist" theory and practice with another when we try to refashion it with respect to other cultures in a manner which fails to respect their own internal complexity and diversity. Progress in this area can only really be achieved through dialogue, testing and exploration. Here is an example from the teaching I undertook in Pristina. At the start of the second training programme I spent two half days introducing the students to some foundation thinking about psychoanalytic theory and practice with a particular emphasis on understanding trauma. I spoke about the method of free association, the conscious and unconscious mind, and how we work at the boundary between the two. I related this to a theme which I knew preoccupied this group, of whether it is better to forget or remember painful experiences in the service of healing. Later the students spent some time in small discussion groups with their tutors thinking about the work they had done, and in the feedback from one group a student said, "We discussed your ideas about forgetting, remembering and free association. At the start we were more in favour of a strategy of forgetting, but by the end of our discussion we felt that it was better to be able to talk freely amongst ourselves about these things". This comment alerted me more fully to the political context in which these ideas were being received. These students belonged to an ethnic population which had experienced severe repression at the hands of the Yugoslav state and had opted to create its own unofficial or "parallel" welfare and educational system. Psychoanalysis also has little currency in the wider culture. Talking freely and associating freely as citizens had simply not been a choice in their lives in the manner which we

take for granted in Western liberal democracies. The concept of free
association, or freedom to think, in the context of inner life and
psychological treatment clearly has a quite different set of
resonances and meanings under these circumstances. What exactly
it means, and what use might be made of it under the social,
political and psychological circumstances now emerging in Kosovo
is not something which can be easily theorized or predicted outside
a process in which such meanings are discovered through dialogue
and exposure to alternative possibilities.

From trauma towards loss and mourning?

Here are the reflections of the second author who visited in
November 2001.

My first impression of flying in to Pristina airport on a cold
Sunday afternoon was of the fact that all the ground crew were UN
soldiers. There was an abundance of tanks and other armed vehicles
and all the soldiers were armed. Once through customs, where I
received no questions in relation to my visit, the overwhelming
atmosphere was that of any other arrivals setting. Families,
children, lone travellers, and professional/business looking men
all hustling to collect baggage and get out as quickly as possible to
waiting loved ones, colleagues, taxis, strangers who would ferry
them quickly to awaiting hotel rooms and to whatever business had
brought them to this recently war torn land.

I was collected, along with four medics from Denmark, by the
IOM mini bus, and we were driven for about twenty minutes and
delivered to the Grand Hotel. The foyer was a bustle of UN soldiers
and other international workers. There was a sense of purpose and I
anticipated that I too would soon be one of "them", pre-occupied
with the job I was here to do. Yet at that moment I felt unclear as to
how and why I was there. Why me? What could I possibly have to
offer this world of professional helpers and protectors? This was not
a place for tourists or sightseers, and the hotel had seen better days,
but staff were friendly and efficient.

The university is a five minute walk from the Grand Hotel. The
streets were noisy and busy, the pavements and roads in a state of
considerable disrepair, with the drainage system unable to clear the

gutters of the rain which had fallen during the night. Consequently wet and mud are transferred from pavements into the buildings. The air both inside and outside was constantly filled with smoke from cigarettes—it seemed that everyone in Pristina smokes, and I encountered no evidence of air conditioning. I had been alerted to the fact that there are regular electricity cuts throughout the day, affecting the lighting and heating, although the university and many shops and restaurants had their own generators. These were immediately put into use once the lights went out, adding significantly to the noise level out on the streets.

I had been provided with an outline of the programme which the students had followed. Each had been required to work with one family who had experienced some kind of difficulty, not necessarily as a direct result of the war. Each family was visited by the student at least twice, with the student usually accompanied by one or two (sometimes more) of their fellow students who worked as a reflective team. Each family was asked if they would agree to the sessions being video recorded (IOM had provided the University with the necessary equipment).

The students were required to write up each visit and to produce a geneogram and an event line. They were asked to relate their work with the family to the theory, concepts and ideas to which they had been introduced during the teaching part of the programme. All written work was available in Albanian, and translated into English.

The room was set up with tables at which staff would sit, with a desk and chair directly in front of for the presenting student. Towards the back of the room, behind the presenting student, was a row of chairs where other students could sit during each presentation. On a table to the side of the student was a monitor and video player, and the interpreter (there were two who took turns) sat to the side of the presenting student and the staff table.

The stories of the families with whom these thirty-nine students had worked were varied, complex and, in most cases, traumatic. Each student introduced the family, usually referring to the geneogram, and showed parts of the videoed sessions (where videoing had been possible) to emphasize or demonstrate a point. Staff would interrupt for points of clarification. Before making this trip I had been briefed by colleagues who had contributed to the teaching of the programme. I was alerted to the effect which listening to the stories of the families might have upon me, in that they would be traumatic and moving. This felt rather like a government warning "listening to the stories of the victims of war can damage your mental health", which stimulated in me a sense of anticipation about what I was about to encounter and experience and how I would deal with my feelings.

Essentially the students' work was directed to encouraging and providing a safe space for the families to talk about their worries and pre-occupations. In some cases the families had reservations about the meetings, having experienced the media interviewing them shortly after or even during their traumatic times. It clearly made a huge difference to the families to realize that the students themselves were Kosovar Albanians. In some cases the families were members of the student's own extended family network. I thought about ethnographic research studies, where the researcher is a part of the research population and study. I thought of these Psycho–Social Counselling students, who were being trained to work with victims of the atrocities of war, who themselves were also victims of the atrocities of war. In training programmes in the UK it would be inappropriate for a family to be seen professionally by a member of their own family. I became aware during the presentations that those students who presented such work had seemed to be less detached from the narratives of the family story.

Here is an example. A student presented his work with a family, to whom he was distantly related.

> The family comprised a thirty-five year old man (the student's second cousin), the man's mother, his wife, his three children, and his fifteen year old niece. The man and his younger brother (the father of the fifteen year old) had both been KLA fighters. They had been hiding in his house when Serb police entered his village. He and his brother fled the house through the garden and were hit by what the man described as "a grenade". The brother was killed and the man lost an eye and is now disabled. The man blamed himself for his brother's death, as he remembers telling his brother to follow him through the garden. In talking of his work with this family the student had tried hard to help the man to feel less responsible for the death of his brother. He spoke of the man's brother choosing to follow him through the garden.

During this presentation, one of the staff of the Assessment Commission asked the student for clarification of "the grenade". Was it perhaps a land mine? The student was adamant that it was not. It was a grenade, thrown by a Serb. It seemed to me that this had been an important question, although I had no idea why. After the session I asked the staff member to explain to me the importance and relevance of his question. He explained that many Kosovar Albanians had mined their own land in order to protect their homes from the Serbs. It was possible that the man's feelings of responsibility for his brother's death might have been because he had been killed by a mine buried by the man himself, rather than by a grenade thrown by a Serb. However, it had seemed intolerable to the student to consider that his own second cousin might have been even accidentally responsible for the brother's death. Unless it is possible for the counsellor to put such an hypothesis to the man, even if his is an accurate account, it is unlikely that this man will be able to address his feelings of guilt and move on to some resolution of his grief.

I knew little of the students' own situations as I listened to their work. I knew that a couple of the men had been members of the KLA during the war, but I did not know which ones. I knew that some students worked as teachers, some were continuing with their studies, some were working as social workers. As they presented their work my curiosity was aroused in some cases in respect of the student's own position and experience, which seemed to be pertinent to how they viewed the families' difficulties. For example, a student presented a family, comprising father, mother, daughter aged ten and son aged six.

The family had moved from Kosovo to Sweden where they had lived throughout the war. They had then returned to live with paternal grandparents. The daughter had attended school for the first three days and then refused to go again. She had explained to her father that she had witnessed a teacher slapping a boy who had not completed his homework. Despite finding an alternative school, the girl refused to attend any education and insisted that the family should return to Sweden. Both parents wanted to stay in Kosovo, and their son was doing well in school. The girl continued to refuse to go to school and eventually the father decided that they should all return to Sweden.

As the family's story unfolded in the presentation, it became clear to me that the daughter was a very powerful member of this family, and I asked the student of her own hypothesis of what might be happening in this family. She was clear that the difficulties had been caused by the incident with the teacher slapping the boy in class, and that this incident had reinforced the girl's fears of returning to a land of violence and danger. This seemed to be a sensible and valid hypothesis. I shared my thoughts about the power this girl held in the family and that it seemed to me that the decision to return to Sweden was a shared one, made by the father/daughter couple. I wondered how this family would make other decisions as and when they arose. The student seemed stuck with her hypothesis, and unable or unprepared to consider an alternative understanding. Listening to the presentation, and to the student's responses I found myself feeling torn between my own under-standing, knowledge, and experience of family dynamics, and wondering why this student seemed to be so wedded to her hypothesis. The complexities informing her work became apparent to me later that day when I learnt that she herself is primary school teacher who holds very strong views against corporal punishment of children, and that she holds positive and optimistic beliefs that Kosovo can move on from the war and that danger and violence should now be things of the past.

In my position as chair of the assessment panel I felt, on one level, that I needed to challenge the stuckness of this student. On another level I felt that this was unsafe. The student's hypothesis was sound, if unsophisticated; any desire or expectation on my part that her thinking should be deeper felt too persecutory, given the context we were in.

This is just one example of several where I had felt a need to continue the teaching of the programme instead of sticking to my brief of Assessment Commission chair. In other contexts back in the UK where I have chaired similar panels I have not felt the need to take on a teaching role within the assessment. I began to reflect upon what was different in the current setting. I think that I was excited by their work and by the programme, and the students, without exception, presented as committed, enthusiastic and thirsty for any droplet of wisdom from the lips of the staff panel. It felt that they were at the very beginning of the work, despite having completed the year's programme and having learnt a great deal. It seemed to me that they were ripe for the programme to continue and I wanted to be directly involved in its continuation. I was frustrated that there wasn't an opportunity for this to happen. Despite the excellence of the programme and the sound clinical fieldwork which the students had done, they really were at the beginning, both in the sense of their work as qualified psycho–social counsellors, but also in the sense of the country's national elections which were taking place later that week. I experienced a real feeling of beginnings and moving on, which would have had a special meaning for those who had lived through and experienced the most difficult times in contrast to myself, who had observed from a distance.

At the end of the week of presentations, after the certificate ceremony and the celebratory party which followed, I reflected upon the work and my experiences of it. Unlike my colleague the previous year, I had not felt that I was present at a war tribunal. Perhaps there was something about the extra year's distance from the war which made a difference to the intensity of the work presented. The stories of the families were indeed moving. The trauma experienced by fathers, mothers, husbands, wives, brothers, and sisters who had watched as loved ones had been shot, blown up, beaten, raped, were painful to hear, but it was possible for me to concentrate on "the work". I have thought often of the stories I heard, but I have not found myself dwelling on the detail in the early hours of the morning. I have wondered if I have just blocked it out because it is too painful to bring back, but I think that it is more to do with the present position of the student group. Things had moved on a great deal in the course of one year. This was supported in a conversation I had with the Head of the IOM programme, who had also been present at the Assessment Commission the previous year. He experienced this second cohort as being more detached from the emotional impact of the details of trauma which the families brought. It felt that he, and some of the teaching colleagues, had developed a special bond with the first cohort of students which was different from their relationship with this second group. This might be consistent with a "first child" bonding, but I think it was also about the time distance from the circumstances and experiences of the war.

My lasting thoughts of this experience are of a group of Kosovar Albanian students and staff, working in difficult conditions of power cuts etc., who are committed to providing opportunities for their fellow citizens to recover from their traumatic experiences in ways which enable them to get on with their lives as productively as possible. As someone coming into the programme at the last moment, I felt strangely attached to the group and to the work. It felt difficult to walk away and I had a sense of unfinished business.

Final thoughts—strangers to ourselves

Most of us who work with refugees have not been refugees, any more than we have been severely traumatized by war, fire, accident or other catastrophe. We would not hold that it is necessary to have been so in order to provide an effective therapeutic response. Yet, we would hold that that there are powerful obstacles in certain areas of psycho–social life to our capacity to extend therapeutic understanding beyond the terrain of the familiar. Fear (and we know how readily fear is turned to hatred) of the stranger, the alien, the intruder, the outsider—the refugee—with all their visible markers of difference, need, dependence (or is it parasitism?) remain so embedded in our culture (that word again) that often we do not know that we do not know how to begin to listen to their experience. Actually, to do so is merely to enact the first principle of all sound therapeutic work. To achieve this entails abandoning the known and familiar and becoming, in some measure, strangers to ourselves.

CHAPTER THIRTEEN

Working with psychosocial counsellors of refugees in their country of origin: exploring the interaction of professional and other discourses

M. Kemal Kuşçu and Renos K. Papadopoulos

Local and international experts in context

Kosovo is a community identified very strongly with the refugee experience for at least the last decade. As a country in turmoil for a long time, refugeedom, displacement, dislodgement, and migration have been central experiences for most of the ethnic groups in that territory. During the NATO air strikes, in particular, the number of refugees was estimated to be well over 800,000. Such an estimate does not give the complete picture of dislocation because many others had to leave their homes to move around within the province. Thus, in some way or another, leaving home has been familiar almost to everyone in Kosovo. Many of those who returned to their homes, after the NATO intervention, found little remaining. The returnees searched the memories of the past in the ruins of their homes and of their neighbourhoods. Often, they found little of what they had left behind, before fleeing. Being at home did not mean that they now had a home.

Returning to their communities of origin, by and large, has been an experience different from what was expected. For many survivors, Kosovo is a lost community where one tries to trace the memories of the past on a daily basis. Not only personal explanations, but also communal ways of talking about these experiences, have been dominated by a yearning for an invisible collective past, which has been supplemented by an equally ungraspable vision for a future. Those who have been trying to touch the imagined secure ground of home seem to have captured some premature or illusory certainty. In Kosovo, home has become an imaginal entity of collective yearning for a clear understanding of the past and for a safe grip on the future.

The dense atmosphere of uncertainty is not limited to the indigenous population of Kosovo. In relation to the local population there is a disproportionally high number of international experts who are residents or visitors in the country. These "internationals" find it hard to work within these undefined conditions. The confusion and uncertainty that reign in Kosovo now, during its current period of reconstruction, affect directly these professionals as well. Every newcomer expert has to deal not only with this state of bewilderment but also to create a newly defined professional agenda for him or herself in order to cope with these formless conditions in Kosovo. Moreover, in constructing an agenda for themselves, the international professionals inevitably have been creating new ways of conceptualizing the refugee experience for the locals, as well.

Therefore, the new reality in Kosovo lies somewhere between these two imagined uncertainties, i.e. of the local past and the present assumptions of both the Kosovars and the foreign experts. This can be a painful state for someone who is trying to make sense of the realities in Kosovo today. The everyday lay and professional discourses grow intertwined together.

In this context, the role and position of the local professionals have an extremely important resonance; such persons stand in between the present and the past as crucial mediators who can contribute substantially to the creation of more appropriate means of working with refugees as well as with their other compatriots who have been affected by the shared turbulent past. However, such local professionals are not only few but also have to be recognized by their own community, in the context of the overwhelming presence of "international experts".

The first author's first visit to the region was when he was invited to offer a training module in systemic family therapy as part of the Psychosocial and Trauma Response (PTR) project of the International Organization for Migration (IOM). This project included a programme of training psychosocial counsellors at the University of Pristina, in conjunction with the Tavistock Clinic, London. He completed his training in family therapy at the Tavistock Clinic and his tutor there, the second author, invited him to participate in the training programme of this project. Subsequently, the IOM contributed to the creation of mental health centres in Kosovo and the graduates of the training were employed as psychosocial counsellors; the task of overseeing the supervision and in-service training of the graduates was offered to the second author who then appointed the first author as the resident, *in situ*, supervisor. The first author is a Turkish psychiatrist and family therapist and the second author is a Greek Cypriot clinical psychologist, family therapist, and Jungian psychoanalyst. The first author lives in Istanbul and the second in London. Our personal friendship and close collaboration offered the local trainees a model of inter-ethnic reconciliation and mutual respect. Although each one of us has our own different cultural and historical connections with the region, our very presence in Kosovo together offered a working example of operating with shared understanding of and personal commitment to our common projects.

The first author felt closer to the region in terms of sharing the same historical Balkan experience, in addition to having members of his family originating from those territories. Thus, working in Kosovo activated personal searching not only for the stories of others but also for making sense of his own personal experience in the context of all these parameters. The second author, although in terms of his origin he is geographically remote from the Balkans and has no family roots in that region, as a young student, with a UNESCO scholarship, had studied in Yugoslavia in the sixties and has remained intimately familiar with the country, speaking Serbocroat, and having close personal friendships with Yugoslavs of all ethnic backgrounds, including Kosovar Albanians.

Both of us developed a close familiarity with the local professionals and their predicament and this chapter discusses some of our observations from our experiences in this work, especially with reference to the discourses of the professional communities in the context of the wider parameters within which they are located.

Cultural dimensions and collaboration dynamics

Any project which aims to create a new local professional agenda, inevitably will also introduce new elements in that culture. In Kosovo, the class of local interventionists *de facto* has been creating new possibilities of explaining and understanding the past and present. However, this group of people with their unique position and expertise of cultural proximity, have to survive within a delicate tension between local and outsider imagined and actual realities.

In effect, this group of local professionals has become the gate-keepers to resources. Most visiting experts expect these colleagues to make decisions about key aspects of their collaborative projects. However, this collaboration always has conditions attached. It is like saying, *tell us who needs help and how we can offer it . . . but tell it to us in our own terms*. Inevitably, conditions are present in all situations and there is a variety of conditions that are associated with such collaboration—from the most open and liberal to the most restrictive and imposing.

Collaborating with "the internationals" has additional dimensions for the local professionals who, themselves, have also been refugees. Their perception of the others' needs in the context of their own overall predicament can be a most difficult task. Their painful effort to be judiciously impartial and objective, at times forces them to go against their own experience and better judgement in order to avoid being (or perceived as being) prejudiced or biased. Moreover, it is not easy to expose their own needs to their visiting colleagues; on the one hand, they certainly wish to co-operate on the basis of equality and trusted exchange but, on the other hand, unless their differences are acknowledged and respected, it is likely that the collaboration will take a skewed direction. The fact is that they are not equal, in all respects, and especially in relation to vital experiences and existing resources. Their local roots place them in the role of participant observers where both the participating part and the observer part are extremely demanding, partisan, and exclusive. Moreover, when they themselves have been struggling to cope with their own feelings in the face of their family and community tragedies, it is not easy to continue operating on abstract professional principles and it is difficult to plan and provide professional services on an "objective" level. Pride, grief, despair, shame, guilt, embarrassment, disorientation, disillusionment, anger, pain, and a host of other feelings and reactions cannot and should not be put aside; yet, it is not easy for such feelings to be accessed in appropriate ways when colleagues endeavour to work together in the planning and implementation of such relevant projects.

From our experience, we have found that creating a safe context to allow this kind of sharing and soul searching to take place, has happened mostly in informal settings and "outside" the "work venues". What should not be forgotten, of course, is that despite the obvious differences between local and visiting experts in terms of a range of primary and secondary factors, a ground of undeniable equality is that of basic humanity. Paradoxically and tragically this dimension of potential equality is often forgotten in the hustle and bustle of professional attention to the correct implementation of projects. At this level, the foreign experts have themselves a substantial amount of complex material to unravel and connect with: their clusters of ambivalent feelings about rescuing and saving the locals, their own personal motivations for undertaking this work, their relationship to the many dimensions of this work, to name but a few. One-sided "sharing" of the locals' predicament with the internationals is not always helpful as it tends to foster the inequalities, dependence, and many other difficult factors in their interaction.

One particularly difficult and indeed tragic phenomenon that is, unfortunately, not uncommon in these types of collaboration is the sour ending of enthusiastic beginnings. More specifically, this happens when, under the intensity of such situations, visiting experts, overwhelmed by their own emotions and compassion for the suffering of the local colleagues idealize them and exaggerate their abilities; in turn, the locals professionals, under the pressure of their own suffering and immense relief as a result of the visiting experts' presence and compassion idealize their new friends and saviours. Such conditions are most conducive to the emergence of misunderstandings and disappointments when the excitement of mutual admiration begins to wane under the weight of practical realities and pragmatic necessities. The euphoria of compassion (in its true sense of the word), the lack of personal and therapeutic boundaries, the exultation generated from sym-pathia (co-suffering), the uniqueness of the moment and mutuality, all these construe a most powerful cocktail of emotional circumstances that can blind well-meaning and competent people, tricking them into ignoring the most elementary precautions. Customary and routine monitoring, setting clear objectives, assessment of staff abilities, acknowledging elementary feasibilities, all tend to be ignored and forgotten. In the cloud of this archetypal cluster, such mundane activities appear demeaning and even insulting. Yet, this mutual affinity can also, of course, be most useful in enabling people to heroically surmount obstacles under the most adverse conditions; however, often such situations end up with resentment and bitter recriminations, not dissimilar to post-divorce reactions. This type of tragedy is particularly painful because potentially compatible and successful partnerships are terminated and the protagonists switch from mutual adoration to mutual accusations. This phenomenon was described by the second author elsewhere (Papadopoulos, 1998, 1999a) and it is endemic to these kinds of international collaboration.

Mindful of this particular difficulty and other similar soul-destroying traps, we have managed to identify their early signs and to minimize their deadly effect.

During the actual training sessions, we have frequently experienced situations when personal emotional reactions from the participants to certain material required us to change track, gently pause the training and provide a containing space for the reactions to be acknowledged and validated. Moreover, we always felt it important at some stage to plough back into the training of these experiences, thus enabling the participants to become enriched rather than embarrassed by their eruption.

In all these situations, no preconceived guidelines or recipes can be of substantial use; what is required is sensitivity and respect at all levels in a unique way to the given situation and to the individuals concerned. It is not easy to operationalize ways in which to convey respect in a tangible and effective way in these contexts. This is particularly so because it involves a wide variety of dimensions, including personal feelings, professional pride, political sensibilities, cultural sentiments, religious leanings, family loyalty, all enwrapped in distressing and distressed anguish.

Running separate groups (in addition or as part of the training programme) for local colleagues (training organizers) and training participants to focus on their own feelings and reactions to the violent turbulence in their country, does not address the issue completely. Such groups are not wrong and their usefulness should not be ignored. However, over and above that, sensitivity and respect are required at all times because emotional eruptions emerge at unpredictable times, places and circumstances, regardless of how much work has been done with them. Creating separate space for this kind of work is important but human responses cannot be compartmentalized and it is not, by any means, easy to maintain a respectful sense of proportion and appropriate balance between human exchange and professional facilitation.

Maintaining balanced perspectives and a sense of proportion is difficult and toilsome in situations such as the current one in Kosovo, where violent political polarization and uncertainty had been chronic, where the brutal outbreak of hostilities created such levels of devastation, and where now, the yearned for peaceful time for reconstruction remains still violent and uncertain, especially in terms of a political future for this territory. Yet, this is precisely what is required in order not to perpetuate further violence in subtler shades and forms in the context of our professional interactions.

As part of their personal journey, the local professionals keep on redefining the complexities of their own predicament in the context of their daily practices. The proximity of their local and professional identities is both a source of unique strength as well as of confusion and anguish. Yet, although we know that surgeons are not encouraged (if not actively discouraged) to operate on members of their own families, in places such as Kosovo with such scarce resources, applying such reasonable principles would be impractical, if not, indeed, unethical. Therefore, under these circumstances, vigilance, sensitivity and respect are the necessary tools that one should be using to go forward.

There are different and shared challenges that local and international experts face in maximizing the positive facets of this complex situation and in minimizing the negative ones. In our joint work, our own acknowledged personal, professional, and cultural similarities and differences have been an additional source of help in this arduous and potentially hazardous undertaking.

"Dominant-discourse-vacuum"

The second author observed that under conditions of substantial upheaval and considerable uncertainty there is a tendency for the development of what he called, a "dominant-discourse-vacuum" (Papadopoulos, 2000b, p. 91). This is the condition when usual ways of accounting for major events in society and human suffering no longer provide adequate accounts and explanations. It is in these times that society tends to turn more eagerly to "experts" expecting them to provide some kind of satisfactory explanation that would encompass the complexities, contradictions and new realities that emerge. In the case of mental health experts, "the conditions of a dominant-discourse-vacuum, ... [create] pressure either to attempt to impose such a discourse or to succumb to the easy option of pathologizing human suffering" (Papadopoulos, 2000b, p. 91). A dominant discourse that is often imposed in these situations is an exclusively political one (usually of extreme polarization), which ignores or dismisses any other human and humane considerations. Mental health professionals are certainly not the main instigators of such an imposition but, wittingly or unwittingly, participate in the solidification of its dominance. What they are often responsible for introducing is the pathologization and medicalization of human suffering (cf. Losi, 2002; Summerfield, 2001). This means that it is easier for them to fall back on simple formulations of what they know best and to exclude any painful ways of interconnecting their professional discourse with wider socio–political and historical contexts.

There are several facets of the "dominant-discourse-vacuum" in Kosovo today. At the political level, the main rhetoric of the Kosovar Albanians had been dominated by the politics of polarization and the movement for independence. The dominant discourse was absolutely clear and unanimously embraced by all. Now, following the NATO intervention, the actual connection with the Yugoslav federation has been severed but not the formal political one. Internal political conflict has replaced the unity which was dictated by the polarized conflict with the Yugoslav administration, dominated by a Serbian presence. This transition is most uncomfortable for all. Whereas at the formal level of political structures the discourse of reconciliation has been introduced, by no means is this a dominant discourse in the wider Kosovar Albanian society today. No alternative rhetoric has yet replaced the clarity of the earlier militant one and this vacuum is felt very painfully. As Losi reported characteristically, one Kosovar Albanian said, well after the war:

> While the Serbs were still here, everything could be blamed on them. Now that young women are disappearing from the streets, we need to accept the idea that there is evil also among us. [Losi, 2002]

At the professional level, before the war there were very few mental health professionals in the province and the dominant discourse was that of medicalized psychiatry and institutionaliza- tion. Now, with the influx of hundreds of aid agencies, with most of them introducing their own brand of trauma response, there has been a plethora of approaches creating a Babel of theoretical schools, resulting in a "dominant-discourse-vacuum".

One of the most important implications of the "dominant- discourse-vacuum" in the work we do in Kosovo is that, given the overall context, there is a very strong tendency by local profes- sionals to adopt unquestionably one of the imported discourses by outside experts as their own dominant one in their own services or organizations, blissfully ignorant of its standing within the wider professional community (of local and visiting experts) in Kosovo or in the world today. In our contact with various services and organizations we have often come across this uncritical phenomenon.

The local psychosocial counsellors (graduated from the IOM training courses) have the unenviable position of being at the crossroads of their newly acquired professional identity, alongside their local experience of their own suffering, as well as their need to relate to their international colleagues. This means that they struggle to mediate between all these discourses in their continuous search for dialogue at different levels within the wider community of professionals, both local and international.

Otherness

In order to understand the perspective of the international view of assessing local needs, one has to reflect on the outsiders' experience in context: Being an outside trainer can be considered partly as an ethnographic experience in the land of the *other*. Like all ethnographic experiences, this undertaking carries different modes of translation and interpretation of the host culture (Clifford, 1986). However, the position of outside experts is hard to define in Kosovo solely on the basis of these modes of encounters. International experts' visits inadvertently constitute injections of new meaning not only to the work carried out in Kosovo, but also in the very perception of the existing local needs.

Cross-cultural expertise inevitably instigates a certain alienation *sui generis*, where the outside experts search for a secure exoticism. In other words, over-sensitive to the "cultural differences", international experts may attempt to avoid importing their own standards and seek to locate and grasp the *other*. However, inescapably, they can only recognize something if it fits within their own scope of comprehension; this means that the outside experts are locked in a paradoxical pursuit in so far as on the one hand they look for something new, outside their own culture, an *other* (Papadopoulos, 2002b), and yet, on the other hand they can only register something that can be comprehensible and explainable in terms of their existing repertoire of understanding, experiences, theories, vocabulary and views.

This paradox relates to the post-colonial debate (Bhabha, 1994; Breckenridge *et al.*, 2000; Sanborn, 1998) which throws new light on the reliability of what westerners have been hearing from non-western sources. This debate clarifies that what westerners thought that non-westerners have been saying to them is not necessarily what westerners thought it was. In other words, there are many possibilities of distortion in this encounter. It has been argued that non-westerners had been more attentive to their own needs and interests than originally anthropologists thought and, therefore, they used to modify what they said to westerners, fashioning it according to their own needs and perceptions. At times they would say things to please the westerners (according to their own impression of what would be pleasing to them), to tease them, or even to mislead them. This distortion took (and still takes) many other forms: westerners heard only what they wanted to hear or were capable of hearing. Also, the power inequality makes open communication between these two worlds extremely difficult, regardless of the good will and intentions of both interlocutors. Although it is not appropriate in this chapter to open up the thorny issue of post-colonial perspectives of international aid and collaborative projects, it is, nevertheless, of paramount importance to note its relevance here.

The communication between international experts and local professionals also evokes an aesthetic dimension where certain stories and certain voices within these stories attract the outsider more than others. Thus, new categories of priorities emerge as a result (Losi, 2000). Unavoidably, a reductive technical tone appears within the international perception as they hear and interpret the experience of the local suffering and the expressed needs. After all, the needs will need to be translated into comprehensible language by the international authorities and into feasible projects that will attract funding.

It is not only the content of the stories that shapes the tone of the outsiders' interpretation of the local experience. Also, the different style and structure of the personal narratives challenge the strong need of the international expertise to find a coherent story in Kosovo. In the face of the devastating events of the past, this seems to be hard to achieve (Papadopoulos, 1997).

At some point during the first author's work, he became particularly observant of the structure and outlook of the counsellors' narratives. Although other international colleagues were concerned about the low standard of reporting by the counsellors, he was intrigued by its uniqueness rather than its standard, according to accepted western professional criteria. At the same time he was also reading the works of Ismail Kadare, the famous Albanian author. He was then struck by the similarity between the two types of narratives—the local counsellors' and Kadare's. There were similarities between the two ways of describing an event. These textual similarities were not restricted to the content and the structure of these narratives, but also extended to the very style of punctuation and the general tone, which wove the fabric of the counsellors' reports. More specifically, both the counsellors and Kadare tended to narrate long and epic stories with complexity beyond the usual western case reports; both tended to use strong and categorical statements and ended with dramatic phrases such as "...these were what I saw and heard...".

This observation made the first author realize that the otherness of the local narratives is not easy to unveil in Kosovo. In their own unique ways, these narratives enabled meanings to appear and disappear within them. We have therefore understood that one way international experts can address this phenomenon is by adopting the approach of *therapeutic witnessing* (Papadopoulos, 1997, 1998). This means that instead of attempting to introduce anything active, it is important to allow a listening in depth which is more than simply hearing the words; attention and absorption into the world of the other is essential in order to become sensitive to facets of stories which are not usually accessible. This process amounts to witnessing not only the locals' experiences but also the very process and anguish involved in attempting to construe their experiences.

Narratives and professional positions

Each community has its own ways of talking about its experience. The stories unfold within the imagination of the storytellers and their audience. New common realities are constructed and co-constructed between those who tell and those who listen. A similar condition applies also to the field of psychosocial work. The therapeutic exchange has been seen as a *conversational* and *narrative* event (Andersen, 2001; Crossley, 2000; McLeod, 1997; White & Epston, 1990) One of the aims of our work in Kosovo has been to assist our counsellors to make use of this existing cultural resource of narration in their work with families.

In Kosovo, being a counsellor is not only based on a wish to help others, but it is also a socially given role. Most of the trainees had told us that they were the main listeners of the stories in their own communities or families even before the war. Their unique role in their communities facilitated their work substantially. Despite the strong cultural background of using stories for supportive conversation, they experienced new dilemmas while preparing their clinical reports for their local colleagues. They found it extremely challenging. This was so because this time, they had to deal not only with the outsider's presumptions and interpretations, but also they had to cope with local professionals' other agendas.

This means that by becoming professionals "officially" in their own country, our trained counsellors were facing this additional difficulty—they had to enable the emergence of new categories, which are the product of the interaction between the reductive tone of the translated psychosocial discourse and the local narratives. More specifically, terms such as *stress* or *trauma*, which have been imported by the international experts, tend to acquire a reductive and individualized meaning by focusing on the experience of an individual and not on the community. Inevitably, such terms have affected the ways that the local narratives are now told. This means that a new form of individuality has been created as a result of this new professional discourse and our counsellors had to adapt their own roles in the context of these changes.

In Kosovo, at a cultural level, an individual account usually is not sufficient to describe and explain an experience. In other words, events can only be explained through a collective discourse. However, in the everyday practice of local professionals this has been changing radically. This contributes to the establishment of new and false medical categories where the individual stories have become disconnected from the collective experiences and narratives. The diagnosis of trauma-related conditions is constantly established on the basis of personal vulnerability and located within a biological domain where the survivors receive combinations of long term psychotropic treatments during long hospital stays. A woman, who was diagnozed as being traumatized and treated for two years with psychotropic medication, described her condition as *grief* during our conversation. Moreover, this grief had clear collective parameters and as an individual this woman was now struggling to make sense of it, especially in view of the fact that she had been diagnozed as suffering from a traumatic mental affliction.

In these detached contexts, there is a lot of hard work that needs to be done in order to create the reality of the psychosocial realm as a viable and workable entity; an entity that truly integrates the psychological with the social, the intrapsychic and the collective, the individual human suffering within the context of socio–political realities.

The realm of the psychosocial in practice

In view of the above, in Kosovo there is a difficulty in delineating what is the precise meaning of "psychosocial" for the local communities, for the local professionals and hence for the international trainers, as well. There seems to be a tendency to consider everything that relates to life adversity on a material level as "social". Despite the strong tradition of social cohesiveness in the community, the diagnosis of so-called "social" cases is usually reserved for certain life adversities. For example, having witnessed a traumatic event is not considered *social*, whereas suffering from material adversity and poor financial conditions is considered social. In general medical practice, the new category of *psychological* is used without a clear definition and in a separate way from the wider social and political discourses.

The combination of psychological and social creates a challenging picture for the counsellors who are trying to find a common tongue between a collective story and local professional practice for psychosocial work.

The overwhelming nature of the work, the extent of the local needs, the conditions within the services, and the uncertainty at the political level, create an almost impossible task for every professional in Kosovo. It is difficult to isolate cases in terms of neat "referrals"; instead, whenever one responds to such a referral, one finds a whole community in need behind it where it is difficult to isolate the individual or family referred. Such complexity imposes overwhelming demands on professionals especially in view of their overloaded schedules. These conditions, which are also affected by the mixture of discourses, force our counsellors to conceive of new pragmatic approaches to their work both on the theoretical and practical levels. They are forced to modify existing conceptualizations and practices. Within such a context, psychosocial work is defined as everything outside the realm of existing services or approaches. In one instance, we have observed with bewilderment and admiration how our trained counsellors (when they felt that the referred family was in a difficult predicament and its members were unable to communicate clearly their needs) resorted to discreetly gathering information and enlisting the help of members of the extended family and even neighbours.

It is easy to criticize both international experts and local counsellors for their failures, which are many. As we know, it is impossible for any conscientious foreign expert to act merely as a technician who is simply translating objective expertise into local application, free from local conditions and considerations. Admittedly, at the level of humanitarian aid this is not very problematical. However, when it comes to the field of psychosocial work, this application and adaptation is by no means easy. More specifically, even the use of seemingly neutral and "technical" terms such as *trauma* and *stress* is fraught with daedalic complexities and it has far reaching implications. It is not only the technical definition of trauma itself, in terms of various theoretical approaches that matters here, but the very way it is used in everyday practice in the context of all the inter-linked systems of individuals, groups and discourses, without, of course, excluding the dimension of power and access to resources.

Today in Kosovo, everyone is talking about the importance of psychosocial work, without offering a clear view of what in any real sense it tries to capture. Everyone believes that it is important to take on board issues such as culture. But still, there is very little evidence of how this phenomenon is understood by the different parties in the various services and organizations. Is culture an incidental epiphenomenon or part and parcel of the core phenomenon? This uncertainty encourages the alienated and uncritical adoption of the technical jargon used by the visiting experts and the "professional literature", without needing to struggle with its complexity. In a cynical way, we could argue that the operational definition of the "psychosocial" as used by many services in Kosovo is what the foreign professionals do, whereas the locals get on with attempting to work as hard as possible with the real difficulties on the ground and with all the untidiness of what is social and what is psychological.

At this point, one assumes that formal procedures and techniques of assessment and evaluation might provide some degree of certainty or structure. There is a general wish that the invention of such objective formulas will clear the confusion and dictate to local counsellors what to do in each given situation and how to discern the unique psychosocial angle. How much to investigate the family's housing predicament, how many members of the extended family to contact in order to piece the story together, how many other services to liase with in order to co-ordinate the best possible "treatment"/"help" package for that family. The painful complexities and the "dominant-discourse-vacuum" tend to privilege the adoption of the visiting professionals' abstract formulas. Stories then become mechanical gatherings of information, and human conditions are reduced to the level of caseworks. Finer facets of discourses then disappear and life and work become tragically oversimplified and devoid of healing potentialities.

Yet, we have found that this power that is given to the "internationals" on a plate, can be used creatively in order to initiate explorative conversations, whilst containing the prevailing anxiety. It is according to this principle that we view positively the potentially constructive contribution of international experts. It can certainly have an empowering effect on local colleagues to facilitate their own creative integration of local and imported discourses.

Psychosocial work as a tool for conversation

The work in Kosovo, like any other work in this field carries personal and collective agendas intermingled together. But for the local counsellors and the ones who are visiting or working with them such a statement needs further analysis. For the local counsellors, being a professional means not only listening to existing stories in the original communities of refugees but also listening to the unique and individual voice of each person they encounter. For the newcomer, the confusion on the ground gives shape to a particular milieu. Working in the original communities of refugees amounts to searching for different voices, which in their own ways gather and disappear. Soon, one discovers that such work can become feasible if we view it as a license for initiating conversations.

This means that instead for looking for suitable objective professional tools to enter into the realities at different levels, we could approach this work in terms of enriching the meaningful exchange of stories, and to begin with, within the different parties in the different services. How did they come to work there? How has their service and its ethos developed? How was it for them as individuals in the early difficult phases? What were their experiences during the war? What losses did they have? And then again, what theoretical frameworks have they found useful? How did they get on with those international experts from that agency? A respectful and open unfolding of human conversations, without losing sight of the task at hand, can open up wider discourses within which new meanings can emerge for both interlocutors. Yes, we shall deliver our project, but first, we really want to understand and learn. The challenge of such work is not limited to the painful memories of the past but also to the stories of the present and the future. In this way, both international and local professionals can enable re-storying and restoring of dislocated, dismembered, and compartmentalized worlds.

Conversations of this kind can create bridges between different stories, roles, practices, discourses and worlds. As Kadare wrote, the builders of such bridges shall carry the different tongues, dialects, and tones and make "... their calculations in eleven languages, not counting dialects" (Kadare, 1997, p. 26).

CHAPTER FOURTEEN

In the aftermath of violence: therapeutic intervention in Kosova[1]

Jenny Altschuler, Majlinda Angoli, Merita Halitaj and Ifakete Jasiqi

F lora, contacted the "One to One" Counselling Centre in Kosovo shortly after the war had ended. She was worried about her eldest son, Ronny, then aged nine. He was extremely fearful, experienced nightmares and wet himself at night. It was immediately clear to the counsellor that there was much that Flora was not saying, and she struggled to know how much to encourage her to speak or whether to respect her need for privacy.

Over time, as she saw Ronny becoming less fearful, Flora began to share her own story. Avoiding eye contact, she talked about how her husband had left their village to join the fighting, leaving her and their four children alone. Physically unharmed, their nights had been spent in fear, trying to protect one another from Serb bullets and NATO bombing. On returning, her husband said little of what had happened to him. From the changes in his behaviour, she was sure he had seen and been part of some terrible events. He seemed very angry and depressed. Their farm had been destroyed, he was unable to find work, and she struggled to know how to help him.

Watching the counsellor's reaction, Flora then told another part of the story: how after the war, when drunk, he had raped and kicked her, and then isolated her from the rest of the family. Ronny was often singled out as the target of his father's rage and there were nights when Flora would wake him to protect them both from his anger. As such, their fear was compounded by the physical exhaustion of yet more broken nights. She felt deeply ashamed about what had happened and wanted reassurance that what she had said would be kept secret.

This story reflects the most serious challenge facing Kosova today: how to make sense of personal and family distress following years of war, political oppression and uncertainty. Drawing on systemic theory, this paper will describe the work of a project aimed at addressing the aftermath of socio–political violence, in a context of increased reports of violence within the home. In so doing, we will highlight the value of intervening therapeutically at several levels, individually, as a family and at the wider level of the community.

Drawing on our different positions, the paper also addresses context at another level, at the level of culture. This includes discussing the questions we have had to face in exploring the meaning of translating ideas about therapy from one culture to another, in a situation in which there have been years of political oppression. The team consisted of Jenny, the UK based trainer and consultant to the project, Majlinda, the Albanian mentor and project supervisor, and Merita and Ifakete, the Kosovar counsellors and managers of the "One to One" centres in Prizren and Peja, respectively.

Political and gendered violence

Political violence has profound, long-term effects on its victims. Perpetrated by the very agencies entrusted to protect and maintain order, it creates a context in which meanings are blurred, where the shift from protection to violence is obscured. All too frequently, this leads to the development of a sense of helplessness and hopelessness that can so easily be transmitted from generation to generation (Sluzki, 1993).

Any attempt to understand the current situation in Kosova needs to include some understanding of the sexual–political power structure of the country, where the birth of a boy was often celebrated by the firing a gun, and the birth of a girl, with tears. The traditional text of *Kanuni I Leke Dukagjini* places responsibility on men to protect the honour of wives and other family members, and revenge any hurt caused to them (Gjecov, 1989). Whilst few abide strictly by these rules today, it positions rape as a sexualized weapon of war, as an attack on the family and whole community (Agger, 1994). The sense of shame evoked adds a further layer of disruption, fear and uncertainty, to the process of coming to terms with the multiple losses of loved ones, treasured family homes, and sense of security (cf. Lee *et al.*, 2001).

Despite considerable international aid, the war set in motion a negative cycle of events: at the time of writing (January, 2002), estimates of unemployment vary from 60 to 80%. There is widespread poverty, compounding the sense of victimhood, despair and powerlessness many experience. As elsewhere, however, in Kosova violence has not been confined to the political context, where the perpetrators can be separated from victims as "Others", as the political enemy. There are growing reports of brutality at home, of violence towards children and gendered violence within the family (Sala, 2000; OSCE Press Release, 2000). It has been argued that current increased reports of violence may relate to the need for men to assert themselves in the only arena in which they are still able to exert power, in intimate relationships within the home.

However, it is difficult to know how much gendered violence has been exacerbated by war, or whether the war enabled women to voice the abuse they have been experiencing for years: there are no legal structures to deal with violence towards women and children, and until recently, few women questioned their right to a life free from violence. In an attempt to redress this, a series of conferences and public awareness campaigns have been initiated to highlight the "voice of those who cannot speak" (Sala, 2000, p. 2), the voice of the women and children who have been abused. However, legislation is but one step in the process: even where formal structures legislate against violence, as in the UK, the sense of shame evoked by violence often makes it enormously difficult to speak out.

An extensive analysis of the interconnection between political and gendered violence is beyond the scope of this paper. However, what appears to be shared is that at the time of any violent act, the initiator experiences a sense of entitlement that exceeds any feelings of responsibility for the physical and emotional well-being of the other. Although not all inequalities in power result in violence, an imbalance in power is required for a violent act to occur (Jenkins, 1991). In both situations, a core therapeutic issue is where responsibility is placed: all too often, those at the receiving end are burdened by feeling responsible for the abuse, compounding the physical and emotional suffering they experience (Serra, 1993; Shaw et al., 1996; Goldner et al., 1990; Vetere & Cooper, 2001).

Trauma and displacement

Traumatic events have primary effects not only on the psychological structures of the self but also on the systems of attachment and meaning that link individual and community. [Herman, 1994, p. 33]

Any attempts to address the impact of trauma on the lives of both individuals and families, needs to address the fragmentary consequences of trauma, the disconnection of the very bonds sustaining individuals, families, and communities.

In trying to understand the consequences of war, we need to reflect on how ideas about ethnic difference have acquired and retained social significance (Hall, 1996). This includes some under-standing of how historical and political events have shaped the experiences of those who have survived the war and may be contributing to reprisals in the present (Salvatici, 2001). Although years of political resistance can have an empowering impact on the local community, ongoing political uncertainty has had a cumula-tively traumatizing effect on the lives of many. During the war, more than a million Kosovar Albanians were forced to flee their homes to live elsewhere, in the often unsafe transitory camps or in strangers' private homes. However for many, this sense of displace-ment was not new, but part of a process of dislocation predating the war (Lafontaine, 2001). Under Serb occupation, there was restricted access to professional training, destabilizing the society and access to community resources. Lack of recognition of their political rights created a sense of alienation within their own country, a "diasporic space" (Brah, 1996) of disconnection and displacement, with the dream of returning to an idealized state, less constrained by harsh political reality.

Inevitably, this dream has not been fulfilled. Instead, many have been confronted with evidence of destruction and loss, often accompanied with feelings of shame, the shame of having been unable to protect families and homes, the shame of knowing that daughters and wives have been raped. In a society that celebrates bravery, *Trimeria*, families are still struggling to come to terms with the times when it was impossible to be brave, when some acted as informers, or when actions in battle led to the death of fellow combatants. These feelings may also have been compounded by not knowing how to mourn the loss of those who have not returned, those who may still be in prison. Nonetheless, this belief in the possibility of reconnection and return has helped many survive and strengthened their capacity to shift their eyes from the past to the future.

Contextualizing personal shame and suffering within the wider socio–political context, enables people to begin to see their experience as part of a wider collective process. Positioning individual experience within the wider system of relationships means moving beyond the level of the individual and family, to include reconstruction and reconnections with the communities in which they live (Papadopoulos, 2001a).

Stage 1: Establishing an initial project in Albania

From early 1999, the British public were confronted with television images of the disasters facing Kosova: the killings, rape, mass graves, and the sight of evermore men, women and children fleeing burning villages to escape further violence and devastation. Under the umbrella of the Disasters Emergency Committee, UK aid organizations worked together to provide food, blankets, clothes, and medicine, with the added intention of assisting and building the infrastructure of the countries taking in most of the refugees, namely Albania and Macedonia. As stories of intense emotional suffering began to emerge, it became clear that practical help was not enough, and that women and children were most at risk.

In partnership with the OSCE (Organization for Security in

Europe), and an Albania based counselling centre for women and girls, the UK based charity, the One to One Children's Fund, established a crisis centre in Northern Albania, with the aim of helping women and children make sense of what was happening to them. In liaison with the charity, Jenny Altschuler was asked to play a role as trainer and consultant in the planning and establishment of the project. Headed by Majlinda Angoli, an initial centre was established, staffed by Albanian counsellors who had, three years previously, begun working with women experiencing violence at home. A shared language and largely similar culture to their Kosovar clients, helped in developing a sense of trust, of *Besa*, in a context where trust had been shattered.

Women and children who were identified by staff in the camps as at particular risk were brought to the centre, where they were cared for, able to wash their clothes, cook, talk, and, most importantly for the children, to play. Access to medical treatment was provided, a service particularly crucial for the women and young girls who had been raped and/or pregnant. Individual and group counselling, art and play therapy provided the opportunity to begin dealing with the psychological consequences of what they had experienced both personally and in witnessing the suffering of others.

Transferring the work to Kosova

As the war ended, many refugees returned home, and the project moved to Kosova. Embracing a commitment to engage with the wider context, intervention has been focused at three levels: direct work with individuals and families in the centre; outreach work; and in contributing to community regeneration, with networking and training local counsellors.

Coming home and being confronted many with frightening flashbacks of earlier experiences, re-traumatized the returning refugees. As a result of the fighting and NATO bombing, towns and villages had been devastated. Although the international community contributed generously to rebuilding homes and roads, this has been far from sufficient. There were and still are serious water and electricity shortages. Harsh winters have added to the difficulties people have had to face. In the absence of their men, many families have been forced to remain in limbo: for some time after the war, many remained in collective centres unable to provide their children with much needed stability, support and supervision.

Schools have had the task of helping children make up for their loss of formal education during the war, and many are finding it difficult to study in a structured way as they are still struggling to make sense of what they witnessed during the fighting. Coupled with this, there have been reports of increased rates of juvenile aggression, both at school and on the streets (OSCE, 2001).

Most pervasive, however, has been the way in which families have been split apart by the aftermath of violence. More than two years on, in those families where members were raped, daughters, mothers, fathers, and mothers-in-law are still locked apart by feelings of guilt and shame.

Centres have been established in two areas substantially devastated by war, in Prizrin and Peya. Whilst locating a venue for the centres in these areas, and establishing appropriate organizational structures has been a challenge, staff recruitment and training has presented more complex dilemmas. Under Yugoslav administration, few Albanian Kosovars were trained in the helping professions: until recently there was no psychology training, psychiatric training has been primarily organic in orientation, and counselling training has only recently been established. So, not only does the society face a difficult task in addressing the aftermath of civil war but it does so in the context of limited psychosocial resources. With the exception of one psychiatrist, none of the staff of the Centres had prior counselling or psychotherapy training: both centre managers had trained initially as engineers, and began working as counsellors after the war. Recruitment has therefore involved assessing the potential to use in-service training to take what is often experienced as a harrowing role, as well as the potential to be able to support colleagues in demanding circumstances.

In the absence of local trainers, the Albanian counsellors have played a central role as trainers and mentors. This has been consolidated by additional input from the UK, (Tavistock Clinic), Croatia, (the Society for Psychological Assistance), and Israel, (the Carmel Institute). Fifteen Kosovar trained counsellors now work in the centres and provide outreach facilities to local communities, school and NGO's.

A: Centre-based work

The physical environment of any therapeutic centre plays an important part in establishing a context of safety: each centre feels very much like a home, with a kitchen, bathroom, therapy rooms and sleeping accommodation for those in crisis. The aim has been to create a space in which people can reflect on their experiences, commemorate their dead, and begin to look to the future. Focusing on the implications of experiences for ongoing interpersonal relationships, women and children are offered individual, group and family therapy.

Some of the stories shared describe the tremendous support people have been able to give and receive from one another. However, others reflect the devastating effects the war has had on interpersonal relationships, the sense of fragmentation and discontinuity between their past and present lives. In some situations, the consequences of what has happened may be reversible, but elsewhere they are or seem to be irreversible.

There have been frequent reports of intrusive thoughts, sleep disorders, high levels of anxiety, impulsive behaviour, guilt and loss of interest in life. Suffering is rarely only an individual experience but part of a process in which each person's experience continually influences and is influenced by their interpersonal relationships. Many struggle with difficulties in relating to family members and friends and avoid discussing the past. Others seem almost compelled to repeat their experiences over and over, be this with words or drawings. Shkute, aged fourteen, finds herself locked into reliving the events she witnessed: eleven members of her family were killed, and ten others wounded before her very eyes. Four of those killed were small children. Markya, aged sixty-one, was brutally attacked, and is now severely disabled. She is still haunted by images of those who did not survive the attack, images of her son and daughter-in-law being killed in front of her.

A core aspect of the work is psycho–educational, providing clients with an explanation of the potential physical and emotional effects of trauma on themselves, and practical input on the physical management of anxiety. Taking an ethical, non-neutral position and focusing on cultural rights, the centres provide a refuge for those who want to speak out about being raped and face threats or ostracism from home. Three of the rape cases heard at the International Court of Justice at The Hague were treated within this project. Influenced by work on rape and other forms of family violence elsewhere, the aim has been to help women establish a new way of seeing themselves, of recognizing that they are not to blame, and placing their experience within the wider context of the war (Smith, 1993; Lupton & Gillespie, 1994). Holding on to such experiences alone can have the effect of encapsulating the fear of being exposed, increasing the sense of dislocation and self-blame. For some, talking in a group and hearing others' experiences can reduce their sense of isolation. However, this has had to be paced carefully to avoid negating the women's own experience, which may include powerful feelings of blame.

Whilst group work has been used to reflect on issues related to political violence, it has been more difficult to address family violence in this way. In the UK, most members of psychotherapy groups are strangers to each other: people are helped to make sense of their experience away from the presence of those with whom they usually interact. This is rarely possible in Kosova where participants are likely to be neighbours and even family members. In a recent seminar on group work, run by Gabrielle Rifkind, one counsellor explained how as a woman, talking out about violence may result in being ostracized by one's family or subjected to yet more violence: one is obliged, "to serve all, and to be abused by all, including one's mother-in-law". Rather than trying to stop violence at home, women tend to feel they need to survive violence with honour. There are clear parallels with work in the UK where fear for the safety of those who speak out can paralyse family members and professionals alike. The traditional text's dictum to seek revenge for unjust actions may compound fears that speaking out might result in yet more violence (Berishaj, 2001). This counsellor cannot speak for all women, but she highlights the risks of crossing the boundary of privacy in speaking out against violence.

Putting experiences into words can be enormously therapeutic, but there are also times when stability depends on silence, when memory cannot be restorative (Frosh, 2002): much of what has been experienced may be too frightening to voice. With children in particular, nonverbal methods of working have played an important part of the work, including music, games and drawing. For example, Liridon, aged six, arrived at the centre quite frozen. He was present when his parents and five other family members were killed. He survived by hiding between his grandmother's legs, the blankets concealing him as she was beaten and punched by soldiers. His first drawings were black pictures of houses burning: he used no colour, with the exception of a little red to indicate blood and flames. As he began to feel understood, he was able to use more words to communicate, and his drawings gained greater colour and complexity. For others, drawings have provided a way of expressing feelings which have remained largely "unlanguaged", and the therapy rooms are lined with drawings of tanks, of monsters with guns and idealized houses with flowers.

Studies looking at childhood resilience across a range of stressful situations including family separation, living with significant levels of family disharmony, illness, and political and environmental disasters suggest that three factors contribute to helping children deal with these events: namely access to confirming relationships; the opportunity for self reflection; and access to some area of personal competence (Garmezy & Masden, 1994; Jenkins & Smith, 1990; Gordon et al., 1999; Gorrell Barnes, 1999; Rutter, 1999). As far as possible this is born in mind in working with children, with considerable emphasis on developing a trusting relationship both with centre staff and family members, planning activities that enhance self-competence, and creating opportunities for self-reflection. Linked with this, children have also been helped to think about their survival skills and who they could turn to in any further emergency. As with interventions following disasters elsewhere (Osofsky, 1997), structured exercises like sentence completion, telling a shared story and role-play, have also been used to help children explore their experiences. Throughout, the counsellors have tried to help the children understand that they are valued, that they recognize how much they have been hurt, and that, as children, they have a right not to be hurt. However, unstructured play has also been crucial, and, where possible, a counsellor has tried to stay close enough to listen and respond to what the child is saying or not saying. Even when working individually, the focus has been on relationships, on how past and present patterns of behaviour influence beliefs and behaviours. For example, the rest of the family might be brought into the room with such questions as "if your mummy was here, what would you want her to say to you now?"

Where possible, work with children has been linked to work with families, helping parents and children make sense of their experiences together. Work with Liridon, above, included helping his extended family reach a decision about where he should live. At the outset, there were plans for him to move between various households. Whilst this reflected the love and commitment of the wider family to Liridon, it was extremely unsettling for him. The family were encouraged to question what these changes might mean for him, and he is now settled within one household, and has a greater sense of belonging.

Some mothers have been able to compartmentalize their own distress sufficiently to remain emotionally available to their children: in such cases, parenting has helped them to restore their sense of competence and order in a world that has been disrupted, and provided a way of looking towards the future. For many who attend the centre, however, the level of trauma has been too overwhelming, and neither parents nor children can find a way of fulfilling one another's expectations. In such cases, family work has not been possible, and it has been a relief for parents to know that someone else can share in taking care of their children. For example, parents' own health problems may have left them unable to connect, or intolerant of their children's behaviour at home or their concentration difficulties at school (Altschuler, 1997). Elsewhere, struggles relate to difficulties in separating, particularly when multiple deaths in the family mean that children are parents' or grandparents' only reason for survival.

As members of the same community with first hand experiences of the war, the counsellors are well aware of parallels with their own lives and how trying to forget the past carries the risk of blotting out the very memories which could provide hope. Despite their own sense of urgency to try to "fix things", they have had to recognize this tension and respect the unique pace of each individual and family. Rather than rushing, emphasis has been placed on creating a safe context, both physically and emotionally, in which people can begin to tell, retell, and rethink their stories.

B: Outreach work

It takes a whole village to raise a child ...(and) ... a whole village to destroy a child. [Osofsky, 1997, p. 326]

Although the war has ended, political uncertainty remains, maintaining the sense of fear and instability for Albanian and Serbian Kosovars alike. This is reflected in confusion about community services. In the attempt to limit the negative cycle set into motion by war, considerable emphasis has been placed on outreach work. This operates at four levels: in direct work with families in the community; consultation to schools; liaison with local NGOs and government institutions; and contributing to public awareness campaigns. However, it needs to be acknowledged that the work is largely confined to working with Albanian Kosovars, an issue which will be addressed later.

Firstly, counsellors work with families in the community. This involves seeing whoever is at home at the time of visiting, and could mean working with a small part of the family or extended family groupings. It requires careful negotiation and respect for cultural traditions and power dynamics: even when families were being seen initially in collective centres, it was been important to respect the family's commitment to *Mikpritya*, hospitality, to respect their position as hosts and their need to be in charge of the process. At times complex ethical issues were raised: for example, permission from the male head of the household is necessary before commencing family work, but this has not always been possible, particularly in cases of rape.

Secondly, consultation and training is provided to local schools, with the aim of helping teachers make sense of teaching traumatized children. Until recently, each school had access to a pedagogue with responsibility for children presenting particular difficulties. Despite mounting concern about increased aggression and juvenile delinquency, most of these posts have been terminated in a cost cutting exercise. Teachers are in a unique position: acting "*in loco parentis*", they are often the person to whom children turn in distress, particularly when parents are physically or emotionally unavailable (Altschuler *et al.*, 1999). Added to this, parents may see education as their children's only hope for the future, compounding the pressure the teachers face. Many feel ambivalent and ill equipped to know how to respond, and lack the opportunity to reflect on the meaning this has for their teaching role. Like their pupils, they are likely to have experienced extreme upheaval during the war, and yet find themselves having to cope with a role that far exceeds the job they were trained for.

In parallel with work in the centre, the consultations often involve a psycho–educational component, outlining the physical and psychological consequences of trauma for children and the potential consequences for learning. Schools have also been encouraged to set in place additional support for staff in meeting the increased demands their current teaching presents. Again, working from within has helped in building a sense of trust in the service: counsellors who were previously trained as teachers have played a key role in consultation to schools.

Thirdly, in the absence of a stable infrastructure, the project has made a significant contribution to reconnecting at a wider community level, with the aim of helping to restore the resources and traditions that have sustained communities through troubled times in the past. This includes playing an active role in the Balkan wide Women's Network, and working towards drawing up a provisional legal document to protect women and children from violence. As Kosova is currently being governed by an international force (UNMIK, i.e. United Nations Mission in Kosova), it remains unclear how any such document can be implemented.

Community reconnection has also involved working with government organizations, such as Social Welfare Departments, and international and local NGOs. Informal referral systems have been established, including practical advocacy work and informing aid agencies of those most in need of material assistance. An example of this work includes the experience of Gana, a seventeen-year old girl, referred to the Peya centre by KFOR (Kosovo Force, the international military force that has been stationed in the territory since the NATO military intervention). Seriously wounded, emaciated and unable to speak, she was helped to recover physically and find her voice. With the assistance of UNHCR (United Nations High Commission for Refugees), she was ultimately reunited with the rest of her family and is currently under the care of the local psychiatric hospital.

As demands for services far outweigh the resources available, outreach work takes place at a wider level, through community awareness programs, in newspapers, on the radio, and television. This has helped to broaden the acceptability of acknowledging the psychological difficulties of post-war life, how violence can affect children, and suggesting ways in which parents can help children understand what has been happening around them. The relative anonymity of radio call-in programs has uncovered additional areas of concern, including male rape. Nothing happens in isolation. This work has required considerable networking and relies on the willingness and courage of broadcasting stations and editors to address these issues.

C: Training and staff development

An overarching theme of the project has been the commitment to community work, to facilitate and strengthen community services.

A new mental health and social welfare strategy is currently unfolding. However, until recently, few Kosovars had been trained as mental health professionals. Consequently, training has played a crucial role, and has been aimed at providing core counselling, psychotherapeutic, and consultation skills; at developing an under-standing of the impact of migration and severe trauma on family life; at extending understanding of child development, aggression, and psychological resilience; and at developing skills in assessment and community networking. Particular attention has been paid to helping people dealing with loss and separation, family violence and school related problems, including ways of working individu-ally, with families and in groups. In addition, training has focused on the meaning of the work for the counsellors, in the attempt to help people connect personal and professional learning, and minimize the risks of "burn out".

The training has consisted of a series of short intensive modules, run by mental health professionals from the UK, Israel, and Croatia. The most recent training has placed particular emphasis on networking and strengthening local capacities for working with children and their families. Participants were therefore drawn from the One to One centres, local Social Welfare departments, local NGOs as well as international organizations like the Red Cross.

However, this has been consolidated through ongoing in-service training and supervision run by Albanian counsellors. Despite obvious differences in their experiences in recent times, they share a common language, culture, and a sense of what might be supportive to families in maintaining their sense of cultural and ethnic identity (cf. Falicov, 1998).

Attended by all staff, training sessions have focused on team building, creating an opportunity to share ideas, and addressing the professional isolation and uncertainty of working in difficult and complex territories. Discussions often return to dealing with the fear and anger evoked by certain cases, and clients' wish to know about the counsellors' own experiences during the war. Inevitably, there is much that may not be shared and we have all had to take decisions about when it might or might not feel safe to talk. Issues of how to harness influences in a therapist's or counsellor's own life divide professional opinion. There may be times when the issues triggered by particular families may feel overwhelming: bearing witness to events that touch personal experience can mean that the counsellors are at greater risk of secondary traumatization, raising ethical issues about how to pace personal and professional issues in training. However, understanding personal experience can be a tremendous support, aiding therapeutic skill, and helping to extend one's understanding family patterns (Gorrell Barnes et al., 2000; Hildebrand, 1998; Shamai, 1998). With this in mind, we have tried to ensure that there is access to support outside of training sessions and that discussions return to a more cognitive understanding, to theoretical constructs, and the implications for clinical work.

In many ways, the Kosovar counsellors face a most difficult task. Like their clients, ethnic prejudice has limited their education and working opportunities. They too were separated from their families during the war and experienced displacement as refugees. One counsellor talked about walking across rugged mountains for three days, carrying with her the image of her house being burnt. Some returned home to find their whole family, including their dog, had survived. But others came home to hear that a brother, sister, parent or child had died.

Yet, they are now in a position of supporting others and helping others to deal with their anger and despair. In situations of ongoing uncertainty, such work can provide some measure of control, mediating personal hardship (Shamai, 1998). However, it can also bring to the fore personal and professional confusion, vulnerability and fear. The counsellors are often stopped on the street and in the shops, with people wanting advice, to talk or cry. Unavoidably, they are part of the community, and yet their roles caste them somewhat outside, into an expert position. Surrounded by tremendous suffering, initially, the staff decided that the centres needed to be open all the time. Although this worked well enough initially, as the impact of the work became increasingly overwhelming, this could not be sustained. However, it was a struggle to recognize that caring for others over such a sustained period of time required caring for oneself as a counsellor: only after considerable consultation was an agreement reached to close the centres over weekends.

Each centre has a manager with clear responsibility for the budget, planning the program and ensuring accurate records were being kept. However clinical supervision is largely peer based. In a context in which authority has so badly been misused, issues related to management and authority have at times been problematic. Opting for peer supervision has in many ways been an attempt to ensure all staff retained their own voice. Instead, Albanian counsellors have continued to act as mentors and supervisors, with additional consultation from UK based staff. Although this has worked relatively well, in situations of uncertainty, feedback is crucial. There have been times where the absence of a local supervisor has compounded the emotional strain of the work and a decision has recently been taken to appoint a local counsellor as clinical supervisor.

Finally, staff support is not only about words: as the consequences of trauma may live on at a non-verbal and physiological level (Williams & Banyard, 1999), the counsellors have found their own unique ways of supporting one another—by singing together at the end of each day, be they Kosovan songs, international pop, or opera.

The way forward

The war has ended but much remains unresolved. Kosova is still being governed by the international UNMIK administration.

Following recent elections there have been positive moves towards forming a national government, with wide ranging plans for a more coherent mental health service. However, events such as the recent unrest in Macedonia and the ongoing war crimes trial in The Hague continue to create an environment of insecurity for Serbs and Albanians alike. Reprisals are a tragic reality and Serbs still living in Kosova are fearful for their safety. Inevitably, there are questions about the potential effectiveness of any psychosocial programme in minimizing the consequences of violence. In concluding the paper, we will discuss the way forward, highlighting how cultural differences have impacted on some of the core aspects of the work.

i) Gender and the role of men

The project's aims state the need to address the impact of violence on women and children, children including both boys and girls. All the counsellors and all four authors of this paper are women. With the exception of assistance in establishing and funding the project and some outside trainers, men play a limited professional role within the project. Outside of some family work and consultation to teachers, they are relatively absent as clients as well.

This is important as war constructs gendered roles in oppositional terms—with men as violence and action oriented, and women as supportive, compassionate, and victims. Boys and girls have been walking the streets, surrounded by KFOR tanks, with armed male soldiers at every corner. Throughout the conflict, it has been the figures of women and children that have been flashed across our TV screens to represent the horrors of war. As victims and the repository of traditional and family honour, it is the women who are required to fulfil moral codes so that their rape becomes the ultimate betrayal of both family and community. Although the impact of the war on women should not be underestimated, they are invariably caste as victims, obscuring women's roles in the process.

Within the project, part of the difficulty has been about engaging men in therapy. Many feel a strong sense of responsibility and shame for what has happened to their family, and knowing someone else is able to support their wife and children can be an enormous relief. The downside is that where they are not included, they have been left to deal with their concerns alone, adding to the isolation they experience. Their absence is particularly worrying in working with couple violence, as it excludes an awareness of the voice of men, and the sense of sadness and shame that may be experienced by the person who lifts their fist to hit. Moreover, returning women to a context in which there has been little change to the cycle of violence maintains the message that those with the least power, women and children, are responsible for stopping the violence. It also excludes the voice of men who may be worried about the way in which women deal with anger towards others in the family.

This is one of the tensions we have struggled with as a group, both in training sessions, and in case discussions. Some of our debates have included sharing our differing beliefs, for example, the belief that given more opportunity, men would refuse to engage in what would be seen as "women's work", or that women would be unlikely to trust sufficiently to talk in the presence of men. Despite this ambivalence, there are increased initiatives to engage with men's experiences more fully. Such dilemmas are not confined to Kosova, and remain questions for women's refuge movements elsewhere as well. The issues are complex and we have had to recognize how our debates reflect culturally constructed ideas about power, anger and protection.

ii) Knowledge and cultural diversity

In a context dominated by prejudice and oppression, we have needed to think carefully about the meaning of translation. At one level, translation has been about language: in collaborating in writing this paper it has meant us having to find words in English that convey as much of what the concepts mean in Albanian as possible, and having to trust the translator with assisting us in that task. Trust has also been important at a second level, in helping people put what has been experienced into words, and recognizing both the value and the risks this might hold. So too, we have needed to find a way of trusting one another to confront the ethics of transferring knowledge gained in one context to another. To teach what has been learned about trauma, gender, and psychological resilience in the UK or Albania as a "truth" would be misleading, ethnocentric or even oppressive, potentially compounding the sense of dislocation and disconnection. But to withhold these ideas could be equally unethical. For example, in the UK, it has become increasingly acceptable for children to talk about their feelings in the presence of their families. However, it is unusual for Kosovar families to discuss children's psychological reactions to events openly. There are also cultural taboos against speaking about the dead in certain ways, challenging current Eurocentric models of helping children make sense of what they have seen and heard. Respect for cultural difference has been a cornerstone of the work, but this can be complex when some of the ideas that do not appear to fit are the very ideas we feel transcend cultural difference.

No culture is static and ideas about childhood and the family evolve in response to new situations. However, it is at times of crisis when so much has been lost that we turn more readily to predictable patterns of relating: any new challenge can be seen as a threat to known and trusted ways of being. On the one hand, the counsellors are well aware of local cultural traditions. However, on the other hand, exposure to new ideas about psychological development, the meaning of psychotherapeutic help and gender have inevitably altered their views, potentially moving them into a more marginal position in relation to clients and their own social context.

As both trainers and local counsellors, we have learned a great deal from listening to one another and exploring new ways of intervening that could be helpful. To do this, we have needed to find a way of acknowledging our differences, and thinking about how those differences impact on our working together. But we have also needed to explore what resonates for each of us, to explore what it is that we share, rather than trying to seek simple resolutions. We have dealt with this by retaining cultural diversity and the relativity of knowledge as a central theme (Altschuler, 2001; Dwedi *et al.*, 1999; Falicov, 1998). It is difficult to emphasize sufficiently the overwhelming atmosphere of personal, political and professional uncertainty. As trainers, this can evoke the temptation to move towards premature certainty in the hope of reaching clarity and coherence, perhaps idealizing what could be done elsewhere, by "experts". In the context of displacement, questions about external input are complex. Whilst the training and resources within the UK may provide a framework for thinking about traumatic experiences, it has been important for us all to hold on to recognizing that few guidelines to this work exist. Yes, there is an increased literature on trauma intervention, in such places as Israel (Gal, 1997; Ayalon, 1998) and Croatia (Adjukovic & Adjukovic, 1998) but the "treatment packages" for this work is being written by the Kosovars themselves.

Final comments

Psychological professionals are often called upon in their roles as clinicians in dealing with victims of violence: important questions remain of how and whether we can contribute more to addressing conflict prior to escalation. Cairns (2001) has argued that truth commissions are more likely to succeed where some form of political consensus has been reached, as in South Africa. The traditional *Kanuni* text prescribes the need for reconciliation, but to date this has only been invoked in terms of addressing disagreements between Kosovar families and clans. Within the project there have been some attempts to work with ethnic minorities outside of the centre, with the Roma, the Daravich, and even Serbs. However, the conflict is far from over and such work remains very risky. The problem about the past is that it is not in the past at all: the push for revenge is still strong. Many counsellors feel it is too soon: time may heal, but they question whether they and their clients have had enough time.

Undoubtedly, setting up the "One to One" centres has achieved a great deal in altering peoples' lives, in training mental health professionals and contributing to public awareness about the psychological impact of violence on the lives of men, women, and children. But, has this been sufficient? What about reconciliation?

Six year old Liridon's drawings have changed from scenes of aggression to those reflecting other aspects of family life. He easily becomes fearful and needs reassurance from the family who now parent him, from his teachers and counsellors. However, he is also more able to settle at school, to play, and relate to peers. In a modest way, this work has contributed to increasing his family's understanding of the irreversible way in which violence has shaped their lives.

Political resolution is crucial, but this cannot happen in isolation: mental health and impaired social functioning needs to be addressed to return the Kosova region to a stable and productive environment. The work has offered both clients and staff a different way of experiencing themselves, in the attempt to link their past and present lives. How the story evolves will ultimately be linked with the wider context of Kosova, *pas lufta*, after the war.

Acknowledgement

The authors wish to acknowledge their gratitude to the Directors of "One to One" David Altschuler and Rita Eker for making this project possible.

Note

1. The authors have chosen to use the Albanian-sounding spelling of Kosovo.

REFERENCES

Abramson, H. (2000). The Esh kodesh of Rabbi Kalonimus Kalmish Shapiro: a Hasidic treatise on communal trauma from the holocaust. *Transcultural Psychiatry, 37*(3): 321–335.

Abt, T. (1983). *Progress Without Loss of Soul. Towards a Wholistic Approach to Modernization Planning.* B. L. Mathews (Trans.). Wilmette, Illinois: Chiron, 1989.

Adjukovic, M., & Adjukovic, D. (1998). Impact of displacement in the psychological well being of children. *International Review of Psychiatry, 10*: 186–195.

Ager, A. (1994). Mental Health Issues in Refugee Populations: a Review. Working paper for the Harvard Center for the Study of Culture and Medicine, Harvard Medical School, Department of Social Medicine.

Ager, A. (1999). *Refugees: Perspectives on the Experience of Forced Migration.* London: Continuum.

Agger, I. (1994). *The Blue Room.* London: Zed Books.

Aitken, S. C., & Herman, T. (1997). Gender, power and crib geography: transitional spaces and potential places. *Gender, Place and Culture, 4*(1): 63–88.

Alexander, P. (1987). *Racism, Resistance and Revolution.* London: Bookmarks.

293

All Equal Under the Act. (1991). Sheila MacDonald, Race Equality Unit.

Altschuler, J. (1997). *Working with Chronic Illness*. Basingstoke: Macmillan.

Altschuler, J. (2001). On working in Kosova. *Context*, *54*: 21–23.

Altschuler, J., Dale, B., & Sass Booth, A. (1999). Supporting children when a parent is physically ill. *Educational Psychology in Practice*, *15*(1): 25–32.

American Psychiatric Association. (1994). *Diagnostic and Statistical Manual of Mental Disorders* (4th edn). Washington, DC: APA.

Andersen, T. (2001). A Collaboration, of some called psychotherapy; bonds filled of expression, and expression filled of meaning. Chapter to appear in a Norwegian book on psychotherapy (Helge Ronnestad, Ed.).

Anderson, H., & Goolishian, H. (1988). Human systems as linguistic systems. *Family Process*, *27*: 371–393.

Appadurai, A. (1996). Sovereignty without territoriality. Notes for a postnational geography. In: P. Yager (Ed.), *Geography of Identity*. Ann Arbor: University of Michigan Press.

Arroyo, W., & Eth, S. (1996). Post-traumatic stress disorder and other stress reactions. In: R. J. Apfel & B. Simon (Eds.), *Minefields in their Hearts: Mental Health of Children in War and Communal Violence* (pp. 52–74). New Haven: Yale University Press.

Ayalon, O. (1998). Community healing for children traumatized by war. *International Review of Psychiatry*, *10*: 224–233.

Bachelard, G. (1958). *The Poetics of Space. The Classic Look at how we Experience Intimate Places*. Maria Jolas (Trans.). Boston: Beacon Press, 1969.

Bagilishya, D. (2000). Mourning and recovery from trauma: in Rwanda, tears flow within. *Transcultural Psychiatry*, *37*(3): 337–353.

Banyard, V. L., & Williams, L. M. (1998). *Trauma and Memory*. London: Sage.

Bard, M., & Sangrey, D. (1979). *The Crime Victim's Book*. New York: Basic Books.

Bateson, G. (1979). *Mind and Nature*. New York: E. P. Dutton.

Bat-Zion, N., & Levy-Shiff, R. (1993). Children in war: stress and coping reactions under the threat of the scud missile attacks and the effects of proximity. In: L. Lewis & N. Fox (Eds.), *Effects of War and Violence in Children* (pp. 143–161). Hillsdale, NJ: Erlbaum.

Bauman, G. (1996). *Contesting Culture: Discourses of Identity in Multi-ethnic London*. Cambridge: Cambridge University Press.

Beiser, M. (1994). *Longitudinal Study of Vietnamese Refugee Adaptation*. Toronto: Clarke Institute of Psychiatry.

Beiser, M., Dion, R., Gotowiec, A., Hyman, I., & Vu, N. (1995). Immigrant and refugee children in Canada. *Canadian Journal of Psychiatry, 40*: 67–71.

Benedek, E. (1984). The silent scream: counter-transference reactions to victims. *American Journal of Social Psychiatry, 4*: 49–52.

Bentovim, A. (1992). *Trauma Organised Systems*. London: Karnac.

Berishaj, A. (2001). Violence following violence. *Psychosocial Notebook— IOM, 2*: 79–88.

Bertrand, D. (1998). Refugees and migrants, migrants and refugees. An ethnological approach. *International Migration, 36*(1): 107–113.

Bhabha, H. K. (1994). *The Location of Culture*. London: Routledge.

Biernacki, P., & Waldorf, D. (1981). Snowball sampling: problems and techniques of chain referral sampling. *Sociological Methods and Research, 10*: 141–163.

Bion, W. R. (1961). *Experiences in Groups*. London: Tavistock, 1968.

Bion, W. R. (1965). *Tranformations*. London: William Heinemann.

Bisson, J., Jenkins, P., Alexander, J., & Bannister, C. (1997). Randomised controlled trial of psychological debriefing for victims of acute burn trauma. *British Journal of Psychiatry, 171*: 78–81.

Blackwell, D. (1997). Holding, containing and bearing witness: the problem of helpfulness in encounters in torture survivors. *Journal of Social Work Practice, 11*(2): 81–89.

Bloch, A. (1999). Carrying out a survey of refugees: some methodological considerations and guidelines. *Journal of Refugee Studies, 12*(4): 367–383.

Bloch, A. (1999). Refugees in the job market: a case of unused skills in the British economy. In: A. Bloch & C. Levy (Eds.). *Refugees, Citizenship and Social Policy in Europe* (pp. 187–210). London: MacMillan Press.

Bloom, S. (1997). *Creating Sanctuary*. London: Routledge.

BMA, Ethics Open document 27.10.01: Access to health care for asylum seekers.

Boscolo, L., & Bertrando, P. (1992). The reflexive loop of past, present and future in systemic therapy and consultation. *Family Process, 31*: 119–130.

Boston, M., & Szur, R. (1983). *Psychotherapy with Severely Deprived Children*. London: Routledge.

Bowen, N. (2000). Trade and livelihood strategies in post-conflict Zambezia province, Mozambqiue. PhD Thesis, Department of Anthropology, and The Gender Institute, London School of Economics, University of London.

Bowlby, J. (1973). *Attachment and Loss, Volume 2. Separation, Anxiety and Anger*. London: Pelican Books, 1985.

Bowlby, J. (1979). *The Making and Breaking of Affectional Bonds*. London: Tavistock.

Bowlby, J. (1988a). *A Secure Base: Parent–Child Attachment and Healthy Human Development*. New York: Basic Books.

Bowlby, J. (1988b). *A Secure Base: Clinical Applications of Attachment Theory*. London: Routledge.

Boyarin, J. (1991). *Polish Jews in Exile: the Ethnography of Memory*. Bloomington: Indiana University Press.

Boyd-Franklin, N. (1989). *Black Families in Therapy—a Multi-systems Approach*. New York: Guilford Press.

Bracken, P. J., & Petty, C. (Eds.) (1998). *Rethinking the Trauma of War*. London: Free Association Books.

Bragin, M. (2001). The role of early aggressive phantasy in the genesis of the sequelae of war, state, and community violence: a cross-cultural perspective. PhD Thesis, New York University.

Brah, A. (1996). *Cartographies of Diaspora*. London: Routledge.

Breckenridge, C. A., Bhabha, H. K., & Pollock, S. (Eds.) (2000). *Cosmopolitanism: a Special Issue of Public Culture*. Durham, NC: Duke University Press.

Britton, R. (1995). Psychic reality and belief. *The International Journal of Psycho-Analysis, 76*: 19–23.

Bruck, P. (1992). Crisis as spectacle: tabloid news and the politics of outrage. In: M. Raboy & B. Dagenais (Eds.), *Media, Crisis and Democracy*. London: Sage Publications.

Bruner, J. (1990). *Acts of Meaning*. Cambridge: Harvard University Press.

Brunner, J. (2000). Will, desire and experience: etiology and ideology in the German and Austrian Medical Discourse on war neuroses, 1914–1922. *Transcultural Psychiatry, 37*(3): 295–320.

Bulloch, J., & Morris, H. (1993). *No Friends but the Mountains: The Tragic History of the Kurds*. London: Penguin.

Burck, C., & Daniel, G. (1995). *Gender and Family Therapy*. London: Karnac.

Burnett, A., & Peel, M. (2001). Health needs of asylum seekers and refugees. *British Medical Journal, 322*: 544–547.

Burr, V. (1995). *An Introduction to Social Constructionism*. London: Routledge.

Cairns, E. (2001). War and peace. *The Psychologist, 14*(6): 292–293.

Camden LEA. (2000). A report on: Meeting the Educational Needs of Somali Pupils in Camden Schools.

Cannon, W. (1914). The emergency function of the adrenal medulla in pain and the major emotions. *American Journal of Physiology*, 3: 356–372.

Carr, A. (2000). *Family Therapy: Concepts, Process and Practice*. Chichester: Wiley.

Caruth, C. (1996). *Unclaimed Experience. Trauma, Narrative and History*. Baltimore: The Johns Hopkins University Press.

Chauvenet, A., Despret, V., & Lemaire, I. M. (1996). *Clinique de la Reconstruction. Une Expérience avec des Réfugiés en ex-Yougoslavie*. Paris: L'Harmattan.

Children Act. (1989). HMSO, 1991.

Clifford, J. (1986). The partial truths. In: J. Clifford & G. E. Marcus (Eds.), *Writing Culture: The Poetic and Politics of Ethnography*. London: University of California Press.

Cronen, V., Pearce, W., & Tomm, K. (1985). A dialectical view of personal change. In: K. Gergen & K. Davis (Eds.), *The Social Construction of the Person*. New York: Springer-Verlag.

Crossley, M. L. (2000). *Introducing Narrative Psychology. Self, Trauma and the Construction of Meaning*. Milton Keynes: Open University Press.

Cuisenier, J. (1991). *Ethnologie de l'Europe*. Paris: Presses Universitaires de France.

Cummins, J. (1984). *Bilingualism and Special Education: Issues in Assessment and Pedagogy*. Clevedon: Multilingual Matters.

CVS Consultants. (1999). *A Shattered World—the Mental Health Needs of Refugees and Newly Arrived Communities*. London: CVS.

Davids, F. (1996). Frantz Fanon and the struggle for inner freedom. *Free Associations*, 38/6(2): 205–234.

Davis, M. (2000). *Magical Urbanism: Latinos Reinvent the US City*. London: Verso.

De Berry, J. (2000). Life After Loss: An Anthropological Study of Post-War Recovery. In Teso, East Uganda, with special reference to young people. PhD Thesis, Department of Anthropology, London School of Economics, University of London.

De Jong, J., & Clarke, L. (Eds.) (1996). *Mental Health of Refugees*. Geneva: World Health Organization/UNCHR.

De Zulueta, F. (1993). *The Traumatic Roots of Destructiveness: From Pain to Violence*. London: Whurr Publishers.

Dona, G., & Berry, J. W. Refugee acculturation and re-acculturation. In: A. Ager (Ed.), *Refugees: Perspectives on the Experience of Forced Migration* (pp. 169–195). London: Continuum.

Donaldson, M. A., & Gardner, R. Jr. (1982). Stress responses in women after childhood incest. Paper presented at the Annual Meeting of the American Psychiatric Association, Toronto, Ontario, Canada May 15th–21st, 1982.

Dowling, E., & Osborne, E. (1995). *The Family and the School*. London: Routledge.

Dwedi, K. *et al.* (1999). Sewing the seeds of cultural competence. *Context*, 44: 21–26.

Dworkin, R. (1986). *Law's Empire*. London: Fontana.

Eisenbruch, M. (1990). Cultural bereavement and homesickness. In: S. Fisher & C. Cooper (Eds.), *On the Move: The Psychology of Change and Transition* (pp. 191–205). Chichester: John Wiley.

Eisenbruch, M. (1991). From post-traumatic stress disorder to cultural bereavement: diagnosis of Southeast Asian refugees. *Social Sciences and Medicine*, 33: 673–680.

Ekblad, S., Ginsburg, B., Jansson, B., & Levi, L. (1986). Psychosocial and psychiatric aspects of refugee adaptation and care in Sweden. In: A. Marsella, T. Bornemann, S. Ekblad & J. Orley (Eds.), *Amidst Peril and Pain: The Mental Well-being of the World's Refugees* (pp. 275–292). Washington DC: American Psychological Association.

Engels, F. (1934). *The Dialectics of Nature*. Moscow: Progress Publishers.

Enriquez, E. (1980). Ulisse, Edipo e la Sfinge. Il formatore tra Scilla e Cariddi.. In: R. Speziale-Bagliacca (Ed.), *Formazione e Percezione Psicoanalitica* (pp. 111–132). Milano: Feltrinelli.

Falicov, C. J. (1998). *Latino Families in Therapy*. New York: Guilford.

Feldman, A. (1991). *Formations of Violence: Narratives of Body and Terror in Northern Ireland*. Chicago: University of Chicago Press.

Field, T. (1985). Attachment as psychobiological attunement: being on the same wavelength. In: M. Rette & T. Field (Eds.), *The Psychobiology of Attachment and Separated*. New York: Academic Press.

Fischer, A., & Good, G. (1997). Men and psychotherapy: an investigation of alexithymia, intimacy, and masculine gender roles. *Psychotherapy*, 34: 160–170.

Fordred, L. (1999). Taming chaos. The dynamics of narrative and conflict. In: *Track Two*, July, pp. 11–15.

Fox, M. (2002). Finding a way through: from mindlessness to minding. In: Renos K. Papadopoulos (Ed.), *Therapeutic Care for Refugees. No Place Like Home*. London: Karnac, Tavistock Clinic Series.

Framework for the Assessment of Children in Need and their Families. (2000). D. H.

Freire, P. (1996). *Pedagogy of the Oppressed*. London: Penguin.

Freire, P. (1998). *Pedagogy of Freedom. Ethics, Democracy, and Civic Courage*. London: Rowman & Littlefield.

Freud, S., & Breuer, G. (1955). *Studies in Hysteria*. In: *Standard Edition of the Complete Psychological Works of Sigmund Freud, Volume 2*. London: Hogarth.

Freud, S, (1917). *Mourning and Melancholia*. S.E., *14*. London: Hogarth Press.

Freud, S. (1920). *Beyond the Pleasure Principle*. S.E., *18*. London: Hogarth Press.

Freud, S. (1924). The loss of reality in neurosis and psychosis. S.E., *19*. London: Hogarth Press.

Freud, S. (1926). *Inhibitions, Symptoms and Anxiety*. S.E., *20*. London: Hogarth Press.

Friedman, M., & Jaranson, J. (1992). The applicability of the PTSD concept to refuges. In: A. J. Marsella *et al.* (Eds.), *Amidst Peril and Pain. The Mental Health and Social Wellbeing of the World's Refugees* (pp. 207–228). Washington DC: American Psychological Association.

Frosh, S. (2002). Knowing more than we can say. In: D. Pare & G. Larner (Ed.), *Critical Knowledge and Practice in Psychology and Therapy*. London: Haworth Press.

Frost, R. (1955). *Selected Poems*. Harmondworth: Penguin.

Gal, R. (1997). *Helping the Helpers*. London: UKJAID publication.

Garland, C. (1998). *Understanding Trauma* (pp. 9–31). London: Duckworth.

Garland, C., Hume, F., & Majid, S. (2002). Remaking connections. Refugees and the development of "emotional capital" in therapy groups. In: Renos K. Papadopoulos (Ed.), *Therapeutic Care for Refugees. No Place Like Home*. London: Karnac, Tavistock Clinic Series.

Garmezy, N., & Masden, A. S. (1994). Chronic adversities. In: M. Rutter, E. Taylor & L. Hersov (Eds.), *Child and Adolescent Psychiatry*. Oxford: Blackwell Scientific Publications.

Gedo, J. E., & Goldberg, A. (1973). *Models of the Mind. A Psychoanalytic Theory*. Chicago: University of Chicago Press.

Gergen, K. (1992). Social construction in question. *Human Systems, 3*: 163–182.

Gibb, E., & Young, L. (1998). Trauma and grievance. In: C. Garland (Ed.), *Understanding Trauma*. London: Duckworth, Tavistock Series.

Giddens, A. (1991). *Modernity and Self Identity*. Oxford: Blackwells.

Gilligan, R. (2000). Adversity, resilience and young people: the protective value of positive school and spare time experiences.

Children and Society, 14(1): 37–47.

Gjecov, S. (1989). *The Code of Leke Dukagjini.* New York: Gjonlekaj Publishing Company.

Glenn, C. (1995). Marx-syst-emic connections. *Context,* 23: 19–20.

Glenn, C. (1999a). Letter to the editor. *Journal of Family Therapy,* 21(4): 444–445.

Glenn, C. (Ed.) (1999b). The political and social context of systemic practice. *Context,* 45, October, 1999.

Gold, S. J. (1992). *Refugee Communities: A Comparative Field Study.* New York: Sage.

Goldner, V. (1985). Feminism and family therapy. *Family Process,* 24: 31–47.

Goldner, V., Penn, P., Sheinberg, M. & Walker, G. (1990). Love and violence: gender paradoxes in volatile attachments. *Family Process,* 29(4): 343–364.

Goodwin-Gill, G. S. (1996). *The Refugee in International Law* (2nd edn). Oxford: Oxford University Press.

Gordon, N., Farberow, N. L., & Maida, C. A. (1999). *Children and Disasters.* New York: Brunner Mazel.

Gorman, J. (2000). *Understanding Post-Traumatic Stress Disorder.* London: Mind Publications.

Gorrell Barnes, G. (1999). Operationalizing the uncertain: some clinical reflections. *Journal of Family Therapy,* 21(2): 145–154.

Gorrell Barnes, G., Down, G., & McCann, D. (2000). *Systemic Supervision.* London: Jessica Kingsley.

Grinberg, L., & Grinberg, R. (1989). *Psychoanalytic Perspectives on Migration and Exile.* New Haven, Connecticut: Yale University Press.

Hacking, I. (1999). *The Social Construction of What?* London: Harvard University Press.

Hale, R., & Sinason, V. (1994). *Treating Survivors of Satanist Abuse.* V. Sinason (Ed.). London: Routledge.

Hall, S. (1996). Who needs identity? In: S. Hall & P. du Gay (Ed.), *Questions of Cultural Identity.* London: Sage.

Hardy, K. (1990). The theoretical myth of sameness: a critical issue in family therapy training and treatment. In: G. Saba, B. Karrer & K. Hardy (Eds.), *Minorities and Family Therapy.* New York: Haworth Press.

Hartman, C., & Burgess, A. (1985). Illness-related post-traumatic disorder. In: C. Figley (Ed.), *Trauma and its Wake* (pp. 338–355). New York: Brunner/Mazel.

Hathaway, J. C. (1991). *The Law of Refugee Status*. Markhams, Ontario: Butterworths.

Heidegger, M. (1962). *Being and Time*. J. MacQuarrie & E. Robinson (Trans.). New York: Harper and Row.

Herman, J. (1992). *Trauma and Recovery. The Aftermath of Violence: From Domestic Abuse to Political Terror*. New York: Basic Books.

Herman, J. (1994). *Trauma and Recovery: From Domestic Abuse to Political Terror* (2nd edn). London: Pandora.

Hildebrand, J. (1998). *Bridging the Gap*. London: Karnac Books.

Homer. (1725). *The Odyssey*. A. Pope (Trans.). London: Grant Richards, 1903.

Homer. (1932) *The Odyssey*. T. E. Shaw [T. E. Lawrence] (Trans.). Gloucester: Alan Sutton, 1986.

Homer. (1946). *The Odyssey*. E. V. Rieu (Trans.). Harmondsworth: Penguin, 1978.

Homer. (1996). *The Odyssey*. R. Fagles (Trans.). New York: Viking Penguin.

Homer. (2000). *The Odyssey*. S. Lombardo (Trans.). New York: Hackett.

Honeyford, R. (2001). Now they are agreeing with everything I said. *Daily Telegraph*, July 15th, 2001.

Horowitz, D. (1999). *Essential Papers on Post-Traumatic Stress Disorder*. New York: New York UP.

Houzel, D. (1996). The family envelope and what happens when it is torn. *The International Journal of Psycho-Analysis*, 77(5): 901–912.

Janoff-Bulman, R. (1985). The aftermath of victimization: rebuilding shattered assumptions. In: C. Figley (Ed.), *Trauma and its Wake, Volume 1. The Study and Treatment of Post Traumatic Stress Disorder* (pp. 15–35). New York: Brunner/Mazel.

Jenkins, J. (1991). Intervention with violence and abuse in families. *Australia and New Zealand Journal of Family Therapy*, 12(4): 186–195.

Jenkins, J., & Smith, M. A. (1990). Factors protecting children living in disharmonious families: maternal reports. *American Academy of Child and Adolescent Psychiatry*, 26: 60–69.

Joseph, S., & Yule, W. (1997). *Post-Traumatic Stress Disorder. A Psychosocial Perspective and Treatment*. London: Wiley.

Joseph, S. A., Williams, R. M., & Yule, W. (1997). Normal and abnormal reactions to trauma. In: S. A. Joseph, R. M. Williams & W. Yule (Eds.), *Understanding Post-Traumatic Stress: A Psychosocial Perspective on PTSD and Treatment* (pp. 5–33). Chichester: Wiley.

Journal of Family Therapy. (1997). *Psychoanalysis and Systemic Approaches*, 19(3).

Kadare, I. (1997). *The Three Arched Bridge*. New York: Arcade Publishing.

Kaiser, T. (1999). Living in Limbo: Insecurity and the settlement of Sudanese refugees in N. Uganda. PhD Thesis, Insitute of Social and Cultural Anthropology, University of Oxford.

Kalsched, D. (1996). *The Inner World of Trauma. Archetypal Defences of the Personal Spirit*. London: Routledge.

Keane, T. M. (1996). Ethnocultural considerations in the assessment of PTSD. In: A. J. Marsella *et al.* (Eds.), *Ethnocultural Aspects of Post-Traumatic Stress Disorder*. Washington DC: American Psychological Association.

Keeney, B. (1983). *Aesthetics of Change*. New York: Guilford Press.

Kibreab, G. (1999). Revisiting the debate on people, place, identity and displacement. *Journal of Refugee Studies*, 12: 384–410.

Kierkegaard, S. (1957). *The Concept of Dread*. W. Lowrie (Trans.). Princeton: Princeton University Press.

Kings Fund Publication. (1999). *The Health of Refugees—A Guide for GPs*. London: Kings Fund.

Klain, E. (1992). *Psychology and Psychiatry of a War*. Zagreb: University of Zagreb.

Klein, M. (1927). Criminal tendencies in normal children. In: M. Klein (Ed.), *The Writings of Melanie Klein, Volume I: Love, Guilt and Reparation and Other Works, 1921–1945* (pp. 170–186). New York: The Free Press, 1975.

Klein, M. (1928). Early stages of the Oedipus conflict. In: M. Klein (Ed.), *The Writings of Melanie Klein, Volume I: Love, Guilt and Reparation and Other Works, 1921–1945* (pp. 186–199). New York: The Free Press, 1975.

Klein, M. (1940). *Mourning and its Relation to Manic-Depressive States* [reprinted in *Love, Guilt and Reparation, and Other Works, 1921–1945*. London: Hogarth Press, 1975].

Knudsen, J. Chr. *Vietnamese Survivors: Process Involved in Refugee Coping and Adaptation* (The Migration Project). Bergen University: Department of Social Anthropology.

Kristal-Andersson, B. (2000). *Psychology of the Refugee, the Immigrant and their Children. Development of a Conceptual Framework and Application to Psychotherapeutic and Related Support Work*. University of Lund.

Kunz, E. F. (1981). Exile and resettlement: refugee theory. *International Migration Review*, 15: 42–51.

LaCapra, D. (2000). *Writing History, Writing Trauma*. Baltimore: The Johns Hopkins University Press.

Lafontaine, A. (2001). After the exile: displacements and suffering in Kosovo. *Psychosocial Notebook (IOM)*, 2: 53–78.

Laing, R. D. (1960). *The Divided Self*. London: Tavistock.

Lebowitz, L., & Newman, E. (1996). The role of cognitive–affective themes in the assessment and treatment of trauma reactions. *Clinical Psychology and Psychotherapy*, 3(3): 196–207.

Lee, D. A., Scragg, P., & Turner, S. (2001). The role of shame and guilt in traumatic events: a clinical model shame-based and guilt-based PTSD. *British Journal of Medical Psychology*, 74(4): 451–466.

Lerner, M. J. K. (1980). *The Belief in a Just World*. New York: Plenum Press.

Leupnitz, D. (1988). *The Family Interpreted: Feminist Theory in Clinical Practice*. New York: Basic Books.

Littlewood, R., & Lipsedge, M. (1997). *Aliens and Alienists: Ethnic Minorities and Psychiatry*. London: Taylor and Francis.

Loizos, P. (1981). *The Heart Grown Bitter: A Chronicle of Cypriot Refugees*. Cambridge: Cambridge University Press.

Loizos, P. (2000). Are refugees social capitalists? In: S. Baron, J. Field & T. Schuller (Eds.), *Social Capital: Critical Perspectives* (pp. 124–141). Oxford: Oxford University Press.

Loizos, P. (n.d.). "Argaki's refugees twenty-five years later". Typescript, obtainable from the author on request. This chapter has been published in Greek for a recent edition of Loizos, 1981. p.loizos@lse.ac.uk .

Losi, N., Passerini, L., & Salvatici, S. (Eds.) (2001). *Archives of Memory. Supporting Traumatized Communities Through Narration and Remembrance, Psychosocial Notebook, Volume 2, October, 2001*. Geneva: International Organization for Migration.

Losi, N. (2000). Understanding the needs of the displaced: some elements on the Kosovo case. *Psychosocial Notebook*, 1: 11–20.

Losi, N. (2000a). *Vite Altrove. Migrazione e Disagio Psichico*. Milano: Feltrinelli.

Losi, N. (Ed.) (2000b). *Psychosocial and Trauma Response in War-Torn Societies. The Case of Kosovo, Psychosocial Notebook, Volume 1*. Geneva: IOM.

Losi, N. (2002). Some assumptions on psychological trauma interventions in post-conflict communities. Chapter in this book.

Lovelock, J. (2000). *Gaia. A New Look at Life on Earth*. Oxford: Oxford University Press.

Lupton, C., & Gillespie, T. (1994). *Working with Violence*. London: McMillan.

Mackinnon, L., & Miller, D. (1987). The new epistomology and the Milan approach: feminist and sociopolitical considerations. *Journal of Marital and Family Therapy*, 13(2): 139–155.

Malkki, L. (1995). *Purity and Exile: Violence, Memory and National Cosmology Among the Hutu Refugees in Tanzania*. Chicago: University of Chicago Press.

Manson, S. (1997). Cross-cultural and multiethnic assessment of trauma. In: J. Wilson & T. Keane (Eds.). *Assessing Psychological Trauma and PTSD*. New York and London: The Guilford Press.

Marsella, A. J. (1992). Ethno–cultural diversity and the international refugee. Challenges for the global community. In: A. J. Marsella *et al.* (Eds.), *Amidst Peril and Pain. The Mental Health and Social Wellbeing of the World's Refugees*. Washington DC: American Psychological Association.

Marsella, A., Bornemann, T., Ekblad, S., & Orley, J. (1994). *Amidst Peril and Pain: The Mental Well-being of the World's Refugees*. Washington DC: American Psychological Association.

Marsella, A. J. *et al.* (1996). Ethnocultural aspects of PTSD: an overview of issues and research directions. In: A. J. Marsella *et al.* (Eds.), *Ethnocultural Aspects of Posttraumatic Stress Disorder. Issues, Research and Clinical Applications* (pp. 105–129). Washington DC: American Psychological Association.

Marx, K., & Engels, F. (1976). *Collected Works, Volume 11*. London: Lawrence & Wishart.

Mayou, R., Ehlers, A., & Hobbs, M. (2000). Psychological debriefing for road traffic accident victims. *British Journal of Psychiatry*, 176: 589–593.

Mazower, M. (1993). *Inside Hitler's Greece: The Experience of Occupation*. Newhaven: Yale University Press.

McDougall, J. (1989). *Theatres of the Body: A Psychoanalytic Approach to Psychosomatic Illness*. London: Free Association Books.

McDougall, J. (1995). *The Many Faces of Eros*. London: Free Association.

McDowall, D. (1992). *The Kurds: A Nation Denied*. London: Minority Rights Publications.

McFarlane, A. (1987). Family functioning and overprotection following a natural disaster; the longitudinal effects of post-traumatic morbidity. *Australia and New Zealand Journal of Psychiatry*, 21: 210–218.

McGoldrick, M. (1994). Culture, class, race and gender. *Human Systems*, 5: 131–153.

McLeod, J. (1997). *Narrative and Psychotherapy*. London: Sage.

Minuchin, S. (1974). *Families and Family Therapy*. Cambridge, MA: Harvard University Press.

Montgomery, E. (1998). Refugee children from the Middle East. *Scandinavian Journal of Social Medicine, Supplementum, 54*: 1–152.

Montgomery, J. R. (1998). Components of refugee adaptation. *International Migration Review, 30*: 679–702.

Moore, T. (Ed.) (1989). *Blue Fire. The Essential James Hillman.* London: Routledge.

Muecke, M. (1992). New paradigms for refugee health problems. *Social Science and Medicine, 35*: 515–523.

Murberg, M. (Ed.) *Catecholaminos in Post-Traumatic Stress Disorder: Emerging Concepts.* Washington: American Psychiatric Press.

Nathan, T. (1986). *La Folie des Autres. Traté d'Ethnopsychiatrie Clinique.* Paris: Dunod.

Nathan, T. (1994). *L'Influence qui Guérit.* Paris: Jacob.

O'Brien, L. S. (1998). *Traumatic Events and Mental Health.* Cambridge: Cambridge University Press.

O'Shea, B., Hodes, M., Down, G., & Bramley, J. (2000). A school-based mental health service for refugee children. *Clinical Child Psychology and Psychiatry, 5*(2): 189–201.

OSCE. (2000). Press release—Symposium on domestic violence, 4th December.

Osofsky, J. D. (1997). Prevention and policy: directions for the future. In: J. D. Osofsky (Ed.), *Children in a Violent Society.* New York: The Guilford Press.

Pandolfi, M. (1994). Pour une ethnopsychiatrie métisse. Au-delà de la folie des autres. *Nouvelle Revue d'Ethnopsychiatrie, 27*: 83–95.

Pandolfi, M. (2000). Disappearing boundaries: notes on Albania, Kosovo and the humanitarian agenda. In: Losi (2000b).

Papadopoulos, R. K. (1987). *Adolescents and Homecoming.* London: Guild of Pastoral Psychology.

Papadopoulos, R. K. (1995). Dilemmas in working with refugees: Clinical service and training. Unpublished transcript.

Papadopoulos, R. K. (1997a). When the secure base is no longer safe: experiences of working with refugees. The 4th annual John Bowlby Memorial Lecture London: The Centre for Attachment-based Psychoanalytical Psychotherapy.

Papadopoulos, R. K. (1997b). Individual identity and collective narratives of conflict. *Harvest: Journal for Jungian Studies, 43*(2): 7–26.

Papadopoulos, R. K. (1998). Destructiveness, atrocities and healing: epistemological and clinical reflections. *The Journal of Analytical Psychology, 43*(4): 455–477.

Papadopoulos, R. K. (1999a). Working with families of Bosnian medical evacuees: therapeutic dilemmas. *Clinical Child Psychology and Psychiatry*, 4(1): 107–120.

Papadopoulos, R. K. (1999b). Storied community as secure base. Response to the paper by Nancy Caro Hollander "Exile: Paradoxes of loss and creativity". *The British Journal of Psychotherapy*, 15(3): 322–332.

Papadopoulos, R. K. (2000a). Factionalism and interethnic conflict: narratives in myth and politics. In: T. Singer (Ed.), *The Vision Thing. Myth, Politics and Psyche in the World*. London and New York: Routledge.

Papadopoulos, R. K. (2000b). A matter of shades: trauma and psychosocial work in Kosovo. In: N. Losi (Ed.), *Psychosocial and Trauma Response in War-Torn Societies; the Case of Kosovo*. Geneva: International Organization for Migration.

Papadopoulos, R. K. (2000c). Distruttivita, efferatezze e terapia. *Anima*, 11: 83–112.

Papadopoulos, R. K. (2001a). Refugees, therapists and trauma: systemic reflections. *Context, the magazine of the Association for Family Therapy*, 54(April): 5–8.

Papadopoulos, R. K. (2001b). Refugee Families: issues of systemic supervision. *Journal of Family Therapy*, 23(4): 405–422.

Papadopoulos, R. K. (2001c). Riflessioni su trauma e lavoro psicosociale. *Psicoanalisi e Metodo* (1).—L'incontro con l'alto. 107–124.

Papadopoulos, R. K. (2002a). Refugees, home and trauma. In: R. K. Papadopoulos (Ed.), *Therapeutic Care for Refugees. No Place Like Home*. London: Karnac, Tavistock Clinic Series.

Papadopoulos, R. K. (2002b). The other other: when the exotic other subjugates the familiar other. *Journal of Analytical Psychology*, 47: 163–188.

Papadopoulos, R. K. (2002c). "But how can I help if I don't know?" Supervising work with refugee families. In: D. Campbell & B. Mason (Eds.), *Aspects of Supervision: a Systemic Perspective*. London: Karnac.

Papadopoulos, R. K. (in press). Narratives of translating—interpreting with refugees; the subjugation of individual discourses. In: R. Tribe & H. Raval (Eds.), *Working with Interpreters in Mental Health*. London: Routledge.

Papadopoulos, R., & Hildebrand, J. (1997). "Is home where the heart is?" Narratives of oppositional discourses in refugee families. In: J. Byng-Hall & R. Papadopoulos (Eds.), *Multiple Voices: Narrative in Systemic Family Psychotherapy* (pp. 206–236). London: Duckworth.

Pattie, S. (1997). *Faith in History: Armenians Rebuilding Community*. Washington: Smithsonian Institute.

Perring, C. (1992). The experience and perspectives of patients and care staff on the transition from hospital to community-based care. In: S. Ramon (Ed.), *Psychiatric Hospital Closure: Myths and Realities* (pp. 122–168). London: Chapman and Hall.

Perry, B. (1994). Neurobiological sequelae of childhood trauma: PTSD in children. In: M. Murberg (Ed.), *Catecholaminos in Post-Traumatic Stress Disorder: Emerging Concepts* (pp. 233–255). Washington: American Psychiatric Press.

Perry, B. *et al.* (1987). Altered platelet alpha2-adrenergic binding sites in posttraumatic stress disorder. *American Journal of Psychiatry*, 144: 1511–1512.

Pilinszky, J. (1995). On the wall of a KZ-Lager. In H. Schiff (Ed.), *Holocaust Poetry*. New York: St Martin's Griffin.

Putnam, R. D. (2000). *Bowling Alone: the Collapse and Revival of American Community*. New York and London: Simon & Schuster.

Pynoos, R., & Nader, K. (1993). Issues in the treatment of post-traumatic stress in children and adolescents. In: J. P. Wilson & B. Raphael (Eds.), *International Handbook of Traumatic Stress Syndromes* (pp. 535–549). New York: Plenum.

Pynoos, R., Steinberg, A., & Wraith, R. (1995). A developmental model of childhood traumatic stress. In: D. Ciccheti & D. Cohen (Eds.), *Developmental Psychopathology, Volume II: Risk, Disorder & Adaptation* (pp. 72–95). New York: John Wiley & Sons.

Ranzato, G. (Ed.) (1994). *Guerre Fratricide. Le Guerre Civili in Età Contemporanea*. Torino: Bollati Boringhieri.

Rechtman, R. (2000). Stories of trauma and idioms of distress: from cultural narratives to clinical assessment. *Transcultural Psychiatry*, 37(3): 403–415.

Rees, J. (Ed.) (1994). The revolutionary ideas of Frederick Engels. *International Socialism*, 65.

Richman, N. (1998). Looking before and after: refugees and asylum seekers in the West. In: P. J. Bracken & C. Petty (Eds.), *Rethinking the Trauma of War*. London: Free Association Books.

Rieber, W. (Ed.) (1989). *The Individual, Communication and Society: Essays in Memory of Gregory Bateson*. Cambridge: Cambridge University Press.

Rustin, M. (2001). The therapist with her back against the wall. *Journal of Child Psychotherapy*, 27(3): 273–284.

Rutter, J. (1994). *Refugee Children in the Classroom.* Stoke-on-Trent: Trentham Books.

Rutter, M. (1987). Psychosocial resilience and protective mechanisms. *American Journal of Orthopsychiatry, 57:* 316–331.

Rutter, M. (1999). Resilience concepts and findings: implications for family therapy. *Journal of Family Therapy, 21*(2): 119–144.

Sala, V. (2000). Let us become the voice of those who cannot speak. *Newsletter, Women's Centre,* September 2–4.

Salvatici, S. (2001). Memory telling, individual and collective identities in post-war Kosovo. *Psychosocial Notebook (IOM), 3:* 15–52.

Sanborn, G. (1998). *The Sign of the Cannibal: Melville and the Making of a Postcolonial Reader.* Durham, NC: Duke University Press.

Sartre, J.-P. (1948). Consciousness of self and knowledge of self. In: N. Lawrence & D. O'Connor (Eds.), *Readings in Existential Phenomenology* (pp. 113–142). Englewood Cliffs: Prentice-Hall, 1967.

Schlenger, W. E., Kulka, R. A., Fairbank, J. A. *et al.* (1992). The prevalence of PTSD in the Vietnam generation: a multimethod multisource assessment of psychiatric disorder. *Journal of Traumatic Stress, 5:* 333–364.

Schore, A. N. (2001a). Effects of a secure attachment relatioship on right brain development, affect regulation, and infant mental health. *Infant Mental Health Journal, 22*(1–2): 7–66.

Schore, A. N. (2001b). The effects of early relational trauma on right brain development, affect regulation and infant mental health. *Infant Mental Health Journal, 22*(1–2): 201–269.

Scurfield, R. (1985). Post trauma stress assessment and treatment, overview and formulations. In: C. Figley (Ed.), *Trauma and its Wake* (pp. 219–256). New York: Brunner/Mazel.

Searles, H. (1978). *L'Effort pour Rendre l'Autre Fou.* Paris: Gallimard.

Serra, P. (1993). Physical violence in the couple relationship: a contribution towards the analysis of the context. *Family Process, 23:* 21–33.

Shamai, M. (1998). Therapists in distress: team supervision of social workers and family therapists who work and live under political uncertainty. *Family Process, 37:* 245–259.

Shamai, M. (1999). Beyond neutrality—a politically-oriented systemic intervention. *Journal of Family Therapy, 21*(2): 217–229.

Shaw, E., Bouris, A., & Pye, S. (1996). The family safety model: a comprehensive strategy for working with domestic violence. *Australia and New Zealand Family Therapy, 17*(3): 126–136.

Shephard, B. (2000). *A War of Nerves. Soldiers and Psychiatrists, 1914–1994*. London: Cape.

Sinason, V. (1987). *Inkstains and Stilletos*. Wirral: Headland.

Sinason, V. (Ed.) (1994). *Treating Survivors of Satanist Abuse*. London: Routledge.

Sinason, V. (Ed.) (2002). *Attachment, Trauma and Multiplicity: Working with Dissociative Identity Disorder*. London: Routledge.

Sinclair, S. K. (1997). *Making Doctors: An Institutional Apprenticeship*. Oxford and New York: Berg.

Sironi, F. (1999). *Bourreaux et Victimes, Psychologie de la Torture*. Paris: Jacob.

Sitaropoulos, N. (2000). Modern Greek asylum policy and practice in the context of the relevant European developments. *Journal of Refugee Studies, 13*: 105–117.

Sluzki, C. (1993). Towards a model of family and political victimization: implications for treatment and recovery. *Psychiatry, 56*: 178–187.

Smith, G. (1993). *Systemic Approaches to Training in Child Protection*. London: Karnac Books.

Spitz, R. A. (1945). Hospitalism: an inquiry into the genesis of psychiatric conditions in early childhood. In: R. Emde (Ed.), *Dialogues from Infancy* (pp. 1–28). New York: International Universities Press, 1983 [Reprinted from *Psychoanalytic Study of the Child, Volume 1*].

Steiner, J. (1993). *Psychic Retreats*. London: Routledge.

Stern, D. (1985). *The Interpersonal World of the Infant: A View from Psychoanalysis and Developmental Psychology*. London: Karnac, 1998.

Stewart, H., Denny, C., & Woodward, W. (2001). Labour cut education spending to 40 year low. *Guardian*, 4.9.2001.

Summerfield, D. (1999a). A critique of seven assumptions behind psychological trauma programmes in war-affected areas. *Social Sciences and Medicine, 48*: 1449–1462.

Summerfield, D. (2001). The invention of post-traumatic stress disorder and the social usefulness of a psychiatric category. *The British Medical Journal, 322*: 95–98.

Summerfield, D. (1999b). Sociocultural dimensions of war, conflict and displacement. In: A. Ager (Ed.), *Refugees: Perspectives on the Experience of Forced Migration* (pp. 111–135). London: Continuum.

Tedeschi, R. G., & Calhoun, L. G. (1995). *Trauma and Transformation. Growing in the Aftermath of Suffering*. New York: Sage.

The Health of Londoners Project. (1999). *Refugee Health in London*.

Thomas, W., & Collier, V. (1999). Accelerated schooling for English language learners. *Education Leadership, April*: 46–49.

Thompson, N. (1998). *Promoting Equality: Challenging Discrimination and Oppression in the Human Services*. Basingstoke: Macmillan.

Thompson, N. (2001). *Anti-Discriminatory Practice* (3rd edn). Basingstoke: Macmillan.

Tyra Henry Report. (1987). London Borough of Lambeth.

UNHCR. (1979). *Handbook on Procedures and Criteria for Determining Refugee Status under the 1951 Convention and the 1967 Protocol relating to the Status of Refugees.*. Genevo.

UNHCR. (1994). *Community Services for Urban Refugees*. Geneva: PTSS.

UNHCR. (1998). *UNHCR by Numbers*. Geneva: Public Information Section, UNHCR.

UNHCR. (1999). *UNHCR by Numbers*. Geneva: Public Information Section, UNHCR.

Van der Kolk, B. A. (Ed.) (1987). *Psychological Trauma* (pp. 63–86). Washington DC: American Psychiatric Press.

Van der Veer, G. (1998). *Counselling and Therapy with Refugees: Psychological problems of Victims of War, Torture and Repression*. Chichester: John Wiley and Sons.

Vernant, J. (1953). *The Refugee in the Post-War World*. London: Allen & Unwin.

Vernez, G. (1991). Current global refugee situation and international public policy. *American Psychologist, 46*: 627–631.

Vetere, A., & Cooper, J. (2001). Working systemically with family violence: risk, responsibility and collaboration. *Journal of Family Therapy, 23*(4): 376–396.

Viñar, M., & Viñar, M. (1989). *Exil et Torture*. Paris: Denoël.

Vivero Pol, J. L. (1999). Stable instability of displaced people in Western Georgia: a food-security and gender survey after five years. *Journal of Refugee Studies, 12*: 349–366.

Vizek-Vidović, V. (1992). Psychological aspects of displacement. In: E. Klain (Ed.), *Psychology and Psychiatry of War*. Zagreb: University of Zagreb Press.

Waldegrave, C., & Tamasese, K. (1994). Some central ideas in the "Just Therapy" approach. *Human Systems, 5*: 191–208.

Webb-Johnson, A. (2000). Loss and the land: recounting the inner and outer. Paper presented at Refugees: Recurring Themes—New perspectives conference, February. London: Tavistock Clinic.

Welch, S. (1975). Sampling by referral in a dispersed population. *Public*

Opinion Quarterly, 39: 237–246.

White, M., & Epston, D. (1990). *Narrative Means to Therapeutic Ends*. New York: Norton.

Williams, L. M., & Banyard, V. L. (1999). *Trauma and Memory*. London: Sage.

Winnicott, D. W. (1982). *Playing and Reality*. London: Routledge.

Winnicott, D. W. (Ed.) (1986). *Home Is Where We start From. Essays by a Psychoanalyst*. Harmondsworth: Penguin.

Winnicott, D. W. (1989). *Psychoanalytic Explorations*. London: Karnac.

Winnicott, D. W. (1992). *The Family and the Individual*. London: Routledge.

Woodcock, J. (1994). Family therapy with refugees and political exiles. *Context, 20*: 37–41.

Woodcock, J. (2001). Threads from the labyrinth: therapy with survivors of war and political oppression. *Journal of Family Therapy, 23*(2): 136–154.

Working together to Safeguard Children. (1999). (pp. 79/8). HMSO.

Wright, T. (2000). Refugees on Screen. RSC Working Paper no. 5. Oxford: Refugee Studies Centre.

Yehuda, R., & McFarlane, A. C. Conflict between current knowledge about posttraumatic stress disorder and its original conceptual basis. Available on the *Trauma Information Pages* at http://www.trauma-pages.com/yehuda95.htm .

Young, A. (1997). *The Harmony of Illusions. Inventing Post-Traumatic Stress Disorder*. Princeton: Princeton University Press.

Yule, W. (1999). *Post-Traumatic Stress Disorder. Concepts and Therapy*. London: Wiley.

Zarowsky, C. (2000). Trauma stories: violence, emotion and politics in Somali Ethiopia. *Transcultural Psychiatry, 37*(3): 383–402.

Zarowsky, C., & Pedersen, D. (2000). Editorial: Rethinking trauma in a transitional world. *Transcultural Psychiatry, 37*(3): 291–293.

Zetter, R. (1991). Labelling refugees: forming and transforming a bureaucratic identity. *Journal of Refugee Studies, 4*(1): 39–62.

Zur, J. (1996). From PTSD to voices in context: from an "experience-far" to "experience-near" understanding of responses to war and atrocity across cultures. *International Journal of Social Psychiatry, 42*: 305–317.

INDEX